Norman Handy

YELLOW SCHOOL BUS

Adventures on a Yellow School Bus from Anchorage in Alaska to Panama

novum ▲ pro

This book is also available as e-book.

www.novum-publishing.co.uk

© 2017 novum publishing

ISBN 978-3-99064-051-7
Editing: Hugo Chandler, BA
Cover photo:
Andrey Bayda | Dreamstime
Cover design, layout & typesetting: novum publishing
Internal illustrations: Norman Handy

www.novum-publishing.co.uk

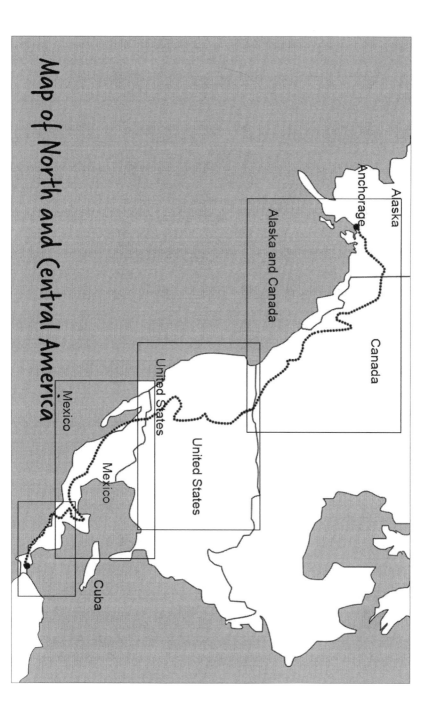

Map of North and Central America

Alaska

Anchorage

Alaska and Canada

Canada

United States

United States

Mexico

Mexico

Cuba

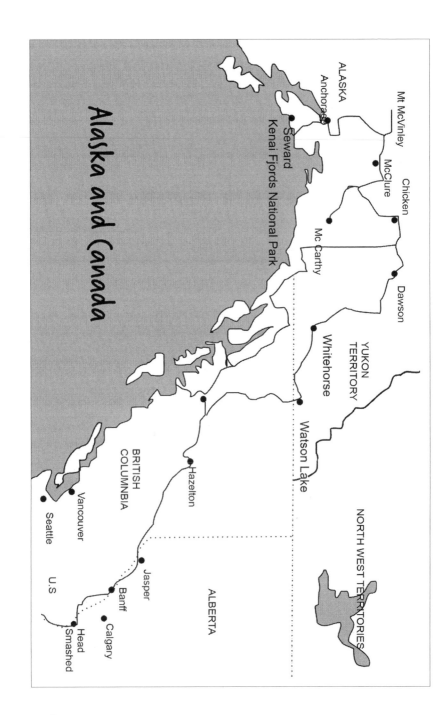

Alaska and Canada

ALASKA
Anchorage
Seward
Kenai Fjords National Park

Mt McVinley
McClure
Chicken
Mc Carthy
Dawson
Whitehorse
YUKON TERRITORY
Watson Lake
NORTH WEST TERRITORIES

BRITISH COLUMNBIA
Hazelton
Vancouver
Seattle
U.S
Jasper
Banff
Calgary
Head Smashed
ALBERTA

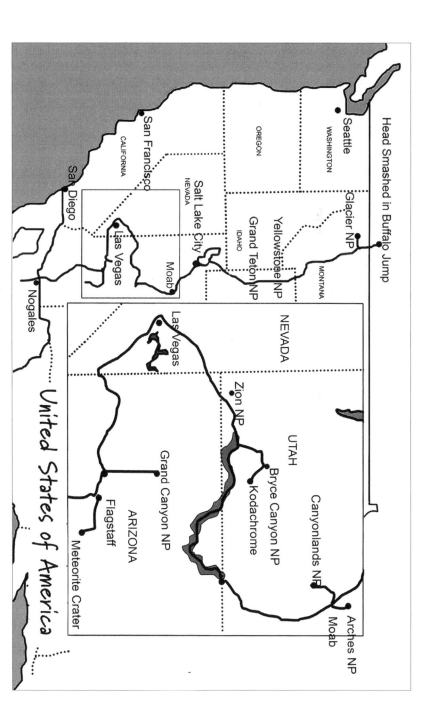

United States of America

Head Smashed in Buffalo Jump

Seattle
WASHINGTON

San Francisco
CALIFORNIA

San Diego

OREGON

Glacier NP

Salt Lake City
NEVADA

Grand Teton NP
IDAHO

Yellowstone NP

MONTANA

Las Vegas

Moab

Nogales

Las Vegas

NEVADA

Zion NP

UTAH

Bryce Canyon NP

Kodachrome

Canyonlands NP

Grand Canyon NP

ARIZONA

Flagstaff

Meteorite Crater

Arches NP

Moab

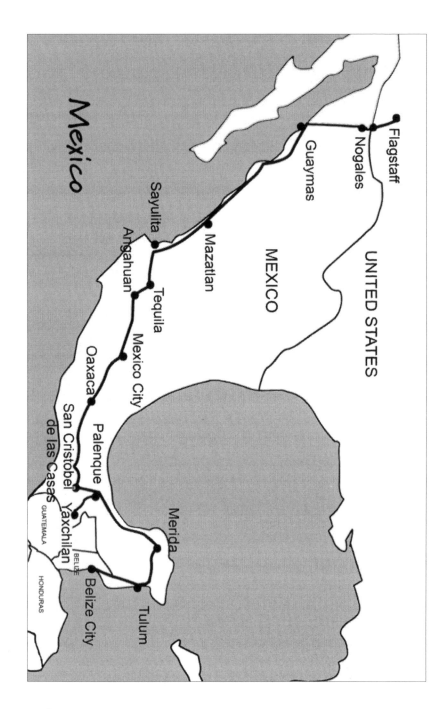

Map of Southern Central America

Mexico
Palenque
San Cristobel de la Cases
Chetumel
Caye Caulker
Belize City
Belmopan
Belize
Yaxichalian
Flores
Panajachel
Guatemala City
Antigua Guatemala
Guatemala
Los Cabanes
Rio Dulce
Livingstone
El Salvador
Copan
San Pedro Sula
Tela
La Ceiba
Roatan
Honduras
Teluogalpa
Pena Blanca
Leon
Granada
Managua
Nicaragua
Costa Rica
San Jose
Boquete
Panama
Panama City

Contents

CHAPTER 1

Alaskan Adventures

I got out of the taxi at the Alaskan Backpackers Inn at seven a.m. I was about to embark on a journey on a yellow school bus down the length of North and Central America from Anchorage in Alaska to Panama City. A large iconic American school bus was sitting in the parking lot alongside the hostel. Next to it was a group of people milling about. These were some of my friends and travelling companions who would be making part or the whole journey with me. The bus had been christened Betsy and was to be our primary mode of transport for the next five months.

There had been a group meeting the day before but I had been unable to attend as I was still travelling to get to Anchorage. Therefore, I had missed the introduction to Betsy. The rest of the group had made their introductions to each other and to Betsy the day before and so I had the disadvantage of trying to pick up everyone's latest news, jobs, and names for those that I did not know personally, already.

I found our leader and driver, Zoë, a Canadian and Seb, her co-driver, a Frenchman from Brittany and introduced myself. We were waiting for one more passenger, Richard, who had not turned up, so having waited an hour, we left a message at reception and set off. We needed to collect supplies so we stopped at a supermarket for an hour.

Before setting off again there was a call to the hostel but still no news from Richard. We set off and as we jerked into motion, a few people who had bought take-away coffees spilt some and complained about the coffee being hot. One of my fellow travelling companions was Gabi who piped up for the benefit of the whole bus that in America they had invented paper sleeves to help insulate the heat from within the cup and lids to stop spillages to protect your hands, as if no one anywhere else in the world had heard of Starbucks, paper sleeves and lids.

Gabi was in her sixties and came from California and she claimed that this was her first overseas trip. Although Alaska is still part of the USA she had flown north and so she was still in the USA. Further the overland journey through Canada back to the lower 48 states was not 'overseas' either so she was wrong on more than one account. But the section of the journey that she was joining us for would be her first foreign trip outside of the USA.

It is an urban myth that only ten per cent of Americans have a passport, as in fact 46 per cent have one (as a comparison, 83 per cent of UK residents have a passport). Overseas travel claims to broaden the mind and educate. However, of all the overseas trips made by Americans, to get a true picture you need to exclude certain trips. A lot of Americans are legitimate immigrants and take multiple trips overseas to visit relatives. Several businessmen also take multiple trips.

The USA is a large country and has a vast number of tourist destinations within its own boundaries so there is a reduced need for overseas travel. Everyone speaks English and the incidence of the ability to speak a language, other than English or Spanish, is very low. Most Americans may recognise the outlines of states and name the state capital of each, but fall short on recognising outlines of overseas countries or naming their capitals. If you also take out trips to neighbouring Canada or Mexico, the number of native born Americans who have experienced another overseas culture is actually very small.

Our first destination was Seward and the Kenai Fjords National Park and we had started down the road leaving Anchorage, which followed a route alongside a railway line, built between 1917 – 23, overlooking Resurrection Bay, named by the Russian fur trader and explorer Alexander Baranof. He was sailing along the coast and was caught in a storm and unexpectedly found shelter in the bay on the Russian Orthodox feast of the Resurrection; hence the name.

Seward was named after Secretary of the Interior William Seward (1861–1869) who negotiated the Alaskan purchase from the Russians. It has an ice-free port and became an important distribution centre for the Alaskan interior. As the city devastated by a massive earthquake in 1964, it has little of the original city left.

The Kenai Fjords National Park sits on the same peninsular as Seward and was set up in 1980 and covers 4,600 square kilometres. At its centre is the Harding Icefield from which 38 glaciers flow. As Kenai Fjords National Park is en route to Seward, we stopped at the Byron Glacier Trail for a walk up the valley to see the glacier.

It was a gentle walk but even at sea level we could see large patches of ice clinging to the mountain slopes rising above us. High above us, at the end of the valley was the snout of the glacier as it tumbled down from the icefield hidden from view behind the mountain tops around us. We checked the hostel for any news of Richard but he still had not turned up.

We drove through Seward and found our campsite along the coast where we would be staying for two nights. It was a warm, dry, and sunny day which made the campsite seem so much more inviting. The tents needed water proofing so we sprayed them as soon as we arrived and left them to dry in the sun.

There was a free day to do whatever was on offer. Several people wanted to take a sea trip along the fjord and hopefully see some whales. I was happy just to wander around town and see Seward along with Roger, an Australian chemistry lecturer on an extended holiday and David, a retired accountant from London. We were dropped off on the far side of town, near the harbour where several other members of the group were going whale watching. We walked back towards downtown along the sea front. After the harbour and its marina, there was a huge RV park with all sorts of vehicles, and judging by the number plates there were vehicles from all over the lower 48 states. Alaska is the 49th, joining the Union in January 1959 and is a long way from the other more southerly states, separated by Canada. There are fifty states in all and the fiftieth state is Hawaii in the middle of the Pacific, which joined in August 1959.

There wasn't much to see of any historical significance in Seward, as it suffered badly from fires and the tsunami following the destruction caused by the earthquake. But it was an interesting walk in bright sunlight. There is history to the town, as it was an important harbour and starting point for many gold prospectors in various gold rushes following the Klondike discoveries in neighbouring Yukon, at Dawson at the end of the nineteenth century. These gold rushes include the Nome, Fairbanks, and Iditarod goldfields and later as prospectors spread throughout Alaska, hundreds of locations were found with gold deposits between 1898 and 1914.

Zoë took me on a tour of introduction to Betsy at the campsite, since I had missed-out on the briefing the day before. She is a traditional big yellow school bus built by Thomas Built Buses, which has its own interesting history. In the economic downturn after the First World War, tram designer Perley A. Thomas lost his job as chief engineer at the Southern Car Works in North Carolina. A few months later he was approached by the Southern Public Utilities Company, a former major client and asked to create a team to renovate several trams that he had designed that his former employer had sold to them.

He contacted his former co-workers and opened the Perley A. Thomas Car Works. Trams were replaced by vehicles, so he expanded and launched his first school bus in 1936. Expansion continued and in 1972 the name changed to Thomas Built Buses and expanded in the commercial market. In 1998, Thomas Built Buses became part of the Daimler group. Innovation followed and by November 2006, Thomas manufactured its last FS-65 conventional bus and retired the product, and produced buses with newer technology and design.

Betsy might be ageing but the Thomas buses have a reputation for being robust work-horses with tried and tested technology and are easy to work on. These buses were exported in droves and can be seen throughout Central and Southern America. In the USA, school buses are painted yellow but in Central America the buses come in all sorts of colours and personalised paint jobs. In Central and South America, they are also referred to as chicken buses, due to the locals often taking their chickens to market on the local buses.

Betsy has had a few modifications but is still easily recognisable as a school bus. She had a modified chassis and suspension to cope with rough roads and low clearance. The back three rows of seats have been converted into a locker for luggage, camping equipment and food storage. Inside there are a range of electrical ports for recharging phones, tablets, and laptops. Otherwise the bus is unaltered from its former role and anyone who has been to school in the USA would have that moment of nostalgia on entering the bus.

We drove back through Anchorage and on to Denali National Park, the home of Mount McKinley which at 6,190 metres, is America's highest peak where we were due to camp for three nights. It was officially renamed Denali meaning 'the tall one' in the local language, but old names tend to stick. It was a long drive day so we left the driving to the drivers and settled into our seats, looking out at the scenery going past, or sleeping.

There were mountains with a scattering of snow on their tops, but as we drove further away from Kenai National Park, the scenery slowly changed to rolling forested hills. In places, there had been wildfires and great stretches had burnt, leaving just blackened trunks pointing skyward. As we approached Denali we could see the mountains covered in snow in the distance.

We stopped at a viewpoint with a braided river below it and views across the landscape to Mount McKinley in the distance. It was named after the American President but he never actually visited Alaska. It is the tallest mountain in the state and is usually cloaked with cloud. Many people come to look at it as it is on the tourists list of things to see in Alaska but few are lucky enough to see it. Down one side is the Ruth Glacier which has carved the Great Gorge. This is 3,000 metres deep but only a little of the gorge is seen as the glacier still fills most of it.

It was early evening by the time we reached the campsite where we would be staying. We drove Betsy through the camp site to our allocated spaces then backed her up from the track through the forest on to a parking space and set up our tents on two neighbouring pitches.

Private vehicles are not allowed inside the park, instead there are a series of shuttle buses and you book the time you want to go. The driver points out things of interest as he drives through the park, with periodic stops. We caught our early morning bus and stopped at one of the designated stops with a café, shop, and toilets, set high on top of a river bank with a view across a braided river. The water levels were low, so there was a lot of light coloured gravel and rocks exposed. It was here that we had our first view of one of the local bears. On the far bank was a brown bear walking along the edge of the river, stopping every now and again to look around and smell the air. We watched until it walked back into the forest and was lost to view.

We got back on our bus and crossed a bridge over the river. There are a few cabins along the way but none are open to the public. They are either left over from the time before this area was a national park, that is prior to 1917 or used by the rangers. Bears are very inquisitive and strong and both doors and windows must be robust to resist tampering. There were heavy steel shutters on some of the windows to protect against bears.

The scenery we were going through had several wide open valleys with rolling hills rising significantly as they get nearer to the central peaks. The bottoms of the valleys have wide braided rivers. As the road climbs upwards, the trees thin to just a few struggling individuals and eventually there are none above the tree line. The grass covering the ground also thins and there are more bare patches of rock and boulders.

The road was purposebuilt to cross some of the best scenery in the park up the Toklat River, to give visitors the best views to appreciate the scenery, sometimes irrespective of cost and the engineering difficulties. That day there was a clear blue sky, no haze, no pollution, and fantastic views of distant peaks with glaciers descending from them from our vantage point high up on one side of the valley.

We had already seen a bear on the lower slopes and up here we saw elk and caribou. It is easy to spot them as there are open vistas with no trees and it was a bright sunny day. The caribou here can be seen individually (as opposed to congregating in herds as in other parks), and can be anywhere in the scenery. One caribou was standing right next to the road with its head planted in a large bush as if it was doing an ostrich impersonation and trying to hide. We got out of the bus to have a closer look and take photos.

While we were doing this, another caribou came gently jogging down the road and passed within an arm's length. Those who heard it and turned around saw this animal coming straight for them. Others had a fright as the first they knew about it was when it rushed past them. Only those quick-witted enough and with a camera at the ready could get any close-up shots.

We arrived at the interpretive centre in the centre of the park where the bus waits for a while before turning around and heading back the way we had come. We saw more bears below the tree line foraging along the river banks as we made our way back. By mid-afternoon we were back at the campsite and we all agreed that it had been a wonderful trip with plenty of magnificent views of the wildlife.

The rest of the day was free and since I had heard trains during the night, I went for a walk in that direction. There was a high, long bridge and just beyond was the railway station. This is where the McKinley Explorer brings guests from the coast and their cruise ships, up into the mountains to visit the park in double-decker railway luxury.

I watched from the river as a train crossed the bridge and slowed as it entered the station. By the time I climbed up the valley side and reached the station, most of the passengers had climbed off and their luggage was transferred by porters. Ever inquisitive, I had a word with the conductor and was allowed on board to view the cabins, the restaurant area and the upper perplex roofed viewing level. It was a modern train with plenty of space but little in the way of decoration. This wasn't needed as the large see-through roof gave panoramic views of the countryside as the train made its way through the mountains to its destination.

That evening we drove out of town to the 49th State Brewery. It is a large restaurant and bar that brews ten types of beer in various styles and strengths up to eleven per cent (which regrettably, was the one beer that they had run out of). Some were named after a local theme such as Solstice IPA or McKinley's Stout or other well-known styles such as Dunkelweizen or Vienna Lager. I tried as many as I could before we finished our meal and I had to go back to the campsite.

The next day was a free day to do whatever we liked. There are several trails radiating away from the campsite, so I first headed to the railway station and the nearby interpretative centre. From here, the Roadside Trail leads off to the sled dog kennels. Here you can wander about the kennels and learn something about their history and their usefulness to rangers in getting about in winter. There is also a dog sled exhibition and demonstration so that guests can get a real understanding of mushing.

I looked around the kennels. Dogs all have characters, and it was clear in these dogs. Some liked to be patted and tolerated the noisy crowd of tourists. Others just slept in the sun, while others hid in or behind their kennels, out of sight. After touring the kennels, I took the alternative but longer Rock Creek Trail to get back. This trail was noticeably quieter and stopping for a moment, I heard nothing except the sounds of the forest. I had met a ranger leading a small group on a flora and fauna walk near the start, coming in the opposite direction but I saw no one else after that. I scanned the trail ahead and stopped and listened for movement. Whenever I was about to break cover across a clearing, I made sure I looked both ways as I was by myself and didn't want an unexpected face-to-face encounter with any large animals especially bears. The local wildlife probably is used to a lot of visitors around here and stay away, but you can never be certain.

You know when you are getting close to your destination as you start to see or hear more people. A lot of people only go for a short circular walk or a short distance up one of the longer trails before turning around again. I had begun to see more people and true enough around the corner was the visitors centre.

I had a picnic lunch at the centre before heading up the Mount Healy Overlook Trail. This was steep in places and didn't look far on the map but seemed a lot further. Again, away from the centre the trail was quiet with just a couple of other walkers, but the outlook is worth the effort. On the return journey, I took the Taiga Trail and the bike path to the Wilderness Centre and finally back to camp. It had been a long day and I would sleep well that night.

We started our drive up the George Parks Highway past the 49th Brewery and for a while we got glimpses of trains running along the far side of the valley, high up the slope. After more than an hour of driving and passing through Cantwell, we turned off the tarmac road onto a gravel track along the Denali Highway to head for our wilderness campsite. The mountains set well-back from the road were covered with snow. As we gently climbed, the trees thinned-out and we had great vistas in all directions. We stopped a few times to stretch our legs and look at wildlife. There were caribou but we saw no bears. There is little traffic along this road and you really get the sense of being in the wilderness.

At mid-afternoon, we arrived at McClaren where the road crosses a river. The settlement is no more than a bush camp, a couple of houses, a cabin and a bar-cum-restaurant. We would be ferried upriver by motor launch to reach our camp. There were only two boats and we would need three trips, so the first boat set off with seven people. The second boat was loaded with our luggage and there was space for two people so Zoë and I jumped in and joined Alan the helmsman and his two dogs that also came along for the ride.

Another boat overtook us going fast and making a lot of waves that rocked us as it shot past. The boat that had taken the first group of passengers was coming back downstream, again fast and I am sure it swung towards us mischievously and spray went everywhere as it shot past and we ploughed through its wake. I was sitting in the bow of the boat and Alan's dog came and sat right next to me. It was obvious that I was in someone else's favourite spot. If I so much as moved an inch away from him, he would move an inch as well. If I nudged him as the boat rocked, he stood his ground and didn't budge an inch. Alan confirmed that I was in his favourite position and he wasn't happy at losing his spot.

We arrived at the campsite and unloaded the baggage. The tents were already set-up with wooden floors and three camp beds in each tent and I shared with Steve, a former English prisoner governor and Laurence, a New Zealander who worked in forestry. This was luxury camping, as all we had to do was unroll our sleeping bags. The toilet wasn't so luxurious. It was a privy with a hole in the ground and no door. There was a wooden baton, so that if it was sticking out, it was occupied and you lowered it after you had finished. It looked away from the campsite up the valley to the glacier and the mountains beyond. It had the best view from any toilet I have ever seen.

The next day was a free day to do as we wished, which was basically either to sit around camp and do nothing or go for a hike. The difficult decision was in which direction. There were no discernible tracks, so you could go in any direction. There was a glacier at the top of the valley and although it was a fair distance I was ready to give it a go. No one expressed any interest in a long walk except for Sigi, a young woman from Austria who ran several chalets in the Alps and who often went off on her own at her own speed, and had already left to walk up the side of the valley. I was ready to go straight after breakfast so I set off up the length of the valley by myself.

There was no obvious path except animal tracks through the scrub and a pair of intermittent tyre marks where an ATV had been across the scrub some time this season. The vegetation at altitude and this far north, is delicate and just one journey in the spring can leave a trace that lasts for the rest of the season.

I forded a few streams and headed up the valley, keeping the main river to my right. The water was cold as it flowed straight off the glacier, and I didn't mind wading through streams up to my knees which I had to do a couple of times as I couldn't find a better crossing-point. The start of the trek was across a wide flat valley floor and easy going until there was a slight rise. There was evidence of a mine with some discarded mining equipment, rubbish, and several spoil heaps but I had no idea what was being sought. After this there was a steep rise right across the valley. I took a dry rocky gulch to the left and scrambled up the slope.

There were no trees here but as I traversed the valley side, there were several small lakes with a milky blue to green tinge, more evidence of some mineral that had coloured the water which had been investigated by the mining company that had dug into the mountain just below. Another scramble and past the next promontory, I either had to head up the side of the valley or down to the valley floor. I opted to keep my height and any views of wildlife and scrambled diagonally up and across the slope only to regret it later, when I had a marvellous view of the glacier ahead but no easy path down.

The glacier had pushed a lot of material into a terminal moraine across the valley and then retreated to form a lake in front of the snout of the glacier. The meltwater had built up until it had carved a route through the far side of the moraine and was slowly draining the lake. Up on the surface of the glacier were darker ribbons of rocks, tracing the lines where smaller glaciers had joined to make one large glacier and lateral moraines had joined together to form medial moraines running the length of the glacier. The lake was a milky colour due to all the fine silt in it from the meltwaters flowing off the glacier. Bobbing about in the lake were a few icebergs that had calved from the main glacier.

I had reached my goal and planned to return the way I had come, but from my vantage point high up on the valley side, the valley floor looked a lot flatter and easier walking so I carried on down to the bottom. I had descended through the gulch and had started to walk across the flat section. I noticed a caribou to my right and one to my left so I aimed for a spot between them. Then, angling their way down the valley slope towards exactly where I was going was a caribou and calf. Just as at that moment there was a noise behind me and I turned to see a caribou running at me from where I had just come.

Common safety advice is that you are recommended to avoid wildlife, but what happens when they come at you? I remembered that you back off from bears and run from moose but what about caribou? They are meant to be timid like deer, and usually avoid people… and these must have seen me but were still coming my way. There were some other trekkers way off to my left, so seeking safety in numbers I quickened my pace and headed straight for them whilst keeping an eye on the movements of the caribou.

The walkers weren't part of my group but they had seen the caribou and stopped to watch them. We exchanged greetings and hiking plans. I wanted to know how easy the route was that they had taken to get here, whilst they asked about paths higher up the valley. Meanwhile the caribou went their separate ways and seeing a gap, I was off again, heading towards the camp.

I rounded the last bluff but from my low position on the valley floor, I wasn't sure in which direction the camp was and I couldn't see it. I only knew for certain that it was next to the main river. And it had started to rain. The problem was, which of the many channels would become the main river which I would be unable to cross. I didn't want to end up on the wrong side of the river so I stayed well to my right for another kilometre or so, before turning at a point that I hoped was perpendicular towards the main river.

As luck would have it, plus what I like to think of as having a good sense of direction, I was just a hundred metres off-track and I gratefully waded the last stream to arrive back in camp. I was the last one back. It had been severe weather at the camp all day and everyone was huddled in the mess tent, drinking tea to keep themselves warm, so I kept quiet about the weather further up the valley which had been bright and sunny for most of the day and only became cold, overcast and raining as I got nearer to the campsite.

We were waiting for the launch to take us downstream to McClaren but we had the choice to paddle. The severe weather had eased off, and after a straw-poll of who wanted to paddle and who wanted to go by launch, there was a consensus of people opting for paddling in canoes, so we ended up three to a canoe, two paddlers and a passenger in the middle. The luggage was loaded onto the launch and we were left to set-off in our canoes in our own time.

The first canoes soon disappeared out of sight and we were the last to go, Zoë in the bow, me as helm at the aft and Bonser in the middle. Bonser was an easy going accountant, originally from London but who now lived and worked in Manchester. The canoe in front of us had Anja from Germany in the bow, Tracey from Australia in the middle and Steve aft. Their canoe team was short on paddling skills and it swung all over the place, plus they didn't recognise approaching shallow water, until they were on top of it, whether they could have done anything about it or not.

Several times we caught up with them, only to see Steve standing in the water, pushing the canoe across a gravel bar. We stayed close, not because it was a difficult river; it was shallow, not too fast moving and there was only one way to go, but just in case they needed help. Besides which, it was a great comical scene, seeing the problems that they had; but at least they were enjoying it and there was no rush or danger.

It wasn't all plain-sailing as the river braided several times and approaching an island, I steered towards the left-hand channel, only to see too late that it shelved into shallow water. It was too late to paddle out of it and the current took us past the start of the island. We shouted at Steve's canoe not to follow. We beached the canoe and all got out and I stood in the water up to my waist and lined the canoe back up the slough and around the tip of the island, before we all got back in and set-off again in the main river. Steve had not gotten much further as they had beached on a sand bar, which was the same one that I had seen and that had persuaded me to go left in the first place.

I have paddled canoes many times but I am not used to being helmsman with two people in the boat. If Zoë leaned to the right, a natural position when paddling on that side, then Bonser would lean to the left to see downstream. That meant that I had two heads to try to see around and had to lean even further and the change in weight distribution affected the way the canoe handled. Ideally the weight should be nearer the back but with just three people and no baggage as ballast, Bonser was sitting forward of centre and Zoë in the bow. She has a physically demanding job driving the truck and undertaking mechanical repairs so, as a result she has a great physique, but is quite muscular for a girl.

I was only wondering about weight distribution and innocently asked how much she weighed, which I realised straight away is not a question you should ever ask a woman. I got an indignant reply, but thinking quickly and hoping to redeem the situation with a bit of humour, I said that she must have misheard and that I was asking what her favourite flowers were. And with Bonser as a witness I was not going to live this down.

Eventually, back in McClaren we dragged the boats onto land and changed into some dry clothes. Most people opted to upgrade to a bunkhouse, but a hardy handful of us pitched our tents for the night, including Bonser and I, without our tent buddies, so with just one person in a tent, there was no shared body heat and it would be a chilly night. But we weren't that eager to camp yet, to be both under canvas and to cook for ourselves, so we all had an evening meal in the restaurant.

After our wilderness camp and thrilling canoe journey it was going to be a long driv day to reach Wrangell-St Elias National Park. This is the largest national park in the USA; six times the size of Yellowstone which is the best-known park, and which people already think is big. Four major mountain ranges meet here, and the park includes nine of the sixteen highest peaks in the USA, including Mt Blackburn and Mt Sanford. The high country is covered with snow all year round, resulting in extensive icefields and there are huge chains of glaciers within the park. Numerous sheep and mountain goats live around the craggy peaks, whilst the park is also home to caribou, moose and brown and black bears.

We stopped off at the visitor centre to get tickets and view the information boards to see what is in the park. From a ridge, just beyond the main building we could see two of the peaks in the park, standing side by side, Mt Drum and Mt Wrangell. Both are volcanoes but Mt Drum is a stratovolcano, with explosive lava forming a steep sided cone, whilst Mt Wrangell is a shield volcano, made-up of flows of lava and shaped like a low dome. We can see them but it would be another two hours before we reached them and our campsite. On our way, we passed the oil pipeline that runs the length of Alaska from Prudhoe Bay on the Arctic Ocean over hundreds of kilometres of tundra, to Valdez on the southern coast of Alaska.

What interested me was the 313-kilometre-long railway line built from Cordova to Kennecott to service a vast copper mine, high in the mountains. This is one of the copper deposits with the highest grade of ore in the world. We paused in Chitina, a small settlement with a café, a community store, a hotel and at most, a dozen houses, before continuing along the road that goes through a cutting. This was originally cut for the railway to reach and cross the Copper River Bridge, which is more than 450 metres long, spanning the wide, shallow, muddy river and then climbing up the far side.

After the bridge, the road heads east on the north side of the Chitina River, along the track bed of what, at the time of construction, was the world's most expensive railway, across the Kuskulana Bridge, built in 1911, above a deep gorge. A bit further on is what has survived of the Gilahina Trestle Bridge, 268 metres long and up to 27 metres high, also built in 1911. The road reaches McCarthy and our campground whilst the old railway route continues up to the Kennecott Copper Mine.

Before the railway was finished, a sternwheeler was designed and built in the lower 48 states and then dismantled and freighted north. It was carried across the mountains by dog-sled teams and reassembled above the Abercrombie Rapids. Then it worked the river to transport goods up the Copper and Chitina Rivers to start building the mine, until the railway arrived with the first locomotive in September 1910 (in fact there were three sternwheelers eventually doing this job). The railway cost USD23 million but profits from the copper mine topped USD100 million between 1911 and 1938; more than a billion in today's money.

Our campsite was an area covered with boulders and a few scraggy trees doing their best to survive. There were magnificent views of the snow-capped mountains in the distance, but nothing else. It was hard to find a flat pitch without clearing a few rocks first and it was cold. To console ourselves we walked to McCarthy and looked around. It is a fascinating place full of wooden houses in true western clapper-board style, plus a bar of course, although the prices reflected the cost and distance to haul goods into the town.

Zoë had brought her violin and she played a few tunes as live entertainment for both us and the other customers. We left late in the evening and walked back to our tents. The path was easy to follow as this far north at the height of summer it doesn't get dark, just twilight around one or two in the morning before brightening up again.

There were various activities on offer such as ice climbing, glacier walks, a flight over the glacier and hiking but my primary aim was to do the historical mine tour. I caught the first shuttle up in the morning from the campsite and bought my ticket for the first mine tour. The smaller buildings, easier to renovate and maintain, were all in excellent condition.

However, the main ore-processing plant, a huge building standing more than fourteen storeys high, built up the sloping hillside overlooking the glacier, still needed quite a bit of work on it to make it look as good as the other buildings. I absolutely love industrial economic development and the trip around the power plant, the huge ore processing plant and offices was fantastic, but I won't bore the reader with any details, other than to say that it is a great destination to spend a day. But there is a magnificent view of the whole plant, the glacier and some of the peripheral mining sites from the top.

I had asked my guide which of the surrounding mines was the best preserved and I was directed to a site in the mountains behind the ore plant. The track was a steep gradient between dense shrubs on both sides of the path. I had no view other than the blue sky above, the greenery on both sides and the grey gravel of the track, and occasionally a glimpse of the mountain ahead, where the track turned a bend. The enjoyment of any trip is not just reaching the destination but also the journey to get there and this seemed a particularly uninteresting trek, with no prospect of improvement. It wasn't a popular choice either as I had seen no one else on the track. So after nearly an hour of walking with no prospect of better views, I turned around.

My alternative plan was to trek alongside the glacier up to another mine site. On the map, it was a greater distance but the gradient was gentler and I had magnificent views across the glacier. I could see tiny black specks on the mostly white ice that were people going ice-climbing or having a walk on the glacier. I met several people coming down but I saw no one ahead of me or following me on the trail behind, and this wasn't surprising as it was getting late in the day and most tourists were making their way back to their hotels in nearby communities. There were only a few of us hardy souls ready to brave camping nearby.

The trail broke through the tree line and from here-on were uninterrupted views across the valley, up and down the glacier and of the many peaks around. At the mine-site there was an information board with some photos, discarded rusting equipment, foundations of buildings and areas that had been levelled or piles of debris but no buildings. With the limited information from the information board and some imagination, I made a mental image of what the site might have looked like while it was being mined. The ore was carried by cable car from the mine site to the main ore processing site, but nothing of this remains, other than a few lengths of discarded cable.

I made my back down the valley the way I had come. At the main Kennecott Mill site, some of the buildings had closed for the day and there were noticeably fewer people around. It was after five p.m. and although I had not missed the last shuttle, I decided to take the old wagon trail from the mill to McCarthy and on to the campsite. It would be about another hour and a half to walk but it was not my turn to cook that evening, so I had the time to spare.

I passed the cemetery on the outskirts of the mine site. Most of the tombstones were only made of wood and the lettering had faded so much as to be indecipherable. A few tombstones were stone but there were not enough stones with legible messages to create any sense of the place from the dates and brief epitaphs. From the cemetery onwards it was a pleasant if lonely walk in the forest, always on the lookout for bears. From McCarthy, I knew the way home from the night before, and crossing the bridge over the river I was rewarded with a picture of a moose just standing in the water a few metres downstream of the bridge.

Driving back across the Copper River we had a brief stop to view the fishing boats used during the salmon run. The whole area is a hive of activity for the few short weeks when the salmon are running. It is a race against nature to capture as many salmon as possible before the salmon season finishes and the endless winter sets in. This is the last chance for people who live in these remote inhospitable regions to preserve salmon for the winter for themselves, or to provide them with something valuable with which to trade.

Then it was a long drive with an overnight stop in Tok. On long drive days, some people slept, some read or just gazed out of the window. To while away the time, we had a game based on Forfeit. A word would be called out and everyone had to do the action. Thus, a call of bear meant that we had to raise our arms with our hands open as if they were claws and to look menacing. A call of moose and we had to put our hands up to our head with our fore and big finger raised as if they were antlers. A call of condor and we had to put our arms out sideways and pretend to soar.

The sight of responsible adults making strange shapes with their hands must have been something to behold but it was amusing and helped to pass some long and otherwise tedious drive days through unchanging forests. Many people may note that condors are not native to Alaska but are large birds' native to South America, so how had they become part of the Forfeit game?

Earlier we had seen some large birds and someone had asked what they were. No one knew but as a joke, I shouted out that they were condors and subsequently any large unidentified bird was called a condor, and so it was used as one of the call-out words for the Forfeit game. We never did establish what the forfeit was for not getting the right action associated with the call, but it was good enough to see people joining-in and making the required shape and laughing good naturedly at those who got flustered and got it wrong.

Originally Tok was a camp for the workers constructing the Alcan and Glenn Highways in the 1940s. It is also where the Alaska Highway crosses an arm of the Pan American Highway. The Pan American Highway is not a single route but several major arteries that connect the far north of the Americas to the far south.

One branch starts in Anchorage which is the road that we were on and meets another branch that starts in Prudhoe Bay. They meet in Dawson and at Carmacks they split with the easterly route going to Watson Lake and the westerly branch going via Whitehorse and the Alaska Highway to reach Watson Lake. There are multiple choices here, but one branch heads east to the Great Lakes and then south to San Antonio in Texas. The westerly route heads south via Calgary and Denver to San Antonio.

The road crosses into Mexico down the eastern side of the country to Mexico City, then Oaxaca and along the Pacific coast towards Panama. We would be following the western route of the Pan American Highway until reaching Yellowstone National Park, where we would make a diversion to Salt Lake City, but pick it up again in Mexico.

Tok is best known today for its association with dog sledding as well as dog breeding, training, mushing and the Tok Race of Champions Sled Dog Race, one of the oldest in the Alaska held each March. Our camp site at Tok was well spaced-out, under some trees and surprisingly quiet. The facilities were modern and clean, with ample hot water. As for the group, for some reason Zoë and Bonser had a cake fight. I forgot how it started but it was good-natured and fun to watch, but if you weren't careful and you watched too closely, you might get hit with some icing ricochet. It was fun to watch and relieved some of the boredom of a long driv day. It was a shame to waste food and I helped myself to some of the larger recognisable pieces of cake out of Zoë's hair and off her T shirt.

Also, en route we stopped at Chicken. When the town was incorporated, the residents wanted to call it Ptarmigan but couldn't agree on the spelling so they called it Chicken instead. This is the site of an early gold rush and there is a large dredger on display in the centre of town. Plus, with a name like Chicken, there is plenty of scope for puns on chickens everywhere. There is a large metal statue of a chicken in the middle of the community. A finger post lists various sister communities, throughout the world with the distance from Chicken. Roosterberg, Belgium, 4,305 miles, Chickaboogalla, Australia, 6,765 miles, Chicken Gizzard, Kentucky, 2,951 miles, Eggamfaaker, Austria, 4,696 miles and Cluck, New Mexico, 2,535 miles, to list just a few.

CHAPTER 2
Gold Rush

We crossed the USA–Canada border at Little Gold also known as Poker Creek and travelled through the rugged landscape along the 'Top of the World Highway' for 130 kilometres to reach Dawson City, scene of one of the most famous gold rushes of the nineteenth century. The road to reach it is known as the 'Top of the World Highway', as it is one of the most northerly roads in the world and its route follows the crests of several ridges and mountains, giving views down the valleys on either side, making travellers feel that they really are on top of the world. We pitched our tents at the campsite in West Dawson and that evening, we took the ferry into town and watched the cabaret at Diamond Tooth Gerties Casino, an old western style casino and entertainment venue that prospectors a century ago would recognise as they spent their hard-won gold.

Afterwards we stopped off at the unimaginatively named Downtown Hotel and had a Sour Toe Cocktail. This is a challenge to drink your choice of alcoholic drink, but the catch is that there is a preserved human toe in the bottom which must touch your lips. The tradition grew from two boasting and competing river captains, and it really is a human toe. You get a certificate and my number for this attempt was 63,656. I got a reduced price as this was my second attempt, as my first attempt was a few years earlier and looking back through the records, we found my name to prove it. My earlier number was 43,554.

Dawson takes us back to the times of the Klondike Gold rush. Large parts of the town are preserved as the original prospectors would have known it. The group was due to visit Dredge No 4, one of the original mining rigs, but as I had visited this twice already on other trips, I did my own thing. I took a tour of the cabin where Robert Service lived, the famous bard of the Yukon who wrote popular poetry and walked through the forest behind the cabin, that he used to wander through whilst composing. On the hill slopes, high above the cabin is a cemetery which has a fascinating array of late nineteenth and early twentieth century funeral architectural styles. Many of the gravestones have the town or city of origin of the deceased and the geographic spread of the places of origin show from how far-and-wide the prospectors came.

I finished my tour of Dawson with a walk down the river, to visit the British Yukon Navigation Company's former shipyards. On the river bank in Dawson sits the SS Keno, a wonderfully preserved sternwheeler from the gold rush which is open to the public. In contrast, the shipyard is where the remains of four other sternwheelers, the Zealandia, Julia B, Seattle #3 and Schwatka, lie abandoned. These had been pulled out of the river and were left here more than sixty years ago. They are slowly decaying and some look just like a jumble of sawn timber rather than a boat.

Further along is another sternwheeler graveyard with boats dating from 1898, the Mary F Graff, the Victorian and the Tyrell which are equally interesting and disappointing, as they are pieces of history that are slowly falling apart and the forest is slowly growing back around and through the piles of sawn planks.

In contrast to the fine weather of the last few days, it had started to rain during the night, but as this was to be a drive-day, leaving Dawson and driving 530 kilometres via Carmacks to Whitehorse, the capital of the Yukon Territory, the weather wouldn't bother us. We said goodbye to Seb who was taking a few days off, to go to a wedding in Vancouver, so Zoë would be looking after us by herself and doing all the driving for a few days. Whitehorse is a wonderful place to visit and spend some time, but we were just passing through. We set up our tents in the Robert Service Campground outside of the city, in the rain.

We also put up a large communal tent to give a dry area for the cook group. It was more of an awning than a tent, as it was open-sided, but it kept the rain off. Whenever we camped and were due to cook for ourselves, the food was prepared by the cook group. We were all split into groups of three or four and took it in turns to cook. The cook group has a budget for their meal, decides what they are going to cook, and buys the necessary ingredients at one of the stops during the day.

Already on the bus, in the back locker, were boxes with standard ingredients such as herbs and spices, a few tins, tea and coffee and a few basic items such as rice or pasta, so it was only the fresh vegetable and meat ingredients that needed to be bought. The cook group also needed to ensure that there was enough to serve a breakfast and if a picnic lunch was needed, that there was enough bread, sandwich fillings and fruit for people to make a packed lunch after breakfast.

Not everyone can cook but out of a small group of three people, there is always one person with an idea and plenty of helpers to chop and stir. Some more ambitious groups served a dessert, as well as a main course. Some breakfasts were cereals only, and other groups cooked scrambled egg or egg bread. No one was ever critical and nothing inedible was ever served. We were also lucky in that no one had any food allergies. Anja was a vegetarian, not for conscience reasons but because she didn't like the taste and texture of meat. But her dietary requirements were simple to meet, as she was content to have the same meal as the rest of us, but just cut out the meat.

Had there been any other food intolerances we would have run out of saucepans, chopping boards, gas rings or space over the fire. There might be problems with those on strict dietary requirements such as vegans or those with lactose or gluten intolerance, but people ate what they were given. Personally, I am careful about my diet at home, but I am prepared to eat anything whilst on a trip, as it can become very difficult for the cooks to satisfy all requirements.

It was still raining in the morning as we packed away our wet tents and set off. We had a lunch stop at Watson Lake. Here is the Northern Lights Centre where there is a film show and interpretive centre for visitors to discover everything they ever wanted to know about the northern lights or aura borealis. Just across the road is the Signpost Forest where there are over 80,000 signs from all over the world, nailed to the trees and posts, erected specially for the purpose. There are street signs, road signs, house signs and all-sorts. For a small fee, you can add your own sign and plenty of people do, and hence it will continue to grow. It has an international following, and people bring signs from their home town from all over the world, to put up.

That evening we pitched camp in the forest on a bank above Watson Lake. I was part of the cook group and had set up the tables and was preparing the meal with Bonser and Anja. Anja was great to have in the cook group as she sorted out her own meat-free meal with no fuss. She also ensured that we didn't go over budget. In the supermarket when the cook group is shopping, it can be all too easy to keep putting things into the basket. Anja would keep a tally of the bill and warn us if we were getting close to the budget limit. The cook group composition would change periodically, as people joined and left the trip. Individuals' shopping habits differ and several times over the next few weeks cook groups would need to be reminded that there was a budget limit and that it was not a target. Some more expensive brands or products would have to be substituted with cheaper items or thoughts of a dessert ditched, to stay within budget.

Betsy had been parked facing uphill nearby to ease unloading and she needed to be turned around. From experience, she doesn't start well on a chilly morning when she is low on fuel and facing uphill. It was after supper when Zoë tried to move her, but she was already too cold to start.

Zoë borrowed some diesel from the warden to fill up the tank. There was a lot of effort and improvisation of funnels and tubes to get the diesel into the tank which meant diesel went everywhere but at least some went into the tank. With our fingers crossed she coaxed the engine into life and turned Betsy around. Telling the story only takes a few lines but it took most of the time between the end of the meal and bedtime. It was worth the effort as it would have meant a long delay to our planned departure and luckily the engine turned over first time the next morning.

Before we set off Roger made a big blunder, but he wasn't to know, and we all learnt something very important. We were tidying up, washing up the breakfast things, putting chairs away and doing a host of morning jobs and he was helping the cook group. Zoë is a coffeeholic and can be like a bear with a bad head until she has had her morning fix. Rather than instant coffee she had her own special supply of coffee grounds, for camping mornings when there is unlikely to be a shop or hotel nearby to get quality coffee. She had made her own coffee and had left it on the table to cool while she went to do another job.

Roger picked it up, being the last item on the table which needed to be stowed away and asked a few people if it was theirs and getting no positive answer, and feeling that the mug was cool, he threw the contents into the undergrowth and washed it up. Zoë returned and wanted to know where her coffee mug was. Roger owned-up to the crime (he was still washing her mug so he could hardly deny it) and we all learnt a valuable lesson, namely that that (insulated) mug was hers and you didn't touch it unless you no longer wanted to live.

The engine started first time but there was still a delay but not for long, as we needed to find a garage to replace the fuel we had borrowed the night before. It was another long-drive day before we would reach our intended campsite at Stewart.

On a long drive, we would stop every so often, every two hours for a comfort break, stretch our legs, do some shopping or for Zoë and Seb to take turns driving. We were driving along a forested valley in the mountains and had pulled off the road for a break. This was in the middle of nowhere and we had at least twenty minutes, so I wandered up the road just to stretch my legs, keeping an eye open for wildlife.

We got back on board and had just started when ahead of us was a black bear, calmly walking along the side of the road in our direction. We stopped and pulled our cameras out. It was very obliging and calmly walked right past us, giving us all great photo opportunities from the comfort and safety of the bus. And the fact that I had been out there in that very spot, just minutes before, sent a shiver down my spine.

We turned off the Pan American Highway and down a side road to Stewart on the Pacific coast. We had a great campsite at the purpose-built Bear Creek RV Park with wide, flat grassy areas, several picnic tables and a permanent wooden open-sided shelter all to ourselves. There were hot showers and laundrette facilities and an opportunity to thoroughly clean both ourselves and our clothes.

The plan was to drive to Hyder which is found on the edge of the Misty Fjords National Park just over the border in the USA. There is Fish Creek to visit, which is renowned as a place where brown, grizzlies and black bears come to catch and eat salmon. Further up the same road is the magnificent Salmon Glacier with magnificent views from the road. The road doesn't go anywhere but such are the borders and the coast that as you leave Canada and enter the USA you must then reverse the process to get home. There are no US border controls but you must go through Canadian border controls to be stamped out to leave and repeat the same process to return, even if the road doesn't go anywhere else than up to the glacier.

At Fish Creek, there are safe elevated viewing walkways and platforms along the river and we were there early in the morning. The waters are clear and there were dozens of different types of salmon moving slowly in the shallow waters. There was an occasional burst of activity as salmon spawned and thrashed about. There were dead salmon as well, that had already spawned and had died. The quantity of salmon both alive and dead explains the popularity of the place for bears. We stayed for over two hours but saw no bears.

We followed the road up into the mountains beside the Salmon Glacier with spectacular views. At the top, we parked the bus and had a few hours to go hiking wherever we wanted. Sigi walked off towards the glacier by herself and most people chose to walk in the same general direction to explore the glacier. I was feeling fresh so rather than just walk to the glacier and then retrace my steps, I walked in a loop along the valley, then crossed it to see the glacier up-close and go back down the valley to the bus.

It was afternoon when we returned and stopped again at Fish Creek and stayed for another two hours in the hope of seeing bear, but alas we were unlucky. We vowed to return after our evening meal as most bear activity occurs in the morning and evening. We passed through Canadian customs and followed procedures. We told them that we would be returning that evening, hoping that the process might be a little quicker if we had already been processed but no luck as the shift would change and the new team would have to go through the entire process with us again.

Hyder has a local custom, like the Sour Toe Cocktail in Dawson, which is to be is 'hyderized' in the local bar. This entails knocking back a shot of some ferocious 120 per cent proof local alcohol and receiving a certificate. Luckily and unlike Dawson, no toes were involved. I was in two minds about bears or being hyderized, but having not seen any bears and doubting that the bears would turn up, I opted for the hyderisation so I was dropped off at the Sealaska Inn in Hyder and would be picked up again in two hours.

The two hours stretched to four and I had plenty of time to explore every road in Hyder and to be thoroughly hyderized. The delay of course was because the others had spotted a bear. They had dozens of great photos and had watched it until it had eaten enough salmon and had disappeared back into the forest. Meanwhile I had my certificate proving that I had been hyderized, and I was feeling the effects of the alcohol and was slightly unsteady on my feet as we went through Canadian customs yet again.

We left Stewart early the next morning and returned to the Pan American Highway. We stopped en-route about mid-morning at a small village. Seb had returned from the wedding in Vancouver and on his return trip by bus to re-join us, his bus had made a stop at the village. It wasn't on the tourist trail but it was an authentic First Nation village complete with a row of totem poles, each of which told a story if you know how to read totem poles. If you didn't know there were plenty of guides to help you on the matter. There were also a couple of interesting wooden churches but neither were open to the public.

We spent lunchtime at Hazelton to visit the Ksan Indian Village. This is a collection of traditional buildings, community halls, cabins and more totem poles, carvings and a museum, housing many artefacts. Fascinating for those with an interest in history or culture and personally I do like to visit ethnological exhibits. There was also plenty of thick green grass to lie on in the sun, for those less interested in ethnography or to relax on after touring the site.

Our afternoon stop was at Moricetown, not much to look at in the town, but on the river, was a sudden constriction of hard rock where the river narrows to a fifth of its former width to squeeze down some rapids and a short canyon. It was a good place to fish and there were many local fishermen who smoked their catch at the side of the river. There were also a couple of fish ladders to help the fish to swim upstream to their spawning grounds, to ensure that there are always enough fish in the river for the locals.

We went through Smithers and on to Burns Lake campground. Simpson fans will recognise the names but I would be fascinated to know whether this place has any connection with Matt Groening or whether it is just a big coincidence. My money is on the side that there is a connection, as his parents are called Homer and Margaret. He has two sisters, Lisa and Patty and was born and brought up in Portland, Oregon, just a few hundred kilometres down the coast.

The main road runs parallel to a railway line and occasionally crosses it and we were held-up at a red light on a level crossing. A Canadian National train came past pulled by two locomotives, pulling a freight train with double-stacked US sized containers (European containers are 40 feet long and 8.5 feet high, American containers are 48 x 9.5 feet). My longest train to date was 156 double-stacked wagons so I just had to start counting.

As soon as it looks like it won't be a new record, I stop counting. And this train was short by North American standards, not even a hundred wagons.

We entered the Jasper National Park set deep inside Alberta's Rockies. The city of Jasper itself, is surrounded by mountains, making this an incredibly beautiful place to visit; famous for its amazing scenery. We found our reserved pitches in what is claimed to be North America's largest campsite. The site is set in the forest and split into sections, often fenced, or separated by streams.

Trees separated each pitch, giving some sense of privacy but sharing a common cul-de-sac access, thereby creating groups of four to eight pitches. Each section is appointed by letters with each section having up to a hundred numbered pitches. There are several stories of people in our group going to the shower block or toilets and not being seen again for two hours as they struggled to find their way back to the right campsite.

Various options were available in Jasper for those seeking a thrilling adventure, such as taking the Tramway up Whistler's Mountain, hiring mountain bikes or less adventurous activities such as going shopping. A popular choice was hiking in a nearby valley and as there was a majority who wanted to do this, Zoë drove the bus out to Maligne Lakes. We stopped at the bottom of False Lake, so called as when river levels are low, it disappears. The base rock is limestone and porous, so the water drains away when there is insufficient water flowing into it to keep it topped up.

There was a crowd at the side of the road taking photos of a black bear. First survival instruction is not to get out of your car. The coach driver ahead of us stopped and opened his door to tell people to get back into their cars but no one did. There are a lot of stupid people in the world wrapped up in their city life, without any sense of danger and it would have served them right had they been attacked, as it would improve the gene pool but then the poor bear in its native environment, acting on instinct, would have been shot by rangers.

At Maligne Lakes we split into smaller groups, depending on the length of walk that people wanted to do. On one side of the valley, the trails were closed as there had recently been bears seen in that vicinity so Bonser, Zoë and I took one of the longer trails up to the top of the mountain opposite. We chose a gentle path to get near the edge of the tree line, but then it was a steep ascent to the top. It was damp and windy but at least the cloud base was high enough to give views down to Maligne Lake and across the valley. Back in the trees we took a different route, shorter and steeper which would have been hard work going up but was a lot easier going down.

I had cooked the night before, so I had some spare time, so on the way back to camp I asked to be dropped off in Jasper, so that I could look at the town and then walk back to camp. After shopping in town, I was walking along the side of the road back towards the campsite when I came across some caribou, quietly grazing next to the main road and standing directly in my way. They showed no likelihood of moving so I had to cross the road and make a diversion higher up the slope through the forest to avoid them. This was also my moment, coming back to camp, where I could see the bus, a big yellow school bus is unmissable and I could hear Tracey's distinctive laugh on the other side of a fence and a stream, but I just couldn't find the right path back for another twenty minutes.

The road south out of Jasper towards Lake Louise is the Icefield Parkway, which passes the Columbia Icefield and there are many wonderful vistas; a lot to see and it is very popular, so we left early. The Columbia Glacier tumbles down from the icefield, just one of six major glaciers leading from the icefield and the source of the Athabasca River. The river formerly ran west to the sea, but following intense glaciation its direction of flow was altered, and it now flows east through Lake Athabasca, and the Great Slave Lake to join the mighty Mackenzie River, past the Great Bear Lake and then forms the Mackenzie Delta that empties into the Arctic Ocean at Inuvik 6,200 kilometres to the north.

Our first stop was at Athabasca Falls before seven a.m. and it was already getting busy with tourists and several coaches were already parked in the car park. There are some hard rocks that have resisted erosion and form a ridge across the valley bottom. The Athabasca River has cut a narrow, vertically walled gorge through this rock and at the top of the gorge are some waterfalls. They are not big but they are in a beautiful setting and there is plenty of noise and spray to add to the experience.

It was a perfect day for sightseeing, a brilliant blue sky with an occasional white cloud. The road follows the wide milky-white river off to our right. The river's edge and lower slopes are forested whilst towering above us were tall mountains with snow covered peaks; glaciers tumbling down off the ice field and steep grey rocky cliffs. We pulled off the road for a break and to take in the fresh, clean mountain air.

The visitor centre opposite the Columbia Glacier is on everyone's list of places to stop and is heaving with tourist coaches and throngs of people. Tours are on offer for people to be taken up onto the glacier in ice buses. It was crowded and commercial so we spent only a little time here and opted to carry on to Bow Summit.

This is the highest elevation of the Icefield Parkway with a view across Peyto Lake, claimed to be the bluest lake in the Rockies. There is a short trail through the forest with information boards which takes about an hour. This is the watershed between east and westerly flowing rivers and the road then dips down several steep gradients to Lake Louise.

This is a well-known ski resort in winter and again heaving with tourists. Lake Louise itself is pleasant but very commercialised, which spoils its natural wonder. All in all, I was disappointed with Lake Louise, but I am glad that I have seen it and don't have to ever go again. We stopped at another lake just as blue as Peyto Lake and finally late in the afternoon left the Icefield Parkway to enter the Banff National Park and found our campsite in Banff.

Banff is one of Canada's most popular tourist destinations, known for its mountainous surroundings, with walking trails, ski runs and hot springs so, a wonderful place to visit at any time of the year. The campsite was another big campsite set along a valley beyond Tunnel Mountain. There was a communal mess hut next to our pitches in the trees that would not be out of place as an English cricket pavilion on a village green with windows all around. Here we met Zoë's mother. She was originally from Hungary before emigrating to Canada and moving to Vancouver. She had driven from home to join us for the weekend and she had offered to cook. She is a great cook and we had a traditional Hungarian meal.

There was another free day but we were transferring first thing in the morning from the campsite to a hostel near the Bow River. Some people wanted to take the gondola up Sulphur Mountain but that didn't interest me, so I went for a walk, being dropped off in the town centre and headed towards the bridge at the end of Main Street. There is a park alongside the Bow River that flows from Bow Glacier through Banff. The park peters out and develops into a trail out of town. The river is wide and shallow and flows over some rapids outside of town. On the far side of the valley surrounded by forest is the iconic Banff Springs Hotel, towering above the treetops. It is a well-known sight that many people will recognise, even if they can't name it. It is a giant luxury hotel, twelve stories high, built over a century ago as a must-go-to-hotel for the well to do, who would arrive at the newly built railway station and be transferred by coach and horses.

The trail continues down by the river's edge, then through forests and across the occasional clearing. It passes around the base of Tunnel Mountain and looking back from a clearing you get a magnificent view of it. It got its name from the time that surveyors were working out the best route for the railway. It was originally planned for a tunnel to be blasted through the mountain. A cheaper alternative route was found, but the name stuck.

The trail then heads diagonally up and across the valley slope to follow the top of the river bank. From here looking down towards the river there are several hoodoos pointing out above the tree canopy, part way down the slope. Looking up the valley I could see the Banff Springs Hotel and although it is a big building, it is dwarfed by the mountains towering above the valley on all sides. It looks great from here and no doubt the view from there down this way along the valley would be equally spectacular.

I found a campsite and went looking for a café or shop. I didn't recognise the campsite at first from this angle, as I was approaching it from an unfamiliar direction, but it turned out to be the one that we had stayed in the night before. I knew where the facilities were and where the bus stop was and could have taken a short cut to get back to town, but I was happy to take a different path down towards the river to re-join the route that I had come up out of town.

I had a late lunch in town and then continued along the river going upstream. There is another park that flanks the river until it reaches the far side of town and crosses a bridge over a tributary stream that joins the Bow River. There is a nature trail through the forest and I followed several of the paths in turn. On the far side of the forest was a footbridge over another stream. I had just crossed over when I heard splashing in the stream. There below me through the trees was a moose cow and calf calmly walking along the stream bed. Had I been just five minutes slower I would have had a marvellous view from the safety of the bridge.

The trail leads out of town past the Vermillion Lakes which aren't red but the usual water colour. I walked along this for an hour but the valley floor was wider, the mountains seemed further away and smaller and the scenery didn't seem so spectacular as on the other side of town so rather than go on, I turned around.

On the return trip, I stopped off at the railway station and looked around the original station where guests would have arrived for their stay at the Banff Springs Hotel. There were photos of how the station looked in former years and some information boards. There were some sidings but little of interest. All night in my tent I could hear train movements and whistles as freight trains made their way along the tracks going past the town. I had hoped that while I was here I might see a train but I hadn't co-ordinated my visit with the timetable and nothing came through while I was there.

We had another farewell meal that evening as some people were leaving the group but then we would meet some new faces the next evening. That night I slept well and didn't have to put a tent up as we had transferred to the Y Mountain Lodge hostel in Banff.

There was yet another free day to do as we wished, for those who already knew the bus and rules but there was a meeting for the newbies to be introduced to each other and to Betsy, a chance to ask questions etc. Meanwhile, I had another trek planned, this time up the Bow River on the other side of the valley from yesterday. I set out straight after breakfast and kept to the north side, following the Caves and Basin Trail. The start of the trail was flat alongside the Bow River. I reached the centre but decided I would visit it on the return journey so I doubled back to take the Marsh Loop along the very edge of the river, which was a signposted nature trail in a loop off the main trail.

The river is calm here seemingly with little current. The waters are still and turquoise blue. There were several kayakers and canoeists gently paddling along. Further along the trail I saw horse dung and hoof prints. There was a stable nearby and this was one of their often used paths. Around a corner I came face to face with a string with about a dozen riders. I love riding but this wasn't the style that I enjoyed. It looked as if these were inexperienced riders out for an hour of 'follow the leader'. Some of the horses did the same route several times a day and looked disinterested, unchallenged, almost bored, and very few looked alert, head up with ears pricked. I stood to one side and let them pass.

I was now on the Sundance Trail alongside the river that led up into the mountains. The trail left the river and weaved its way across the valley side, but still at a gentle gradient. There were quite a few people at the start of the trail, but after two hours I didn't see a soul. There was still horse dung and hoof prints but it was a less used track. Set back in the forest were a few buildings, a corral, a couple of horse drawn wagons and picnic tables. This was the destination of another potential horse ride and after this I saw no more dung or hoof prints.

Passing an open-sided shelter complete with toilets, the gentle trail ends and the Sundance Loop begins. This is a steep walk up a narrow path, beside a stream that has cut a deep gorge, with water cascading over rocks. It is picturesque but challenging and rises into the mountains. There is a loop through the forest with steep gradients up and down until it curves back on itself and rejoins the original path and runs back down the gorge. It is an interesting forest walk but you never leave the trees and there are no stunning vistas but pleasant in its own way.

It was a sweltering day even in the shadow of the forest, so I stripped off and washed in the stream and sat on the bank drying in the sun as I dangled my feet in the cool rushing water. Then I set off back down the trail. A short while after passing the horse corral was a junction where two paths crossed. Both were long distance tracks, one up to a mountain north of Banff and the other back to the river and upstream. I had time and I was inquisitive. I didn't have a map with me so I didn't know if it connected with another path to take me back to Banff, so I decided to follow it for an hour and just see where it went.

It was a much less used path; no hoof prints or footprints. There were tyre tracks but these were old. I kept an eye out for wildlife as I walked through the forest. There were a few slopes up and down, but gentle and not a challenge to any vehicle or walker. Other than a collapsed cabin in an overgrown clearing there was little evidence, away from the track that man had ever been here. On the basis that the return journey is always faster than the outward journey I walked on for another half an hour but still there were no signs or other paths, so I retraced my steps.

I reached the Caves and Basins centre and had a look around. I wasn't interested in the spa but there was a temporary exhibition displaying stories of individuals and the country's involvement in the First World War. It is not everybody's cup of tea but it is a period of history I know well and I was thoroughly absorbed until it was closing time and I had to leave, but not before having a flying tour of the last part of the exhibition, under the gaze of a curator eager to lock up.

It was time to meet the newbies who were joining up for the next leg of the trip and to set out for the drive from Banff to the next national park. We could take the main road to Calgary and turn south but we opted for the more scenic drive through some stunning mountains in the Peter Lougheed Provincial Park. Having left the main road, we were passing through a valley with high peaks around us with snow on top with forested lower slopes. There was roadworks ahead and big signs pointing to a diversion and another set of big signs in big letters saying, 'BRIDGE OUT', which until I saw it in reality, I thought were only ever seen in cartoons.

As the day progressed the mountains retreated to become hills and the hills became rolling plains as we left the Rockies behind. The forests thinned and we were crossing a grassy plain. There were cattle grazing on the prairie and fenced areas left for hay, some which had already been cut and wrapped in large round bales, ready for collection. The road ran parallel to a railway track and into view came three Canadian Pacific logo'd locomotives, two in red livery, one in yellow, pulling a mixed freight train of containers, wheat wagons and oil tankers. For a moment, it looked like a contender for my longest train but it fell short. The next train was just a single locomotive so it could never be a real contender and I didn't even start counting.

We stopped at the Head-Smashed-In Buffalo Jump centre and a UNESCO World Heritage Site. This is a cliff stretching across the prairie used for hunting. First Nation peoples have used these for more than 6,000 years to round up buffalo on the high plateau above and funnel them in a herd to the edge of the cliff where they jumped over the edge and died. The carcasses would then be butchered for meat, hides and bone and everything was used. Surplus meat would be dried and surplus hides and other products traded with neighbouring communities.

The Interpretation centre is carefully and tastefully built into the cliff so that it doesn't seem to be very big from the outside and blends into the scenery. However, it is much larger on the inside and houses a mass of artefacts, dioramas, pictures and anecdotes concerning the site. There is also a film about a re-enactment of a hunt to show how it was done. Visitors enter at the base of the cliff and having worked their way up through the museum and armed with all the knowledge necessary can emerge at the top of the cliff and walk along the edge of the cliff and get a feel what a hunt meant. It is also a magnificent view.

We crossed the Canadian-USA border into Montana which was surprisingly simple and hassle-free and continued to our camp-site at Glacier National Park (also called Waterton Lakes National Park on the Canadian side). The cook team lucked out here as we arrived after seven p.m. and had to put up tents first before even starting to cook and it was getting too late to start cooking so after the tents were up we went back into town for some fast food. It was a bit of a misnomer as the settlement is quite small but they had just had a large order so ours was delayed but there was a bar next door with a snooker table and it was a meal that we didn't have to cook or wash up afterwards.

Glacier National Park is located where the Rockies meet the prairies. The park offers wonderful trekking opportunities and has over 700 lakes, the largest being Lake McDonald which is over nine miles long. We had breakfast early so we could get going. I hadn't noticed it on our arrival but there was a haze in the sky and a smell of smoke. There were several forest fires burning in the area and the smoke was drifting about and was not being blown away.

Betsy couldn't enter the park so we had to rely on the shuttle buses provided by the park to get around. With a group of disparate independent travellers like ourselves there are all sorts of tastes to cater for. Some didn't want to go, one was too ill to go, someone just wanted to have a day off to lie in bed, some were always so slow to get ready that you would know not to bother to wait or you would miss the bus, literally and so on so it is not surprising that we broke into smaller groups.

The first bus was early in the morning and it was on a first come first served basis and there would inevitably be a queue. The next bus was some time away and by then there would be an even bigger queue. Some of us were eager to get started so Sigi, plus two new members of the group who had joined us in Banff, Lisa who was also Austrian and Paola, an Italian working in pharmacological research and I were at the bus stop thirty minutes before it was due to leave and there were already sixteen people ahead of us. We were also not sure of the capacity of the buses… whether they were fifty seat coaches, whether they would allow standing passengers or whether they were mini-buses for between twelve and thirty.

My plan was to take the shuttle right to the far side of the park, changing buses where necessary and ignoring stops on the way out and then work my way back. The bus came and frustratingly there were already people on the bus but at least it was a coach able to seat at least fifty passengers. We were lucky to board but all the seats were taken so we had to stand so those who arrived later, thinking that they had only a short wait, were disappointed and would have to wait for the next bus or even the next one after that. The rule for eager, seasoned travellers is always be extra early! Get up in the dark, forego breakfast, pack the evening before, be independent, have a plan… you will have the greatest time window to relax and enjoy yourself and you can always waste time later in the day without any regrets.

We were driven up the road and alongside a lake. Patches of the forest had been recently burnt and large areas were just charred blackened tree trunks pointing skyward, often standing out from bare rock as the leaf litter and undergrowth had also been burnt. Soon we were amongst the mountains with patches of snow huddled in corners out of the sun. Some smoke laid heavy in the air from recent or continuing fires that the wind had yet to disperse.

At the summit where we had to change shuttles we saw our first wildlife, some mountain goats with their large, distinctive curled horns standing near the road grazing without any concern about the cars and buses passing by and turning into the summit centre. We got off and walked straight onto the next shuttle heading down the valley on the far side.

We changed shuttle again at Avalanche Creek and this time we had to wait for the next shuttle. It was here that we saw a group of Amish or Mennonites with the men in broad straw hats, white shirts and black trousers and beards, whilst the women had traditional head coverings, like wimples and billowing dresses that touched the ground. I was surprised to see them, but not about seeing them as I knew they existed but because they were here and that they go on holiday as well, despite the problems about mixing with modernity and needing a shuttle bus to visit the park. Perhaps I do the organisers a disservice as, through experience from the trip, there are now horse drawn transports available also so that they could see these wonders of nature and not have to compromise on deeply held religious beliefs.

It had taken us well over two hours just to get to Apgar at the end of the lake and onto the far side of the park from our campsite. Here was a little settlement with traditional wooden weatherboard buildings, a café, some houses, a school and a wooden sign above the door proudly claiming the dates of 1915–1958 before it was turned into a souvenir shop. Sigi and Lisa wanted to go paddling on the lake so Paola and I watched them hire a couple of kayaks and set off on the water and we shouted goodbye.

We had a coffee and ice cream while we waited for the next shuttle and neither measured-up to Italian offerings. We got off the shuttle at Avalanche Creek and took the Trail of the Cedars up to Avalanche Lake. It followed the course of a stream that had cut a gorge through the valley side. It was a pleasant if undemanding gradient-wise walk through a forest full of cedars. At the top of the trail the mountains retreated and there was a wide forested bowl with a lake.

The shore was stony and shelved gently with the occasional large rock sticking through the calm surface of the water. The water was clear with some tree trunks and tree roots stranded near the shore and others visible below the surface. We sat down and had a late lunch of sandwiches, surrounded by inquisitive and bold squirrels and chipmunks ever-ready to help themselves to our lunch. We tried to get a few good photographs but in every photo, the background was wrong, the animals didn't co-operate or didn't stand still for that vital moment, the angle wasn't right, the light wrong and so on, so we packed our stuff and walked back down the valley.

We took a shuttle back to the summit. We passed a sign saying, 'Bird Woman Falls 462 feet' which works well on more than one level. Going up the valley we got some magnificent views of the road that was hacked out of the rock and built up in other places. It was truly a Herculean task and truly an engineering feat to be proud of, but every now and again the haze from forest fires spoiled the sharpness of the vista across or along the valley.

It was late in the afternoon and so I didn't linger at the transfer-point at the summit but continued downwards. Paola wanted to indulge in her passion for photography, so she said that she would catch the next shuttle. I left her to take some photos in the evening light while my bus passed through the burnt-out forest that we had passed through on the way up.

After a stop at the campground next to the lake I saw a helicopter with a bucket slung underneath. It circled and dropped its load of water onto a small fire. It went back to the lake and refilled and repeated the operation. Being so close to the campsite and infrastructure, this fire, although small was a high priority but it also meant that another fire somewhere else was being left to burn even more trees, animals' homes or special places and throw yet more smoke and ash into the skies.

CHAPTER 3
Old Faithful

Another even earlier start and we were on the road at seven a.m. That meant getting up at six a.m. to have breakfast, wash and pack both your own tent and help with clearing away the kitchen and packing the back locker. For the cook group, it meant a five thirty a.m. start to have breakfast ready for everyone.

We left the mountains again and were driving through the rolling grasslands of the prairies. We were due for a morning break when we had one thrust upon us a little earlier than we had expected. We were flagged down by a woman in a hi-vis vest. There were roadworks ahead and we had to wait for the pilot car to take us through the work site with its various heavy earthmoving equipment, which would be crossing the road to create a new road, while traffic still had to move through the area to support commerce in the community.

There was not a tree, bush or rock in sight, and there hadn't been for a while and there was unlikely to be one for a while longer. Those that needed to go to the toilet just had to go and if you might be embarrassed then best not to look. Lavatorial positions with some cover were restricted to the right-hand side of the road and most people stood with their back towards this area to admire the rolling grass plains stretching off on the left-hand side of the road.

The pilot car turned up, turned around and we followed it off the tarmac and along a gravel track through the roadworks which consisted of a lot of earth moving equipment straightening out the road and making gentler gradients for the next several kilometres.

By late afternoon we were heading into hills again, dissected by valleys with rivers and slopes covered with trees. We turned up one valley and saw a massive bare scar on the far side of the valley. In the valley bottom were various rocky hillocks with little vegetation.

There had been a landslide here caused by an earthquake in 1980 when the side of the valley collapsed into the river below, creating a natural dam. Behind the rock fall was a lake that had filled up from the river. The river had started to cut through the natural rock dam but progress was slow and so the lake survived. Many of the trees that were previously standing on the valley side were now partially submerged and dead with just their upper trunks and branches sticking out of the water and bleached white by the sun.

It was nearly six p.m. as we entered Yellowstone National Park. The park covers 8,983 square kilometres and at its centre is Yellowstone Lake found in the Yellowstone Caldera, a huge super volcano which is responsible for most of the geothermal features and lava flows in the park. It has exploded with violent force several times in the geological past and the last major eruption was over 600,000 years ago and the next major event is overdue.

There are plenty of things to see whether it is grizzly bears, wolves, and free-ranging herds of bison or elk that live in the park. The bison herd is the oldest and largest public bison herd in the United States. There are several campsites, often booked months or a year in advance and there are plenty of opportunities for trekking, sightseeing, fishing and boating on the many lakes.

It is also the home of Old Faithful who is so faithful that it erupts on schedule every ninety-one minutes and on every day of the year, so we went straight to see her erupt. Yellowstone is widely known, especially as it is the home of Old Faithful, but it has other claims to fame such as it was the world's first national park created in 1872 and it has the highest density of geysers, hot springs, fumaroles and mud pots of any area in the world.

We joined the crowds huddled around her on benches set well-back from the girl herself, partially for safety but also partly to ensure that a lot of people could get that photo. The site is surrounded by forest in a large clearing, and in the middle, is a low dome of white wet deposits from the top of which belches puffs of steam. Shortly after six fifty p.m. there was an increase in the amount of steam being given off and then after a few false starts, she erupted and a long stream of steam shot into the air. It was an incredible and unique sight. After a short display and seemingly no time at all, it was all over and it went back to just a few wisps of steam vapour escaping from a hole. Just ten minutes later the hundreds of people in the surrounding crowds had also vanished as if they had never been there and we were due to leave as well to find our pitches at the Grant Village campsite. From the top of the low dome steam still rose slowly into the cooling evening air to erupt again in ninety-one minutes time with no one to see it.

We were up early and ready to roll by eight a.m. It is such an iconic sight, not to be missed that even the usual and predictable slower members of the group surprised us by being ready to go on time. We were going to have a drive through Yellowstone National Park to see some of the incredible sights that the park boasts.

We had hardly left the campsite when we stopped to watch some bison walking along the edge of the road. Looking a little bizarre with their large hairy heads, complete with goatee beards and horns, big shoulders and incongruously their skinny behinds. Added to the spectacle was the position where we had come across them; directly in front of a sign saying 'caution, wildlife on the road'.

The first planned stop was at Biscuit Basin where there are a lot of hot springs whose different minerals formed colourful formations and a mass of steam rising into the cool morning air. There are boardwalks to give better and safe access to some of the springs and the light wind gently blows the steam across the paths, occasionally obscuring where you are going.

On the far side of Biscuit Basin, we continued up Fairy Creek Trail, a steep climb to the Scenic Outlook and it was worth the effort as from this high up we had a marvellous view of Biscuit Basin and the surrounding countryside and steam rising from the basin and many other springs, forming a rough line running directly away from us.

We then followed a trail and took a turn through the forest and eventually down the hillside to pass Mystic Falls and back to Biscuit Basin. We were spread out in a lengthy line with Sigi, Lisa and myself, being the faster walkers in front and Paola taking photos at the back and lastly Zoë making sure that no one was left behind. It gives a leader no end of problems and rib pulling if she 'losses' a client even though it may be no fault of theirs.

Just up the road was Grand Prismatic Springs and the Excelsior Geyser. Access was by a bridge over the river. As you crossed it you had a view of hot mineral water flowing away from the springs and into the river. Biscuit Basin included several small individual springs and by contrast to others, this one was centred around one large pool. Steam rose from the surface and while the predominant colour was blue there were hints of other colours.

There were more sightings of bison before we made an unscheduled stop at Gibbons Falls on the way to the Norris Geyser Basin with its separate Porcelain Basin, Back Basin and another loop further south. These are several spread-out geysers and hot springs with paths that connect all of them, I would have liked to have stayed longer to have a good look at all of them but we were pressed for time. However, being a faster walker than some of the others, I did get to see all of them but it was more of a flying visit than an opportunity to savour, relax and to enjoy the moment.

The travertines at Mammoth Hot Springs are where several springs have been pouring out hot mineral water for aeons. The cascading mineral rich waters have formed deposits over a huge area. The area boasts the tallest geyser with eruptions up to 91 metres (Old Faithful has a maximum of 56 metres) but with its unpredictable and erratic nature, you could wait a long time. There are more frequent small eruptions but a sign nearby tells of the last large eruption which at the time of my visit, was more than a year earlier.

Tower Fall, named due to the tower-like pinnacles of rock at the top of the waterfall, plunges 40 metres into a gorge before Tower Creek joins the Yellowstone River a kilometre downstream. There is a distinctive and thick layer of basalt which formed vertical columns as it cooled on the far side of the valley. Then the Yellowstone River flows over the Yellowstone Falls into the Grand Canyon of the Yellowstone. This is 39 kilometres long, up to 370 metres deep and at its widest, just 1.2 kilometres wide. This is not 'the' Grand Canyon but the name had been recycled onto several different canyons. Nevertheless, it is still a magnificent sight and on our trip, it was our first 'large' canyon.

We were going down the Loop Road heading south which follows the Yellowstone River when we came across a herd of bison feeding in open grassland by the river. We stopped and took photos and then just watched them. On the other side of the road was an elk standing by the roadside and a ranger near-by to ensure that you didn't get too close.

We skirted Yellowstone Lake and finally reached Grant Village and our campsite. The cook group consisting of Clare who lived in London and was between jobs, Paola and Steve, got to work, but the rest of us all helped or 'relaxed' whilst we chopped veg-etables; if you can call chopping vegetables work.

The 'village' was a collection of houses but also boosted a shop, a tourist information office, a laundrette, and plenty of hot water for showers. They were great facilities, all clustered together and a bit of a walk. That won't worry the locals because they drive everywhere but it is a bit of a hike if you are on foot.

The skies darkened and then the heavens opened and a mas-sive downpour followed with thunder and lightning. It was so quick that we didn't have time to erect the awning but just re-treated to the bus, except for the cook group who hadn't quite finished and had been ambitious about having a main dish and a dessert. They finished cooking in the rain and we rushed out in ones and twos to serve ourselves and rushed back to the security of the bus to get out of the rain. It was only the second time in five months that we had to eat on the bus.

The rain eased-off and clouds cleared during the night and the sky was a clear blue the next morning. There was some fog lingering in the trees but this would be quickly burnt off by the sun. We said farewell to Yellowstone and before leaving Montana, we visited the Grand Teton National Park. The first permanent settlers began arriving in nearby Jackson Hole in the late 1880's and soon after, efforts began to preserve the surrounding area led to the establishment of Grand Teton National Park in 1929 to protect the major peaks of the Teton mountain range. The park is named after the Grand Teton, the highest mountain in the range at 4,199 metres.

The focus for visitors is to see Hidden Falls and Inspiration Point on the far side of the lake. This could be reached directly and effortlessly by boat or by trekking around either side of the lake but we had insufficient time to go around the whole lake and see the waterfall. Paola and I took the clockwise route from the visitor's centre, while Sigi and Lisa took the longer anti-clock-wise route, each planning to come back via the ferry service.

Paola and I had just started an ascent up the valley side besides Moose Ponds when looking down below us, in the small lake was a moose, standing in the water. Every now and again he would dip his head below the surface and pull up some weed, then re-surface and chew on the freshly harvested weed, whilst looking about at the scenery around him. Despite the abundant green grass around the edge of the lake he must have thought that the water weed was tastier. And there was another moose making its way down the slope to the same lake. The lakes were aptly named!

We watched for a while and David caught us up and together we watched the moose chew water weed. Eventually there was some movement from hikers on another trail nearer the lake and the moose moved back into the forest so we went on together. The track undulated across the slopes falling occasionally towards the lake and weaved its way through the forest along the shoreline.

After an hour of walking along the lake-edge we joined a trail that headed up a valley from the wharf where the boats moored. We had not seen anyone on the trail around the lake but the trail up the valley was much busier, with people who had taken the ferry, landing at the mouth of the valley and then making their way up to see Hidden Falls. Viewers stood on one side of the stream and looked across and up at the waterfall as a lot of white water cascaded down the vertical rocky cliff that makes up Hidden Falls.

Retracing our steps, we came to a junction and a wide path that leads off into the forest on a gentle gradient. This is deceptive as some way along the track, the path turns and narrows as it weaves its way up the steep valley slopes, often doubling back on itself in a series of hairpin bends. Some people give up here, as it is quite a steep ascent and a long way to go before you get to the top.

Hidden in the undergrowth to one side of the trail were two moose with their rumps facing the trail. They were so well hidden from below that we didn't see them until we were on top of them. They seemed unconcerned about our presence and didn't give us a second look but, judging by the amount of noise we were making they had known we were coming for some time. If they were in this area and not retreating, they were used to or at least tolerant of tourists.

After an hour of climbing upwards the trail levelled off and left the forest for a clearing on top of the solid rock of the cliff top and Inspiration Point. There was brilliant sunlight, blue skies and a splendid view across the lake. The air was clear and we could see right across to the far side and see the boats coming and going between the two landing stages, bringing more tourists, or taking them back.

This was where we decided to have lunch. We had only just opened our rucksacks to pull out our sandwiches when we were assaulted by hordes of bold squirrels who were determined to make their lunch out of our sandwiches. David was good enough to pose and let them clamber around him, so that Paola and I could take some photos of him with squirrels climbing into his pack or up his leg. We lingered a bit longer than necessary and then due to lack of time, we took the boat back across the lake rather than walking back the way we had come.

At Jackson Hole, our campsite was set well outside of the town near a lake. We set up camp but we weren't going to have a group cook. Several people wanted to see a rodeo so Zoë proposed to drive them into town, where they would have an evening meal as well. Those of us who were left in camp could make an evening meal out of whatever was in the food locker. I was torn between seeing the rodeo and going for a walk and reasoned that there may be other opportunities to see a rodeo yet I might not come back to this spot so I opted for a walk.

The people going to the rodeo got changed and left for town. I said goodbye and followed the path down to the lake to a small cove. Sigi had lost her sunglasses earlier in the day on a trip to the beach, so I kept my eyes open for them as well as wildlife. I walked along the shore and watched a couple of pleasure craft go by, some distance from the shore.

On getting back to the track to go back to the camp, I sat on a beach and watched the sun go down behind the mountains. It was peaceful and a delight to just sit with the noise of an occasional bird or ripple of a wave against the shore. Some ducks swam by and the sky turned a mixture of reds and yellows. All this time, and despite the hundreds of people at the campsite, I had not seen another person on the trail down to or along the lake shore.

We passed through Jackson Hole before the shops were open and above the city there were swathes of grass coming down from the tops of the mountains through the trees. In winter, these are covered with snow and make up some of the great pistes that are on offer to skiers, when this becomes a winter resort destination. We left Wyoming and went through a small section of Idaho, known as the potato state as it grows a lot of potatoes. And true enough, right on cue, there were fields of potatoes lining the roadside.

We crossed the state line into Utah and headed to the capital, Salt Lake City. We passed the Bingham Canyon Mine, also confusingly known as the Kennecott Copper Mine among locals, but nothing to do with the Kennecott mine that we had visited in Alaska. Copper ore was discovered here in 1848 but it was 1863 before some minor ore extraction work started. Its real potential was not appreciated until much later. Major production only started in 1906, but further expansion has continued ever since, and explains why this is the largest man-made hole in the ground, at nearly a kilometre deep and four kilometres wide. It produces copper plus lesser amounts of silver, gold, lead, molybdenum, platinum, palladium and as a side product of the process, sulphuric acid. Environmentalists are concerned about lead, arsenic, mercury and other heavy metal contamination.

In Salt Lake City, we stopped at Temple Square to discover something about the Mormons or the Church of Latter Day Saints, as they are more correctly named. We were shown around the magnificent main temple hall and the adjacent older hall. We were told a lot about the beliefs and history. I won't recall it here but it is freely available on the internet for those who are interested.

The city was founded in 1847 by Brigham Young and his followers as they searched for a place to settle and practice their faith away from the violence and persecution that they faced back east. Today only about half of the city's population are Mormons but the city is still synonymous with the religion.

We left Salt Lake City and crossed a causeway over the Salt Lake itself to Antelope Island. This is incorrectly named for two reasons. Firstly, it is not an island as it is connected to the mainland by the causeway. Secondly, the animal that gives its name to the island is not an antelope, as they are only found in Africa. The animal associated with the island is in fact a pronghorn, more closely related to giraffes and okapis than their distant cousins, the antelope. However, the Pronghorn Promontory is a bit of a mouthful and not so interesting, hence Antelope Island.

Pragmatically, the Salt Lake is not correct either, as salinity within the lake varies, depending significantly upon where and when you measure it but again, 'Briny in Places at sometimes during the Year Lake' doesn't have the same ring about it.

The island is treeless and inhabited by a bison herd that wanders around as individuals rather than as a herd. We pitched our tents and had the site to ourselves. If there were other people about we were wary of the amount of noise we made and didn't have any music but when we were by ourselves, by mutual and majority agreement, we had music whilst we cooked and ate.

There were squared-off and levelled areas for tents and as no one else was camping here that night, we could spread ourselves about. Few people want to be cheek-by-jowl if they don't have to be. By habit, I chose a pitch up the hill away from everyone else, so I didn't have to listen to their midnight walks and calls of nature, their coughing and sneezing, whimpering and snoring and neither did they have to listen to mine.

There was a brilliant sunset with vivid red and yellow hues in the sky as the sun dipped below the horizon and sank into the lake. It was late summer and well past the equinox and we were heading south so now there were sunsets, although it was still dusk for a long time into the evening and there was darkness for a few hours every night.

A sound awoke me, but I was not sure what it was in my initially drowsy state. But suddenly I was alert and trying to make out the unusual sounds and break them down into something I could understand. There was something rustling the grass, some deep, heavy breathing and the sound of something tearing up the grass like a gardener might do when weeding. Then the penny dropped as I heard the unmistakeable sound of an animal chewing. I peeped out of my tent fly and sure enough not two metres away was the rump of a bison having a midnight feast next to my tent.

I thought through the options; if it is a moose, you run away and so do they. Bears you avoid confrontational eye-contact and back-off. Regarding caribou, such as I had had running at me at an earlier confrontation at our bush camp at McCarthy; I had subsequently been reminded that if you make enough noise and flap your arms they usually avoid you. Bison? They are big beasts and prone to random stampeding away from unexpected noises and you might feel especially vulnerable if you are lying on the ground in a sleeping bag, looking up at one, just two metres away.

They are meant to be stupid and frightened of sudden sustained noise and activity such as vigorous arm-waving but, had he read the book? I thought that if I left him alone, he would leave me alone and my tent was bigger than he was, so I retreated and lay there, listening to him eating grass until he shuffled away out of earshot... but I kept listening in case he was making a feint and would circle back. I didn't have a good night's sleep that night.

I was awoken at dawn to see the darkness of night give way to a blue sky tinged with red and turning to vermillion across the sky, and then being dazzled by the bright yellow sun as it emerged above the horizon; all in the space of just thirty minutes. We passed a bison as we made our way off the island and I wondered whether it was the same one that had robbed me of my sleep. I am sure it was, because he had the same four legs, big head and a long beard with a smug, satisfied look on his face, having got one-over on one of the many tourists that plague his natural existence.

We continued our drive south through Utah to Moab where the road shared a valley with a set of railway tracks. I kept my eyes open but didn't see any trains. The valley opened out onto a plateau with distant hill tops surrounding us on all sides. There was a sign proclaiming 'prevent wildfires' which seemed a bit incongruous as there was nothing in this patch of desert to burn.

Another sign announced a turnoff to the UMTRA Project, part of the Department of Energy. This stands for the Uranium Mining Tailings Rehabilitation Administration which is spending billions trying to tidy up and make the environment safe after decades of uranium mining for atomic weapons as well as peaceful purposes. We continued until the mountains moved in on the road and the rocks turned red.

We had reached Moab in the early afternoon and our campsite was next to the office of an RV park on the outskirts of town. The ground had been levelled and some soil put on top. The area had been scattered with meadow seeds so that the resulting thick sward which benefited from frequent watering provided a well cushioned and comfortable base, with the added benefit that the pegs were easy to drive home. There was ample hot water and the showers were free for seven minutes, more than enough time to wash thoroughly when you have been used to cold showers or paying for two or a maximum of four minutes at other campsites.

There was a lot to see there so we wasted no time in getting out to Arches National Park, just down the road. To get to the park itself we had to drive up the side of the valley to reach the plateau above. On the way, up to the plateau we had a pleasant view across the valley to the railway track that runs along the far side of the valley, that had not escaped my attention earlier in the day. However, there would be no trains running along this track for a few days.

On the gradient running up out of town, a train had broken down. A coupling had broken and a number of wagons had rolled backwards, leaving the two locomotives at the front coupled to half of the train and the other half separated by a hundred metres. The break-away rear section had been halted by the brake van at the back of the train. There were some maintenance vehicles with flashing orange lights by the side of the tracks, so engineers were on-hand but it wasn't going to be fixed any time soon.

Betsy struggled up the gradient and the hairpin bends and finally made it on to the plateau. It was still a fair way to drive but we stopped at the Balancing Rock. This was as the name suggested, a large boulder balanced on a thin pinnacle of rock. One side was jutting out so much further than the other sides it did look like an impossibility for it to be able to exist.

In the distance, we saw patches of sky peeking through what was otherwise a cliff face. Here were the North and South Arches. We left the bus in the car park for a short walk up to the arches. There are stone arches in other parts of the world but these are some of the biggest. There are other formations such as Turret and Double Arch and it is a wonder how nature can create such beauty.

Becky, a good-natured Australian who had joined us in Banff had bought a stuffed cuddly toy, a rat with a long pink tail with a rucksack on its back, hence its name Packrat. Packrat started turning up in pictures and posing for camera shots in front of some of the best locations for tourist photos. Soon he became a celebrity with everyone taking photos of Packrat with some of the arches behind him, but the finale was still to come.

Further along a wide shallow valley on the plateau was another arch that can be best seen from the road on the far side of the valley or viewed up-front and personal, but needing a trek uphill. It is known as the Delicate Arch. And at sunset, this was a popular time as it is alleged you can see the sun set through the arch. People are ever hopeful of achieving this, but the skies must be clear and depending on the time of year, you need to know the exact spot; turning up and hoping to move about to catch that spot might mean you are stranded on one side of a gorge with the perfect spot just a hundred metres away as the crow flies but several kilometres to reach on foot and no time.

Seb drove the bus up the road whilst Zoë, Paola, David, Laurence and I took the trekking option. It was early evening and the worst of the day's heat had gone so it was pleasant. The arch sits on one side of a U-shaped bowl in plain view, high above the valley and is approached from behind one of the arms of the U, so that there is no glimpse of it until you reach the rim and then standing in front of you in all its magnificence, is the Delicate Arch.

It is not just the arch of rock that makes this a unique arch, but the surrounding walls that would have formed part of the supporting structure have also been eroded, so it is just a natural arch of two columns and the top stone. There were dozens of people here to see the sunset. Everyone wanted a picture of just themselves and the arch. Off to one side standing in a neat orderly line were the hopefuls. They took it in turns to walk forward and stand under the arch for their friends to take that photo, whilst everyone else stood well back.

There was no ranger, no railings and no signs; people had just formed themselves into some form of order. The lack of signs or railings preserved the special feeling of the place, despite long drops and steep slopes. Zoë dropped her water bottle and it bounced and rolled down a long slope, for minutes until it disappeared over the edge far below, so best not to slip just here otherwise you might follow the bottle into oblivion.

We had our photos and after a long day of clear skies there were clouds building between us and the sun, as it gradually moved down towards the horizon. The weather wasn't going to be just right for that perfect sunset photo through the arch, so we set off back down the trail and back to camp.

CHAPTER 4

Canyons

It was another warm and sunny morning as we made our way to Canyonlands National Park. En-route we stopped off at the Island in the Sky State Park which abuts Canyonlands. The Colorado River and a major tributary, the Green River meandered across the ancient landscape and then started eroding its riverbed to form a deep canyon.

The Island in the Sky State Park is one of these former meanders with vertical canyon walls around most of the top, but with a long narrow waist of land to connect the top of the meander to the plateau. There are great views up and down the canyon, the high walls exposing different strata of rocks; the curves of the canyon and the muddy brown waters of the Colorado filling the bottom of the canyon. And of course photos of Packrat with a canyon in the background.

The natural terrain was put to good work by cowboys as the neck was easy to fence and the cliffs of the canyon all around formed a natural barrier. Feral horses would be rounded up and herded onto the Island in the Sky. Then they would be separated and the good ones pulled out of the herd for domestication. Unfortunately, the horses thought to be too weak, old, or feral to be domesticated were competition for the scrubby pasture and would be left to die, stranded on the island.

On 24th May 1869, Major John Wesley Powell, a geology professor and a one-armed veteran of the Civil War set off with four boats and nine oarsmen to travel down and chart the Green and Colorado Rivers. Three months later on 30th August 1869 the expedition finished at what is now the downstream end of Lake Mead. He had lost two boats and three men but had a detailed knowledge of this unique landscape and a story to tell the world.

We visited Grand View Point, the viewpoint over Buck Canyon on the Green River. We walked up a trail to the rim of Upheaval Dome. This is a circular hole in the ground with jagged edges and a small conical mound at the bottom. There are two schools of thought as to its origin. One is that it is a meteorite crater. But this doesn't explain the angled rock strata and there have been no meteorite fragments found, easy to do as they are heavy and magnetic and a valuable ore for steelmaking so people would have been looking for it.

The alternative is that it is a salt dome. There was an inland sea here that became landlocked and it evaporated, leaving a thick layer of salt. Over time, more sediments were deposited on top and the weight of these sediments above the friable salt pushed it down and the salt slowly moved up through a weak point, deforming layers of rocks around it. People like a mystery but to me it's a clear case of a salt dome.

Nearby and another short walk from the road was the opportunity to view another wonder of nature. Mesa Arch is another gently curving rock arch set on top of a cliff. The cliff immediately behind it has eroded leaving a deep chasm between the two. The arch is parallel to and only a few metres from the solid cliff face but it has a drop of over a hundred metres below it.

After a long hot day, it was time to head back to our campsite. There was a treat in store that we had kept secret. It was Lisa's birthday and as a surprise after our evening meal we had a cake topped with candles and we all sung happy birthday. Over the meal we had a chance to chat about what we had planned for the next day. This was a free day, always useful on a long trip, to ensure that should something delay the journey for whatever reason, there is a spare day so that we can catch up and get back on schedule or if nothing drastic had happened, it was a day to relax and do whatever you wanted to do. I had decided to walk into town to see what there was in Moab. It is a functioning town with all the facilities that you might need, but nothing in the way of a traditional old centre with lots of history. I passed a sign announcing Norm's barber shop. I had noticed that I was getting a bit shaggy having left home several months previously and had not had a haircut since, so I just had to go in and have my haircut.

We had agreed to meet up as a group mid-afternoon and go for a walk and a swim in a local swimming hole up a valley that we had been told about by the campsite manager. We found the road and parked Betsy in the car park and then started the walk up the valley. It had been a hot bright day and the valley was hot and bathed in the afternoon sun. The valley started wide at its mouth but soon narrowed. The path was squeezed into the little piece of ground between the walls of the canyon and the stream, which we had to ford a few times as the path wound its way up the canyon. Then we came to the first pool with steep sides, a few rocks piled across the outlet to increase the depth of the pool and a waterfall three or four metres high.

Retracing our steps and taking a rocky path up the other side of the canyon brought you out to the more open area above the waterfall, another pool and some cascades. We changed into our swimming things and relaxed in the sun or sat in the pool to cool off and have a drink or two that we had brought with us.

We were joined in the pool by a local crayfish who was patrolling his patch. He was safe from the pot as he was too small but still his claws looked big enough to give a nasty nip. Those amongst us who were brave such as Sigi and Zoë jumped in from the cliff edge above the waterfall. To get back up for another go was a scramble up the side of the waterfall.

Meanwhile, Laurence went off to look for some petroglyphs that were further up the valley. Paola, Megan and Clare had found a sunny patch near the lower pool to relax in. Tracey was wading across the upper pool with a drink in her hand and slipped and fell in the water. She hadn't intended going for a swim so she was still in her clothes but she stood up again and in true Aussie style had not spilt a drop of her drink.

Back in town we stopped at Milt's for our evening meal. This was a diner originally set up in the 1950's and was virtually unaltered, offering a range of traditional American food. It had been on the edge of town but the town had expanded around it and now it seemed to be in the middle of a housing estate and you wouldn't find it unless you knew it was there. A decade ago it might have seemed old and tired but now that retro is back in fashion it is iconic. It was also a popular place with locals and tourists alike and every table was taken.

Every day we would have a briefing and be told, what we are doing, where we are going and when, and therefore what we needed to pack, whether we needed to make sandwiches for a pack lunch, whether we were camping or in hostels, whether upgrades were available, which would have to be booked in advance and the like. Steve and David had both forgotten and were too scared of Zoë to ask her to repeat herself. I couldn't remember either but wasn't concerned as I would roll with the punches and see what happens.

They were too scared to ask themselves but they put me up to standing in the firing line and asking her on their behalf, provided I didn't mention them by name. I interrupted Zoë doing one of her many chores around the truck and asked for a recap on the next day's schedule. I did my best to listen to the answer but was distracted by the sight of Steve and David trying to hide behind a telegraph pole just two metres behind Zoë while their faces peered out from behind the pole like two naughty schoolboys.

The answer and the next day's plan was that we were to drive 250 kilometres across the desert to Monument Valley. We stopped for lunch at a small town and I went up the road for a walk around town while most of the others went for a burger at the crossroads. There was a supermarket and garage at the main crossroads and I went in, after my walk, to get something to drink such as beer for the evening. It was more than just a supermarket as inside there was a fast food outlet and a bowling alley. Zoë, Seb, Steve and Tracey were spending their lunchtime playing bowls.

On the approach to Monument Valley we stopped opposite another distinctive balancing rock set well back from the road. It was a long thin rock which was sitting on a pedestal whose thickness was just a tenth of the width of the rock above. It was here that the scene from Forrest Gump was filmed where Forrest was told to 'Run, Forrest, run' and this is the road that he runs down.

We arrived at the visitor centre but it was shut, as confusingly, a new one has been built further into the park at the base of the mountains, but the maps and signs had yet to catch up with reality. From the new visitor centre, there are some magnificent views of the buttes and mesas made famous as they were used for backdrops of so many movies, starting with several John Ford and John Wayne movies.

We grabbed our overnight bags from the bus and got into two jeeps for a guided jeep tour around Monument Valley Tribal Park and to see some of the incredible formations. First stop was a native village, more of a string of adobe houses left over from a film set where there were hosts of tourist trinkets to be had and horses for hire. Next, we went by jeep and for me, unfortunately not by horse, into the interior with our guides past springs, more buttes and curiously smoothed boulders to arrive at a native village. Here, there were several hogans or houses made by the Navajo Indians and used as permanent houses.

From the outside, they appear as steep-sided mud domes with a door. Inside you can see the walls were made from sections of timber standing upright with their bases buried in the sand. On top is a lattice work of logs resting on each other and working their way into the centre of the hogan giving the roof the shape of the inside of a pyramid. At the apex was a small hole to allow smoke to escape. The whole wooden structure was covered with mud. This stands for considerable effort as there are no trees in the area so these had to be cut, shaped and transported here from outside the desert.

Inside one of these was a mother and daughter in traditional dress making jewellery and weaving fabrics with traditional patterns. We were told something about the Navajo view of the buttes and mesas, their beliefs and culture, their way of life and how they survived here. They were initially hunter-gatherers that lived peacefully alongside existing tribes. When the Spanish arrived in the 1800s, the Navajo acquired horses, thus becoming a powerful and dominant tribe in the area.

The fabrics, mostly mats and wall hangings were patterned but also told a story and once you knew the language and what the patterns meant, you could 'read' each piece. At night, the jewellery and fabrics were packed away and the hogan was available to sleep in, which is where we would be sleeping that night.

First, we had more of the park to see, stopping at the Big Hogan. This is a natural formation set into the side of a cliff face and resembles a giant hogan cut in half, over 40 metres high, 25 metres wide at the mouth and 10 metres deep complete with a circular hole in the roof, all formed by nature. It had good acoustics and our Navajo guide had brought along a couple of traditional instruments and sang some songs.

There were also other arches, pinnacles and petroglyphs to see before we stopped in the shade of a cliff for our evening entertainment around a camp fire. We had a meal and then were treated to some songs and dancing by Navajos in traditional dress and had an opportunity to join in. We were taken back to the hogans and we could sleep in the open under the stars or choose one of two hogans. It promised to be a warm clear night so along with Steve and Laurence, I opted to sleep under the stars, outside one of the hogans.

In the middle of the night it started to rain. I ignored it as it wasn't too heavy, but suddenly Steve shouted out, "Hey Norman, it's raining, we're getting wet!" and he started to gather his things to get inside the hogan. I tried waking Laurence but he grunted, rolled over and went back to sleep. I had been in the hogan for all of five minutes, but would never get any sleep as Gabi was snoring like a steam engine. I decided it might be better to sleep outside if the rain wasn't too heavy. Luckily it was easing off so I took a chance and went back outside.

We woke up early to see the sun rise and started to pack our things away. I was taking my gear to the jeep when I came across Steve's laptop lying in the dust. He had dropped it during his relocation into the hogan out of the rain last night and hadn't yet noticed it was missing. A little later I found his wallet as well which is testament to his scramble to get out of the rain.

We climbed a ridge and waited to see the sun rise at a spot which was famous for its spectacular sunrises. The rain clouds had thinned but had not dispersed and so it just got lighter and we didn't see the sun come up above the horizon and shine across this amazing landscape. It was more of a bright yellow glow behind some thin clouds so we were driven back to Betsy and crossed into Arizona and through Page. We stopped at the Carl Hayden Visitor centre at the dam that creates Lake Powell, named after Major John Wesley Powell. I wanted to take the tour of the dam but the tour times didn't fit with our schedule but there would be another opportunity for a dam tour later the trip.

Our purpose-built campground with ample facilities was over-looking Lake Powell. There was a gently sloping sandy beach with all kinds of pleasure craft moored out on the water. We cooled off in the pleasantly warm waters and passed the time sunbathing or playing Frisbee and catch ball in the water. Then it was off to see Antelope Slot Canyon. We were the last tour of the day so after the tour group in front had gone we would have the place to ourselves and early evening is the best time when the light is just right.

There was a wide shallow valley up in the hills which suddenly thins to a deep very narrow canyon, sometimes just wide enough for two people to pass before emerging at the base of a cliff into a wide, flat bottomed valley full of sand washed down from the valley above and cut out of the canyon. We got onto our four-wheel-drive vehicles at the Antelope Slot Canyon Tour Company's offices in Page, on seats facing outwards and strapped ourselves in. We set off at breath-taking speed out of town into the desert, off the main road and down a rocky track and finally onto the sandy wadi floor for a bumpy ride, to stop at the entrance to the slot canyon.

The professional photos of the canyon are remarkable, with their subtle play of light and dark, sun and shadow, and a host of reds, oranges and yellows that play off the sandy walls of the canyon. The reality is just as good and vivid. Our guide Lillian who was also the owner of the company that organises tours here took us up the canyon. We stopped often for formations to be pointed out. All the way along there were formations that resembled famous people and locations such as Abraham Lincoln, Monument Butte, George Washington, the Taj Mahal and a host of other well-known landmarks.

The last flash flood had lowered the floor of the canyon by over a metre, so we could stand to see some of the likenesses rather than lie on the ground like last season's guests had had to do. Gabi asked where did all the sand go? Which we had just been told had been washed out of the canyon into the wadi below. It was a wonderful experience but over all too soon. We got back onto the vehicles and we had another mad dash across the desert collecting a few more bruises from being thrown around in the back before reaching our more sedate and in comparison, comfortable Betsy style of transport.

CHAPTER 5

Escape from Vegas

We left Arizona and headed west back into Utah for a long drive. We stopped by some hoodoos on the R12 in the Dixie National Forest and took some pictures of them. And of course, Packrat, on top of the bus, by the tyres, under the windscreen wipers and on the bumper. Some other travellers that had also stopped looked on in bewilderment. What was it that these adults found so amusing about a cuddly toy? It was just something to help pass the time and a bit of light relief on a long drive. I think it was Steve that told them that we are only allowed out with our minders once a month.

We arrived at the visitors' centre at Bryce Canyon National Park at lunchtime and got our tickets and maps then headed off to the start of some of the trails at Sunset Point and as usual, naturally split into smaller groups. I was with David and Paola walking along the rim of Bryce's Canyon. This is not actually a canyon but in fact is a giant natural amphitheatre created by erosion along the eastern side of the Paunsaugunt Plateau.

Erosion has cut into the soft sandstones and created a mass of hoodoos of all shapes and sizes. The sandstone is also multi-coloured from various minerals in the different strata ranging from browns, reds and oranges through yellows to whites. The colours also change in intensity when the sun shines on them and we had magnificent views down on them from the rim of the bowl, especially from Inspiration Point where there is a purpose-built viewing platform. We walked on up the rim to Bryce's Point next to the peak at 2,539 metres.

These three points on the rim and other stops throughout the park are connected by tour bus so it was not surprising that they were crowded, but few people seemed interested in walking from one to the other so the paths in between were in contrast quiet.

It had started to rain, so instead of walking down the trail to see the hoodoos close-up we caught the bus back to Sunset Point, by which time the rain had eased off but it had also thinned the crowds. The plan from here on, was to descend into the bowl to follow the Navajo Loop and Queen's Garden Trail to emerge at Sunrise Point and back to Betsy.

The trail down is dramatic as it is quite steep and follows a cleft void of vegetation with steep sandy side walls as it weaves its way down to the floor of the bowl. At the bottom, it is a gentle walk along a stream bed. We made a short diversion up the Peekaboo Trail to get views of some of the hoodoos and other formations before turning around back onto our planned route. We passed a formation called Queen Victoria and it does bear an uncanny resemblance in outline, to Queen Victoria sitting on her throne.

We climbed out of the bowl and headed back to what we thought was the right way, only to discover that we were lost or not in the right place, although we had a map. We asked directions to ensure that we were correctly oriented and ended up being offered a lift which we thankfully accepted, not because we were tired but because I for one, hate being late and would not want to miss our scheduled departure time and delay the rest of the group. That would be both rude and inconsiderate.

We were dropped off next to Betsy with only minutes to spare, only to find that some of the others had yet to turn up. We had not been able to book camping spaces in Bryce's Canyon and so had had to move on to Kodachrome Basin State Park. It was named by the 1948 National Geographic Society expedition after the new brand of Kodak film that they had used. Its official name was Chimney Rock State Park, chosen after fearing lawsuits from the company by using one of their brand names but renamed Kodachrome Basin a few years later with Kodak's permission. It is a pleasant enough area but after the spectacular Monument Valley the day before and Bryce's Canyon, it would always be a struggle to be in the same league but it had its own charms.

From Kodachrome State Park, we drove into Zion National Park. The Native American Paiute people originally inhabited this area but in 1863 Mormons fleeing religious persecution on the eastern seaboard had been moving west and had settled in the area and had called it their Zion. There are many great treks within Zion with amazing formations and scenery, colours that change, depending on the time of day, cliffs that tower above you and steep trails that never seem to end.

There is a long tunnel to negotiate to get up to the visitors' centre and in the early morning rush hour there was a delay. The tunnel can only handle traffic one way at a time, so it is a bit of a bottleneck but it is the only way in and out of the park by road. All the way up was scenic and could be viewed from the comfort of the bus. At the visitors centre we were free to choose which path we wanted to follow or to just sit and relax in the sun next to the gift shop, café and bar.

I wanted to see as much as possible so I took the shuttle bus up to the furthest extent of the valley before returning to the visitors' centre. I wanted to go up a challenging path to get a view down the valley and with me were David, Paola and Zoë. It was a steep climb and whenever you looked back down the trail, the path hair pinned many times to get up the slope. Paola was indulging herself in her passion for photography and we had to wait several times for her to catch up, but it gave us the chance for a breather on the way up.

After a succession of steep climbs interspersed with more gentle gradients we had reached the top and a leisurely walk along the edge of the canyon. I don't have a good head for heights but I am told that there are some fantastic views across and along the valley with its many different types of rock face, colours and slopes. I was content to view them from the safety of a few steps back from the edge of a drop into the abyssal depths but the views were still fantastic.

We trekked down from our eyrie and drove back through the tunnel to our campsite in Virgin. It was a great campsite overlooking a river with a swimming pool, but as I was part of the cook group with Tracey and Becky, we had to prepare and cook our evening meal so I didn't get a chance to have a swim.

As a member of the cook group preparing breakfast, we had to be up even earlier than everyone else. It wasn't cold but it was still dark and we had a job to do as there is no one worse than a tired hungry camper whose food is not ready at the allotted time. We had decided to cook pancakes for breakfast.

As a team, we were one short as Becky didn't 'do' mornings and was never seen until fifteen minutes before the scheduled departure time but she was never late. I didn't mind as she was easy-going but still did more than her fair share at the evening meal and I was aware of her eccentricities. We all have our individualities but it depends on whether they are disruptive or offensive as to whether they cause resentment and bad will... and whether the individual is aware of their effect on others and can make the necessary adjustments, alternative arrangements, apologises etc.

I was delighted with my ability to toss pancakes. If you get the temperature right and have decent hand-eye co-ordination it is easy to flip or toss a pancake and I did everyone without missing or the pancake ending up as a pile of glop in the frying pan. But then again practice makes perfect but oddly, whilst I enjoy cooking them, I don't enjoy eating pancakes, whatever the topping maybe.

There is maple syrup and then there is maple syrup. The most often found products are made from corn starch and sugar. Having Zoë on board, a French Canadian with a good palate who knew her food, I would only notice the difference when you got the real thing made from maple sap and the cheap generic product to taste, side by side. The real thing may be ten times the price but it is more than ten times better and I was instantly converted to the real thing.

We were on the road by eight a.m. for the drive to Las Vegas or just Vegas as it is popularly known, locally. We drove through the outskirts and along 'the strip' and arrived at lunchtime. We were to have a break from camping for the next two nights and the chance to enjoy a bed. We were early so we drove all along the strip, yet again to the far end past all the well-known names plus a host of others that weren't so well-known but all making money out of the punter in the middle of the desert.

There was a giant Coca Cola bottle, and reproductions of the Eiffel Tower, of the New York skyline and of a pyramid. There was Venice, the Caribbean and ancient Rome represented by Caesar's Palace. We stopped at the far end of the strip for that special photo with Elvis Presley under the Las Vegas welcome sign, along with his twin brother, also called Elvis, who is alive and well and looking very young and posing for photos with anyone who will slip him a few bucks.

We pulled into the MGM Grand where Zoë had been able to spread some of her magic and had got all of us upgrades. Although horribly overcrowded for my taste it still had a buzz. There were shops, fast food outlets, swimming pools with slides and areas for sun bathing and relaxing, so you might never need to leave the air-conditioned comfort of the MGM Grand.

And of course, the whole purpose of the entire city, wherever you looked, there were slot machines and gaming tables and electronic games of chance of every description, to provide you with entertainment but of course also to fleece you of your hard-earned cash. Whether it was the dance halls up in Dawson more than a century ago or the modern electronic one-armed bandit, people have always seemed willing to work hard and then blow it for a fun time.

I was sharing a room with Laurence but he had booked a stretch-limo ride with some of the rest of the group for that evening so I didn't see him. On offer was a ride along the strip with all its neon lights in the stretch-limo with champagne on ice and a party on the inside. The girls had made a heroic effort to dress up with their best flattering, revealing dresses with full make up and had ordered in total, more than a bottle of champagne each. Zoë was dressed in a tight fitting cat suit and nothing else and was stunning. Laurence was the only male on the trip and had had a shower and a bottle of beer

There were seven girls plus Laurence, all out for a good night, plus more champagne bought as the trip progressed, more than the originally ordered bottles. The limo cruised up and down the strip and stopped occasionally to investigate some of the better-known places on offer for the evening. I am not sure that this is a tour for a couple or a family but with a group of friends out for a fun time, this is a must-do activity. I was gutted in retrospect that I had not joined them in what must have been the party of a lifetime.

Meanwhile all I had done was to walk down the strip and found it to be hot and uncomfortable, so I had ducked into various malls and hotels to benefit from the air-conditioning. I had seen some of the sights from the outside, but my heart wasn't in it to do the tourist trail. I had been offered some incredible deals on tickets to shows at a tenth or less of the published prices but despite the outrageous offers, I was not tempted even to see Derren Brown for just USD10. Each to their own.

As night drew in, the neon signs came into their own to light up the strip as if it were still daytime. They are worth a look just for their outrageousness. The sights seen in the day take on a whole new meaning at night and I had to retrace my steps to see the differences between the daylight viewing and the night time viewing.

There had been a light rain during the night and it had washed some of the fine particles out of the air. It was going to be a bright summer's day without the haze. Vegas owes its growth to the Hoover Dam which brought a large supply of construction workers into the area at the same time as the Nevada Government legalised gambling. I had missed seeing the dam at Page so I had booked myself onto a tour of the Hoover Dam and a cruise on Lake Mead created by the dam.

The construction of the dam was started in 1931 and finished in 1936, two years ahead of schedule. Its aim was to control flooding on the lower river, to provide water for both drinking and irrigation and to generate hydroelectric power. There are various tours and combinations on offer and as I had missed out at Page, I went for everything, the visitor centre, the museum, the power plant, inside the dam and across the top.

A lift took us down into the dam itself but we still had a way to go to tour some of the tunnels, both inside the dam and along some of the tunnels through the rock that gave access to all the areas that engineers needed to reach. The turbine hall was massive with turbines stretching off into the distance. There was a dull hum as water rushed through the turbines generating electricity. Power generated here is transmitted across the whole western area of the USA.

The top of the dam used to carry the main road but a new bridge has been built just down river from the dam. Having seen the dam from the land, next I boarded a boat for a cruise on Lake Mead behind the dam which promised views up to the dam from the water. The harbour is a floating harbour a few kilometres away from the dam, reached along a floating walkway on pontoons, as although the dam controlled the water level it can still fluctuate. Judging by the marks high on the rock walls surrounding the water, the current water level was quite low.

The boat was built in the form of a sternwheeler and although the paddles turned, it was only for effect as the major form of propulsion was by propeller. Lunch was included and served as soon as we had left the harbour.

There was a running commentary about the river, the dam, the history of both the local Indians, the early exploration of the area and the building of the dam. It was thorough and comprehensive although there was so much to take in that it was almost overwhelming. The sun was intense and only a few people stayed on deck, most preferring the shade below decks where there was still a magnificent view.

We navigated along the lake and soon we were in a canyon with high walls on either side. Around a bend we came face to face with the upstream concrete face of the dam and high behind it the new bridge spanning the canyon. Earlier that morning I had been up there looking down. Now I was just a small speck on the water between tall canyon walls looking up at the massive face of the dam. It was inspiring for tourists and awesome for engineers and builders.

On the way back to Vegas we stopped at Ethel M's, an up-market chocolate factory set up by Forrest Mars, the owner of Mars. Having made a fortune out of mass produced chocolate, he set this up for the top end market. At the top of the factory he made a home so he could oversee his new project (ever the canny billionaire also for advantageous tax reasons) but his wife insisted on a garden.

This being an arid area, she planted a cactus garden, hence opposite the factory is the Botanical Cactus Garden. It is a fascinating collection of different cacti, each carefully labelled and looked after. It seemed a bit incongruous to have a chocolate factory with a house on top next to a cactus garden but when you are rich you can indulge yourself. In the factory shop, not only does it sell chocolates that are produced at the factory, it also has on offer every colour of Smarties now known internationally as M&Ms. The Ms stand for the founders of the business, Forrest Mars and Bruce Murrie, his business partner whose father was William Murrie, president of Hershey.

After a swim in one of the hotel's several swimming pools on offer, that evening, I walked along the strip to the far end to see the sights that I had missed the night before. It was humming with activity and the smell of eager anticipation of ever-hopeful punters. I never did have a go on the tables or the endless rows of slot machines. But I had even got up in the middle of the night just to see what was happening at three a.m. and the place was still humming with people out on the street, traffic on the roads and punters feeding slot machines.

In the morning, we waited for Seb to return with the bus that had been parked in a truck park on the outskirts of town. On the main floor of the casino, there were still some bleary- eyed punters sitting in front of gaming machines, hoping for a change in their fortunes. We had to wait a bit longer than expected as Betsy wouldn't start, as the fridge had been left on and had drained the battery. It took a while for Seb to get help from another truck driver who had some jump leads to start her.

We left Vegas and followed the famous Route 66 which was first named in 1926. This starts in Chicago, Illinois and travels west through Missouri, Kansas, Oklahoma, Texas, New Mexico, Arizona and finishes in Santa Monica in California. It was a popular tourist route to take but also for migrants from the industrial east seeking new and better lives in the west. It features in John Steinbeck's 'The Grapes of Wrath' with poor farmers escaping the dust bowls of Oklahoma in the 1930's. It also features in several songs, both from the period and contemporary popular music such as 'Get your kicks on Route 66'.

We stopped for lunch in Kingman. We found an iconic diner straight from the 50s called Mr D'z painted pink and blue with a couple of old pickups and several old motorbikes parked outside. Inside was loads of 50s and 60s memorabilia, posters, all types of old coke bottles, old toy cars and dummies dressed as Elvis and James Dean. The menu had traditional root beer and sarsaparilla but unfortunately it had modern prices.

Opposite was a double tracked railway that I had watched while eating my lunch. It was a busy line with several trains going past in both directions, all with BNSF logos, Burlington Northern and Santa Fe Railway, an amalgam of over 390 lines created over 160 years. I started counting wagons but none was bigger than 139 wagons which was some way short of my personal record.

I had noticed something else that I had not been recording. One train had five locomotives at the front (but shorter at 98 wagons) and another had four at the front and two at the back (yet was only just a bit longer at 103 wagons). I realised that it is to do with weight but I would still like to know all the criteria which determine why some trains are made up differently.

There is a new straighter road from Kingman to Seligman via Route 40 but we took the old Route 66. Along its length there are a wealth of themed stops. The first one we stopped at was in Hackberry. It was a general store and outside were 1950s style petrol pumps, enamel signs, old cars in various states of repair, an open-sided garage and an Indian mannequin sitting by the door. Inside were collections of road signs, number plates, pictures of

Elvis, a juke box and dummies in period costumes. It was more of a museum than a café or store. We drove through several other villages, lost in time but our next stop was in a small town of Seligman and it too had several shops with the 50s and 60s period theme of Route 66 when it was at its peak. More old vehicles, enamel signs, etc

Then, in the early evening we reached the Grand Canyon National Park. Carved by the Colorado River, The Grand Canyon is over 440 kilometres long, up to 28 kilometres wide and over a kilometre and a half deep making it one of the largest canyons in the world and allowing it to justifiably call itself grand. The canyon is one of the most famous natural sights in North America and is on everyone's list of places to see. Rather than pitching tents at the camp site we went straight to a lookout over the canyon to see the sun set.

The setting sun bathed the canyons walls in bright sunlight and made the colours even more dazzling. It was a spectacular sight but as the sun dipped below the horizon it was all over. We were awestruck by the breadth and depth of this truly Grand Canyon. We had seen the canyons in Canyonlands but this was so much bigger; so big it was difficult to take it all in.

A few people from the group had opted to take a flight across the canyon and they left before sunrise to be taken to the aerodrome nearby. The rest of the group had a leisurely breakfast and caught the shuttle bus to the main centre. Then we caught another shuttle bus out to where some of the treks started. Thus, I found myself with Clare and Megan walking along the edge of the Grand Canyon towards Hermit's Rest with stunning views of the gaping slash across the landscape, or a big hole in the ground as I had jokingly called it.

There were birds of prey soaring above us on the thermals rising alongside the canyon walls. We passed the site of the Orphan Mine. Dan Hogan discovered copper ore here in 1891 and built a mine to extract the copper ore. He ceased mining in 1936 and built a hotel which became the Grand Canyon Inn which still trades today. Uranium ore was confirmed here in 1951 and as one the richest ore bodies in the USA, was mined here from 1956 to 1969. A 600-room hotel was also proposed to be built here with tiers of rooms down the slope with each room facing the canyon. Luckily this was never built but it is hard to appreciate that an eyesore of a hotel or a mine could ever be built today in such a breath-taking example of natural wonder.

We reached the furthest extent of the trail and caught the shuttle bus back to the visitor's centre. Clare and Megan went to find some lunch and to go shopping and I went for a trek along the canyon rim eastwards. I wanted to see as much of the canyon as I could but then I had discovered that I was suffering from FOMO. I wasn't familiar with the expression but as Megan explained, it was a 'fear of missing out'.

I was also diagnosed as suffering from FORO, a 'fear of running out' so that when estimating how much of something I needed, I would estimate and add on a bit for good measure... hence FORO. Megan had worked in an IT call centre and in a separate conversation, the most common resolution was to ask the user whether they had tried to reboot. It seemed to work quite often. They also had to keep records of the problems that users faced. The most common was where the hardware was working fine and it was politically incorrect to claim operator error so they put problems down to PEBUK...'problem existed between user and keyboard'.

I made my way back to the campsite avoiding the caribou grazing nearby the tents. Laurence is a geocache hunter so with Zoë and I, we went to find a cache that was just a short distance away from the camp. We found the spot with the help of Laurence's GPS but we couldn't find the actual cache. There were several dead trees and the cache could have been hidden in any one of a dozen little nooks and crannies but try as we might, we couldn't find it. It was my first but unsuccessful geocache hunt.

We had a drive day to get further south towards the Mexican border but we had a few more nights in the USA. We were heading south via Flagstaff, the capital of Arizona. Nearby, but not on our schedule was the impact site of a meteor that hit the Earth millions of years ago. Several people had expressed an interest in it and it wasn't too far off our intended route, but no one wanted to suggest a detour to our leader, Zoë. It was down to me again to put my head on the block. They knew I was going to ask and Steve and David positioned themselves behind Zoë, hiding behind a corner of the bus with just their heads peaking past the corner as I proposed a change in plan to Zoë to see the crater.

The detour would take a while and delay our planned arrival at the next campsite. It could also affect the plans of the cook group and therefore, in true democratic fashion it was put to the vote and the majority decision would be final. It seemed as if the motion might not be carried. Some of the non-native English speakers didn't understand what we were voting on until a meteor crater was explained. After the explanation and a revote, the diversion was carried by a narrow margin and we were going to visit the meteor crater.

It is located on a flat plateau and is the only large feature for miles around. Standing on the top of the rim, there is a circular ridge with a deep hole in the middle. The sides have eroded over the years but the bottom is still noticeably much lower than the average surrounding terrain.

Visitors are no longer allowed to walk down into the crater itself but there is an interesting museum, a visitor's centre, together with a test version of the Apollo mission capsule on show. We had a guided tour on the rim of the crater and were told all about the crater and how it was formed and a brief walk along the rim. Not everyone had known what to expect and we only went to see it on the thinnest of majorities but having seen the site, everyone was glad that they had seen it.

We headed on southwards and as we went the scenery changed again. We were heading into cactus country. Along the highway we could see giant cacti with their arms pointing heavenward. Our campsite for the evening was at the Lost Dutchman Goldmine campground, close to the mine itself and within the state park of the same name. The name comes from a story which is a mixture of fact and fiction. The mine is named after German immigrant Jacob Waltz, 1810–1891, who discovered a rich gold mine but kept its location a secret. 'Dutchman' was a common American term for 'German' and a bastardised form of the more correct 'Deutsch'. The location is believed to be in the Superstition Mountains. There are several variants of the story, various locations and different names and many have some truth, just enough to be plausible.

But it's a remarkable story so why let facts get in the way. Just like legends of Inca gold, Atlantis and the Loch Ness Monster, it inspires people to go out and have a look for it. There is certainly gold in the area with old names such as Goldmine Trailhead and Gold Canyon. There is modern mining nearby at Freeport McMoran Copper and Gold, a large open cast mine near Copper Hill.

I would have loved to visit the Lost Dutchman Goldmine but it had closed for the day and we would be leaving in the morning before the first tour. No matter, as I have been in gold mines before but it is always interesting to indulge a passion for mining and engineering with yet another site visit.

We had the campsite to ourselves so we had an excellent choice of pitches and the showers were warm and free. There were plenty of sharp needled cacti about and Becky got caught in one. As Zoë and I went to help we also got spiked. We escaped with a few scratches but I had so many spines that were poking through the soft material of my flip-flops that I had to throw them away. We were all English speakers but some words have different meanings. Flip-flops are a type of sandal but Antipodeans call them thongs which to the English are a type of woman's underwear. In retelling the story over the evening meal there was both some laughter and incredulity as I tried to make myself clear to different nationalities that I had cactus spines in my footwear and not my underwear.

It was a spectacular sunset with a range of colours from red through orange to yellow as the sun set. Shortly afterwards there was an equally impressive moonrise as it rose behind one of the surrounding mountains and bathed everything in an eerie night time glow. I, along with several of the others tried to take some photos. Paola's photos were excellent but mine, without a professional camera with adjustments for low light levels turned out to be just smudges.

Before we even got to the entrance of the Saguaro National Park, the terrain was littered with giant cacti. At the visitor's centre were information boards and displays plus a couple of films. One was interesting but the second was so dull that most people had walked out before it was halfway through. After the visitor's centre, we drove up into the park and had a walk. It was very hot but we preserved and walked up to a lookout across a sea of cacti plants. After the visit to Saguaro we had a new Forfeit action. We kept the game in keeping with the environment that we were going through. We were out of bear country so we dropped the bear and replaced it with a new call out of cactus and we had to hold our arms up to imitate one of the giant saguaro cacti.

We drove on to our campsite next to a lake just outside the border town of Nogales. We were following the same journey that comedians Dara O'Briain and Ed Byrne took which was shown on television as Dara and Ed's Great Big Adventure taking four weeks to travel from Arizona through Mexico and along the Pan American Highway to Panama.

They started in Nogales following the route that Sullivan Richardson took in 1941 in a Chrysler Plymouth sedan car, together with his friends Arnold Whitaker who was the mechanic and Ken van Hee who was the cook. Richardson's Pan American Highway Expedition was then published as a book entitled Adventure South. In contrast, I had started in Anchorage in Alaska and it would still be another two months before I reached Panama but then I would be taking some diversions away from the modern route of the Pan American Highway.

CHAPTER 6
Spirits in the Mountains

We drove to the USA – Mexican border at Nogales. There is a huge fence all along the border to try to prevent Mexicans and all sorts of other nationalities from entering the USA illegally. Despite the fences and border controls thousands of illegal immigrants still make it across and tens of thousands more are intercepted and sent back.

We had to wait at the border as the Mexican border control wanted to search the bus. There was a delay whilst a dog handler was found so that the dog could sniff all over the bus and in the back locker. It was ages coming and eventually a dog patrol van arrived but it was only a cursory check. Having checked the inside of the bus, it was time to check the back locker. The door was opened and there was a tightly stacked wall of luggage, stoves, food boxes and tents without any space. Still the handler encouraged his dog to jump up but all it did was bounce off the tightly stacked bags and camping equipment. The dog tried several times but couldn't get inside so the handler gave up and walked back to the air-conditioned comfort of his van. It was a long drive day and made longer by the wait at the border.

We followed the road via Hermosilla and on to Guaymas on the coast. At last we saw the sea again that we hadn't seen since Alaska but this time it was a much more pleasant temperature. It had been up to 39^0C during the day so it was great to dive in to relax and cool down.

The campsite had a swimming pool but it was small, more of a large bath and not big enough for two strokes before you were at the other side. As we were pitching the tents, a skunk wandered down the side of the camp site over fifty metres away. They have a fearsome reputation for squirting very smelly urine as a defence. Gabi went around shouting at everyone several times to beware of the skunk and to stay away from it as its spray is very obnoxious and difficult to wash off, as if we didn't know what it was or what it could get up to.

I have smelt the result of a close encounter with a skunk and the smell is not so bad. It's a bit like wet dog in that it is unpleasant but a natural smell and you can get used to it so it is less repulsive on later encounters. It is usually the suddenness of the first encounter and the memory that people remember rather than the actual smell. But it is still best to avoid skunks as it is true that the smell doesn't easily wash off so you and your clothes will smell foul for several days afterwards.

Another long drive day was made longer this time by road works and random police checks plus an identity check at the Sonora – Sinaloa state border. The scenery was flat agricultural land and not particularly interesting. It was cooler then the day before with temperatures up to 35^0C. It rained in the afternoon but there was no change in the temperature but at least it helped to keep the dust down.

We were due to camp at Mazatlán, a popular tourist destination on the coast in the grounds of a hotel but first we stopped at a supermarket. We had forty minutes to buy whatever we wanted for drinks and snacks whilst the cook group shopped for the evening meal and breakfast. They hadn't settled on a dish and Gabi had shelled out a lot of ideas but no solid target. Whenever they settled on a proposal and started looking for ingredients, she was very critical saying that she wouldn't buy a brand that she didn't recognise, in California everything is organic and washed for hygiene or that the colour or the shapes of the vegetables wasn't right and therefore made another proposal for the meal.

I went past them in the vegetable aisle as they were debating about buying carrots but they weren't ready wrapped and washed and still had some soil on them. I could see that David was getting very frustrated. Everyone else was back at the bus by the allotted time and we were already running late but with no sign of the cook group. Even had they returned the food still had to be stowed away in the back locker. We sent Zoë back to chivvy them along. When they finally arrived, we didn't stow the food but just left it on some spare seats so that we could get to the campground, pitch the tents and start cooking.

It was dark by the time we had pitched our tents. The hotel had a swimming pool with fine netting above it to keep it shaded during the day. It had been another sweltering day and it was no cooler at night. We ordered a lot of beer and chatted and floated until late into the night.

We drove on forever going south until we reached the town of Sayulita for a few nights in a hostel. The resort is off the main road and it was some 125 kilometres drive down narrow winding roads through some mountains to get from Tepic to the coast. Sayulita is a coastal town situated on the Riviera Nayurit.

It's a laid-back town with miles of sandy beaches and a wonderful spot to relax or get involved in the many water sports on offer as it is a well-known surfing hotspot. After several days of heat, I was looking forward to just relaxing on the beach in the sun but with a gentle sea breeze to make it feel comfortable.

Steve went to have his hair cut. The hair dresser didn't speak English so we helped with the translation as Steve wanted a particular style. Then David, Paola and I went to the beach and hired a parasol and some chairs and sat back and enjoyed the view. Steve came and joined us after his haircut and despite our instructions, I am not sure that the hairdresser had understood or believed what was being requested as it wasn't quite what he had wanted as he was very specific about his requirement. He was sanguine and it would grow out in time.

There were some pelicans that came flying past and a few landed and swam in the sea just in front of us. We saw some of the other members of the group making their way along the beach who joined us for a morning drink. I left early afternoon as I felt that I had had enough sun despite trying to stay under the parasol and went in search of some lunch at the local Oxxo. These was a large chain of grocery stores with coffee machines, ice creams and often hot snacks. And they seemed to have shops at most petrol stations.

Later that evening we were walking through the town after our evening meal and came into the main plaza. In one corner were several horses and riders. A rider would ride forward and turn to stand in front of the other riders and encourage his horse to perform a dance, lifting their legs up high and pausing, then moving sideways, backwards, backwards in a circle, then more dancing on the spot. When one finished the next rider moved forward and did a dancing display, all the time the horse shoes were ringing on the cobbles of the square adding a musical tempo to the display. It didn't seem to be a festival or a tourist display followed by passing a hat round, they were just doing it for fun. Then they all turned and trotted off down the street. We had been treated to a display of expert horsemanship for free.

We drove back up the narrow twisting mountain road and back on to the main road for the 240 kilometres drive to Tequila. There were plenty of road signs saying 'curva peligrosa' meaning dangerous bends until we reached the main toll road that led east through the mountains to Tequila. We knew we were nearing our destination as there were an increasing number of blue agave cactus fields which are a feature of the agriculture around Tequila. We arrived at lunchtime and dropped our bags off at the hotel then walked into the centre of town for lunch. We were due to meet up again opposite the distinctive cathedral in the main plaza to go on a tequila distillery tour.

There are several distilleries that offer tours and we had planned to go to the Jose Cuervo distillery, one of the most famous brands and widely available back home throughout the UK. Being seasoned travellers we were happy to depart from the schedule and ever ready for a bargain so we were easily persuaded to go instead to La Americana distillery, not just because it was cheaper but they would also give us ten shots of tequila to try. As part of the marketing strategy, several of the distilleries have their own transport that picks you up from the plaza. The Rubio distillery has a bus in the shape of a large red chilli pepper, another has a train shaped bus whilst La Americana has a bus in the shape of a wooden barrel.

It was only a short drive and we could have walked but the barrel bus was all part of the fun. We put on our hard hats for the tour and went past a table with the ten bottles of different tequilas that were available to try after the tour. We had a general talk about tequila and then we entered the distillery. Tequila is made from the juice of the blue agave cactus. A clear spirit can be made from other cacti and from blue agave cacti from other areas but in order to preserve the quality and designation of the name, only spirit made from blue agave in this area can be marketed as tequila.

It is the heart of the cactus that is needed and with the leaves cut off it resembles a giant closed pine cone standing on its end, the larger ones may reach up to your thigh. It can take between four and seven years to reach this size. They can be grown in poor soil and steep slopes and rows of them can be seen growing all over the countryside, on slopes too steep to farm, on the slopes of road cuttings, marking the edges of fields and any odd shaped scrap of land.

The harvested cores of the cactus are cooked in giant ovens to release the sugars. They are then crushed and soaked in water and the resultant liquid is left to ferment. We had a sample of cooked cactus flesh and it was remarkably sweet although the fibres were still tough and we were told to just suck the juice and spit out the indigestible fibrous part.

After fermentation, the liquid is filtered and put through a still where the alcohol is extracted from the liquor and again we had an opportunity to savour the pre-and post-fermented liquor. There are various qualities of tequila depending on how and for how long it is stored. Besides the clear varieties that I am familiar with at home there are also coloured versions much the same colours as whisky. It can be drunk straight away or stored for six months, a year or two years which adds to the flavour and of course to the price.

At the end of the tour we had a chance to taste the different ages and colours. I made sure I got my fair share plus a few shots from other people who had had enough. These weren't pub measures but thimbleful measures, just enough to give an idea of the taste. The prices were just a bit below local retail high street prices and they did a roaring trade as people were swept up in the heat of the moment and bought several bottles each.

After the tour, we still had the taste for more so we visited the Jose Cuervo distillery, not to see the process but we went straight to their hospitality suite. It was just off the main plaza and had been built centuries ago in the traditional Spanish colonial style and recently refurbished. There were several courtyards with statues depicting part of the agave growing or distilling process. There was also a large black statue of a crow as 'cuervo' means crow. It was late in the day and the coach loads of tourists that would usually be here had gone so we had the place to ourselves.

There was a myriad of different types of cocktails on offer all based on tequila such as with lemon, mango, or tamarind. The margaritas were perfecta, passion, fusion, exotica, sandia and real plus kiwi colada, festiva and La Enamorada. They were served in different glasses and were all adding to the experience. We all tried several and between us we must have had all of them. Some people were hungry but it was too early for me to eat so I left the group as they walked across the road to a very nice restaurant, La Cholula on the other side of the road for an evening meal and I walked around town with Zoë before we headed back to the hotel.

I hadn't taken any pictures of the town the night before so I was up early and went for a walk back into the centre of town so that I was ready for sunrise. There were a lot of interesting buildings in the Spanish colonial style, murals, local statues, many based on some aspect of tequila production, so featuring cacti and barrels and street architecture with emblems of cacti, but I made sure that I was back at the hotel ready for the scheduled eight-thirty a.m. departure.

It was another long drive day so the passengers relaxed and looked out of the windows or slept. After the visit to the tequila distilleries we had a new Forfeit call out. A call of tequila and we had to raise one hand holding an imaginary glass as a toast.

Besides the blue Algarve cactus that was growing everywhere, we passed a lot of maize fields which is the staple crop in these parts.

We are used to seeing maize that is yellow but here other varieties are grown which are all shades of yellow and there are white and blue cultivars as well. The day had started out bright and sunny but during the afternoon the cloud had built and had let rip with a serious thunderstorm and torrents of rain.

We continued to the small town of Angahuan. On the outside of the town were charcoal burners and despite the rain, there was still some smoke drifting across the road as they plied their trade. By the time we reached the centre of town it was only light rain but there were puddles everywhere and low cloud, making it seem a lot darker than normal for the time of day. This town was inhabited by the Purepecha who suffered under the Conquistadors who massacred a great many of them.

This was a camping night with an open sided roofed area for cooking with beautifully carved wooden columns. There were flat pitches under the trees, but the upgrades were very cheap. Some were modern buildings, able to sleep up to eight and others were more traditional wooden cabins for two or four. Some had toilets and showers and some were without one or the other or both.

I looked around and discovered that there was a one room cabin with just a double bed. It was not big enough for any other furniture other than a chair on the veranda, and no toilet or shower. It had a wood shingle roof and the base was built on small stone pillars raising the base off the ground. It was in some trees, set back from the path at the far end of the row of more recently built cabins. Had it been a modern building I would have camped but it was made of rough-hewn wood and was a converted granary store. It smelt a bit damp but it was wooden and rustic so I took it. All the cabins had names and mine was Trojecito which I later discovered meant 'little granary'.

The small village of Anguhuan is situated near the Paricutín Volcano which sits high above the village. It started as just a crack with some smoke drifting out of it in a farmer's field one morning in 1943 and continued to erupt until 1954 when it ceased as suddenly as it had started. In that time, the volcano and its lava flows engulfed two entire villages and grew into a tall conical volcano that dominates the landscape. All that remains of the original villages are the eerie double church spires protruding from a frozen lava flow which had surrounded the church but had not destroyed it.

There were walking options, a do nothing and stay in the camp choice and a horse riding option so being a keen rider, I opted for the horse riding. It was still dark as we collected our horses and set off down the hill on our ride to see the volcano. Zoë, Becky and I had all ridden before and were comfortable in the saddle. Also with us were Paola, David and Laurence. Laurence was a big chap and it seemed that he had the smallest horse. The stirrups had been adjusted to be as long as possible but it still wasn't long enough. The result was that it looked like he was crouching on his horse with his knees up by his chin and it didn't look comfortable at all.

We had western saddles with large wooden pommels and thick wide stirrups for the feet. My horse was called Conquistador, with a lovely brown coat and a long black mane. He was bright, alert and responsive with pricked up ears. We rode along the face of a lava flow, the final flow before the volcano stopped erupting. There were fields with crops or orchards and then a steep dark bank of ragged lava that had crept across the fields and then solidified just here.

We rode up on to the volcano to an area of black volcanic sand that had been blown out of the volcano and had collected on top of the lava flow to create a black sand desert. It drains very well and no soil has developed so there are only a few bushes with deep roots struggling to survive in the very porous sand.

We crossed the lava fields and came to the base of the steep sided regularly-shaped cone of the volcano itself. We tied the horses up and continued on foot as the sides were too steep for the horses. We took a detour diagonally across the slope of the cone to where there were some jagged rocks protruding from the otherwise regular curve of the cone. Steam and gases were still escaping from deep below ground and swirling around in the gentle early morning breeze. It would not be amiss on a film set for an atmospheric effect in a movie.

Then the climb up the steep-sided cone started. It was a narrow track that wound its way past a mass of small stones and fragments that had been ejected from the top of the cone to fall here and build up the cone with each subsequent violent eruption. The view from the top was worth the effort and I took some time to absorb the view and to recover my breath.

There were good views across the lava field surrounding the volcano, the black sandy parts and in the distance the church surrounded by lava. We took an anti-clockwise circular walk around the rim with a long steep drop on the outside of the cone and a shorter, but still a long drop down the sharp rocky inside slope of the volcano to a pair of throats at the bottom, from where the volcano threw out its gases and projectiles.

Then it was time to re-join the horses. Going down the outside of the cone was a lot easier and quicker than going up. There was a long black sandy slope from the top to the bottom. It was tiring to put your foot down, only for it to slide in the soft sand before there was enough strength or resistance to support your weight. It was easier to run down, given that there was not even time for your foot to sink into the soft volcanic sand before you shifted your weight onto the other foot provided you didn't topple forward. We were careful of course, not to drop anything as it would be a painful chest bursting, muscle burning struggle to go back up the hill to retrieve it.

At the base of the cinder cone, we got back to our horses but before we mounted, we had our packed lunches. Then it was time to ride around the base of the volcano to view the church. The guide was happy for some of us to ride ahead so Zoë, Becky and I had several gallops along the track whist the others walked on and caught us up. Both riders being lighter than me, my horse struggled with the extra weight and I was resigned to never being out in front, an important consideration as the lead horse will throw up stones and mud as it gallops and as second or third, you can end up covered in mud, dust and hit by the occasional stone.

We tied up the horses and walked through a small market selling tourists trinkets, food and drink. After scrambling across some sharp-edged lava we stood in front of the remains of the church. One spire still stood tall and the other was only half the height and since its top was flat, it looked like it had not been completed when disaster struck. Between the two stood a curtain wall but all the other parts of the church had been destroyed and covered with lava and the lava field had inched its way right up the bases of the spires.

In the market, Zoë and I shared a coconut. This wasn't the usual brown matting covered coconut with hard white flesh inside that we see in the UK but a much larger green skinned coconut with a white pithy interior covering the shell, within which is the familiar white coconut flesh, but with a much softer texture. The top was cut off with a single blow from a machete and we were given a couple of straws. After we had drunk the milk, the husk was cut off and the white flesh cut into strips, and put into a plastic bag with some fresh chilli and some lemon juice. This might seem an unusual combination but it was very pleasant and I would recommend it.

Once everyone had returned from the church and the market to where we had tied up the horses, we rode back up the hill to our campsite just outside of Anguhuan. The horses knew they had completed the ride and had quickened their pace, eager to get home. We thanked the guide and he led the horses away to their stables.

There were a couple of hours before our evening meal and we had had only a brief look at the town as we came through yesterday evening in the rain so Becky, Paola and I walked into town. We went to the main plaza and took a long circuit through the back streets to get a feel for the place. There were women dressed in traditional clothes, a dress with a colourful apron over the front edged with intricate lacework and a shawl. We visited the church in the main plaza decked out in a mass of flowers and bunting and viewed the outside of a nunnery.

There was a farmer selling maize from the back of his pick-up which, unlike the yellow maize with which I am familiar, these were blue or purple although I am told that the colour does not affect the flavour. I was later to try different coloured tortillas made from the flour of the different types of maize and can confirm that there is no difference in flavour. It was a Saturday and a popular day for weddings and there were several receptions in full swing with the sound of live local-style music rolling down the narrow streets as we explored, and as always, waiting for Paolo as she was once again engaged in her favourite pastime of taking photos.

The cook group gave a wonderful meal and we chatted around the camp fire afterwards. In Mexico City, we would say goodbye to a few passengers but also pick up more people so space might be at a premium. One of the earlier guests had donated a travel bag of assortments. It took up some space so we decided to open the bag and auction off the contents to people who wanted them and throw the rest away.

It was an Aladdin's Cave of items. There were cosmetics and toiletries which were snapped up in no time. Colin's bag had holes in it and broken handles so he had the bag. Most of the contents were snapped up and I got a peaked hat, as my existing one had faded in the strong sun from dark green to an off white and had started to fray at the edges.

People started to drift away to bed. I helped Zoë with the last few jobs and found that we were the last people awake at the camp site. We made our way to our respective cabins. My Trojecito was the last but-one cabin and Zoë's was the very last cabin. She didn't make it to her cabin until after dawn. One memory that I remember distinctly was going to the toilet during the night. My Trojecito cabin had no facilities and the communal facilities were a long way up the path, around the covered area that we used for cooking. Instead of getting dressed and going all the way back to the toilet block, I nipped out the back of the cabin and found a tree. Zoë had had the same idea and by chance we had chosen the same tree. As my eyes grew accustomed to the dark,

I could just make the whites of her eyes and the white enamel of her teeth as she smiled up at me in the gloom.

Secrets cannot be held for long within a group who are all travelling together but we would do our best. Zoë had got dressed in the dark and in the morning, I found a few items. I didn't want to hand them to her in public as it would set tongues wagging. I was going to the bus anyway so I smuggled them on board and left them on her seat on the bus amongst her other belongings and hopefully no one would notice and I joined the others for breakfast.

We passed back through the town as it still slept at seven a.m. on the Sunday morning and back down the same twisting narrow mountainous road that we had come up two days previously. There were major roadworks in progress to straighten out and reduce the gradients, so this time next year Anguhuan would no longer be a quiet picturesque remote place but would have a major bypass running along one edge and the noise associated with it.

It would bring no lasting economic benefit to the community except making it easier for the youngsters to leave and find jobs in the big cities, thus hastening the community's decline into a small backwater beside a main road. On the far side of the town there was still a lot of smoke drifting across the countryside as the charcoal burners were busy tending their earth kilns cooking wood to create charcoal for cooking. And without the rain that had doused some of the smoke on our way to the campsite, there was a lot of thick smoke drifting across the road.

We went through Uruapan and Patzcuaro with its lake, as we sped on down the main road to reach Mexico City Districto Federale or locally just called DF for short. We stopped at a petrol station with an Oxxo for a natural break and for those with a coffee addiction to get a cup of their favourite brew. It was here that we picked up our armed army escort. They had also seemingly stopped for coffee and toilets, but always with an officer near the cab, all armed, with one man standing behind a large calibre machine gun mounted on the back of the lorry and several wearing balaclavas, not against the sun but against being recognised.

When we set off they followed us and overtook us but stayed a hundred metres in front. On hills which Betsy wasn't good at getting up, we slowed down and the truck would increase the distance between us but it would slow and wait for us to catch up. On straight downhill sections, we speeded up and got up close to the back of the truck and then they too would speed up to match our speed.

This continued all the way along the main road to the turn off for Maravatío where we were planning to have lunch, whereupon we turned off and they continued along the main road. Coincidence or following orders to protect foreigners? we will never know. The town has a beautiful centre with a plaza with a bandstand in the centre. There are covered shopping arcades set under pillars with an open side looking onto the square. Some of the older buildings have fine facades. There were street vendors and a market and everyone was out for their Sunday lunch.

David and I had a huge sandwich with white and yellow cheese, pork, chicken, bacon and beef, plus salad, plus a choice of sauces. We had ordered only one, intending to share it as we knew how big they were. Somehow this got interpreted as one each and so we were served one each, but the price was very good so what we didn't eat for lunch would do for a snack later or for an evening meal. We pressed on past Atlancomulco and Toluca to reach DF in the mid-afternoon.

This is one of the world's busiest and most populated cities with more than twenty million people, making it not only larger than many other cities but also larger than a fistful of countries. It also has a pollution problem as the city lies in a bowl surrounded by mountains and emissions tend to get trapped within the bowl and build up. The weather is rarely sufficiently benign to wash pollutants out of the air or to blow them away so smog can linger for days at a time. We checked into the Hotel Marlowe and I shared a room with Laurence but we had already planned to make the most of the city, as there is so much to see and so little time. After registration, we had planned a tour of the city in what little time we had left that afternoon.

Before we had left there was a knock at the door. It was Zoë asking me whether I wanted to go down to the shops with her for a moment. Surprisingly for me, I got the hint and walked down the stairs with her. There were a few issues to resolve after last night. She started the conversation but the stairwell echoed up and down and along the corridors that led off it so we might be overheard so I suggested that we wait until we were outside.

The intimate conversation between us dodged all over the place. Did we feel the same about each other? It was part apology and partly to test each other's feelings. It can be disruptive for the group if there is favouritism or a situation where the leader is not approachable. It is not the done thing for tour leaders to assault passengers, not professional and might lead to complaints or dissatisfaction. Passengers should not interpret a leader's dedication to her job to get people involved and satisfied, as anything more than doing her job. We ploughed through the issues and we were of similar views and came to an amicable conclusion.

A short while later I left the hotel with Laurence and went out to the Conte de Obispo's formal residence, a beautiful, old building with pretty tiles on the façade, intricate balconies and carved decorations at roof level. Laurence wanted to find a geocache and he surreptitiously eased it out of its hiding place in the railings. It was a tiny cylinder with a screw top, less than two centimetres long and as thin as a pencil. Inside was a tiny slip of rolled up paper to which he added his name and date and returned it to its hiding place for the next geocacher to find.

We passed the National Palace of Fine Arts with its wonderful reception area and further on at a side entrance behind some bars are four meteorites that had fallen from the skies each the size of a settee with details of dates and locations. They are lit up at night but unfortunately with coloured lights which detracts from their scientific significance and makes them look more like Christmas decorations than interesting scientific artefacts.

Next, we walked on to the Plaza de la Constitucion, the main square and dominating it is a massive colonial Hispanic cathedral which was built on the site of the ancient Aztec capital, the remains of which can be viewed alongside at the Temple Mayor and its Museum. It was time for the changing of the guard and a massive flag was being lowered with sixteen soldiers needed to fold it. We watched this spectacle until it was finished and then went to view the inside of the cathedral. It was spectacular, but being a Sunday, services were being held and some areas we could only view from a respectable distance.

There are several other equally impressive official buildings around the plaza, such as The National Palace and the old municipal buildings. There are murals created by Diego Rivera decorating several buildings but we were not able to see any of them as it was getting late in the day. We passed an old building and were invited inside to listen to a poetry recital. I stayed for a while not that I am a fan of poetry, but I found the architecture fascinating. It was an old style colonial house with a central courtyard with arches on two levels looking somewhat like cloisters, overlooking the light-well where the recital was taking place. The arches were supported by wooden frames and the whole structure was leaning at noticeably crazy angles.

The whole of DF is subject to earthquakes and several large earthquakes have occurred over the years. To make matters worse much of the city is built across an ancient lake bed with loose unconsolidated soils. If the foundations are not deep enough and I mean tens of metres down to bed rock, the ground has a propensity, in an earthquake, to take on the properties of a liquid and will become incapable of supporting any weight. Therefore, buildings can sink into the ground during large long-lasting earthquakes in a process called liquefaction. This building was still standing but its foundations had settled considerably and hence none of the arches were the correct shape as the architect had intended but now had to be supported by wooden frames.

Several people were leaving the group so we had a farewell dinner that evening at El Café de Tacuba, founded in 1912 but set up in a 17th century mansion. It has been a classic place to celebrate for decades and has its place in history. It has been featured in Mexican life in other ways, despite the ghostly nun that haunts the building and brings a chill to the room. She is also alleged to move tablecloths but we experienced none of these events. Antony Queen, an employee for over fifty years, played Santos Hermandez in the film Los hijos de Sanchez. On 25th June 1936, Manilo Fabio Altamirano, a lawyer and politician in the National Revolutionary Party was assassinated here.

The food is really very good but I liked the architecture and the environs more than anything and left the table more than once, pretending to be in search of toilets or just plain lost, to see as much of the building and its decorations as I could. Whilst eating we were serenaded by an orchestra of local musicians playing local style music. It was a small venue and there were several of them, at least eight but some were playing and joining in whilst standing in corridors or behind table divides, but the music was excellent. One chap caught the girls' attention as he had an outrageously big bushy moustache.

CHAPTER 7
Ancient Civilisations

Laurence, Paola and I had booked an excursion to see the Aztec ruins at Teotihuacan and as Paola was flying out that evening, we had asked and received assurances that the tour would be back at the hotel before six p.m. which was the latest that she could get to the airport and not miss her flight. The tour didn't get off to a good start as the bus was late to arrive. It also went around a few other hotels to pick up guests and despite being late, some of the guests still weren't ready which I think is extremely rude. Waste your own time but don't delay other people. It was a frustrating start to the day but we had all day and the guide assured us that we would make up time somewhere.

The first stop was Garibaldi Plaza. A wonderful place for an evening out with bars and discos plus a choice of local musicians, mariachis, dressed for the part despite this being early in the morning. It is also home to MUTEM, or the Museo del Tequila y el Mezcal, a museum dedicated to the history of tequila and mescal which is the same drink but the name used when it is not made in Tequila. It was housed in a modern building but we weren't going in to visit.

Next stop was just up the road at another unscheduled stop. This time at the Centro Cultural Universario Tlatelolco, part of the Universidad Nacional Autónoma de México, also known as UNAM. We stood outside and were told about the history of the colonial church that had been built above ancient ruins which have since been excavated and are now open to the public. We were only told about them and although they were just in front of us, we weren't about to go and have a closer look.

When we got back on our bus, there had been some rearrangement of passengers with some that had left us and others that had joined us. We set off and no more than twenty minutes later having stood for some time in traffic we had turned off the main road and weaved our way through some back streets to yet another unscheduled stop, this time at a silversmith. I should have known that there are always extra sites thrown in. I suggest for a cut of the tourist spend, but it may also be altruistic and to allow guests to the country to experience something more than just the big headline attractions.

We had passed some colourful residential buildings clinging to the hillsides as we at last progressed along the main road towards our scheduled destination. It had already gone midday when we pulled into another tourist site and no, this wasn't the entrance to Teotihuacan that we had signed up to see but another tourist market. We were shown Mexican hairless dogs, shown how the carvers create works of art from just lumps of rock, offered tastes of tequila, and shown all sorts of tourist baubles based on the Aztec style of decoration, head dresses, face masks, jewellery, ornaments and so on. I am always impressed at the skill that the artisans show in creating these goods but there is no way that I want to buy one and have it in my house gathering dust.

At last we were dropped off at the Teotihuacan archaeological site for our tour after one p.m. It is a fascinating site with a multitude of square based stepped pyramids with steep staircases to give access to the top. There are two main thoroughfares set perpendicular to each other, the Avenue of the Dead running north – south, and the east – west Avenue. The buildings on the site are all set well apart from each other. The city was home to over 175,000 people and was in its ascendency from 200BC, dominating a large empire until it was abandoned around 750AD.

There is a museum with many of the precious finds with good labelling plus a diorama of the buildings on the site. You can climb up to the top of the main pyramid, the Temple of the Sun and get some amazing views. At the far end of the site is the Temple of the Moon although you are only allowed to climb up part of the way.

The bus picked us up at three-thirty p.m. and dropped us off just ten minutes later for the all-inclusive lunch. Whether this was the usual time or whether the schedule had slipped I was not sure but either way it is very late for lunch if you have been up since seven a.m. Lunch was buffet style and you helped yourself to the large selection of dishes on offer. We were treated to two local performers who were dressed in traditional costumes of feathers and beads who performed a dance with accompanying music. They would also pose with you for an undisclosed amount.

We were then off to see a basilica but it was getting late and Paola needed to get to the airport. There was no way that the tour was going to end at the promised time, especially as there was one more scheduled site to see and I bet another unscheduled tourist trinket shop stop, so Laurence, Paola and I were dropped off at a taxi rank and we headed back to the hotel, where Paola grabbed her bags and went straight on to the airport and we would be leaving the next day.

We left the hubbub of the capital behind and drove out of DF although that was easier said than done as the rush hour seems to be 24 hours. At least we were going against most of the traffic. After two hours, we were back in open farmland with fields all around.

We went through more mountainous terrain with a scant covering of plants and several types of cactus with their arms reaching up to the skies. There were just mountains and slopes and not a field or farm to be seen as we crossed another mountain range. That afternoon it rained again in torrential bucket loads. Along the road there were minor mudslides with their toes spreading out across the side of the road. There were streams rushing down usually dry embankments, bringing with them a ton of washed-out material, the muddy waters flowing on across the tarmac but leaving the heavier stones and small boulders lying in the road. The bus swerved several times in the poor visibility to avoid the larger rocks on the road.

As quickly as it had started the rain eased off and the sun came out as if the storm had never happened. We dipped into lower elevations and reached the city of Oaxaca and signed into our hotel, the Hotel Aurora. The city is low-level with buildings of one and two and occasionally three storeys. It is a beautiful old colonial town with graceful arcades and colourful markets populated by the descendants of Zapotec and Mixtec Indians, who come to sell their colourful woven blankets and shawls in the Zócalo or main plaza around the cathedral. It was these narrow-cobbled streets which gave D.H. Lawrence the inspiration for his novel, 'The Plumed Serpent'.

From the rooftop terrace of our hotel we looked out across the city and the surrounding hills, most topped with communication masts and a large stadium beyond the hotel half way up the hill towards just one of many telecommunication masts and arrays of discs and antennas. Oaxaca's nickname is the 'Land of Seven Moles', pronounced not as the single syllable little black mammal that burrows under your lawn and throws up molehills but two syllables as in guacamole. Each of the province's seven regions produces a unique variation of this spicy mole sauce.

For the evening meal, we walked through some police checkpoints to a local restaurant in the main plaza. We opted to sit in the open in front of the restaurant which seemed an excellent idea at the time, but we were constantly interrupted by street vendors, entertainers and beggars as we had a meal and got to know our three new traveling companions. There was Nicole, an experienced nurse from Sydney, Australia, John, a young lorry driver from Essex and Kate, a civil servant from Wales. Together with Steve, Laurence, Tracey, Clare and myself there were just eight passengers plus Zoë and Seb, for the next leg of the journey.

Walking through to the Zócalo after the meal we came across a tented encampment between the bandstand and the main town hall. This was a protest that had resulted from the abduction and murder of forty-three student teachers. The students and unions have had a long history of struggle for rights and have been very outspoken in the past. This was a protest to demand action. This was the reason for the police checkpoints but I wasn't sure whose side they were on. Were they there to protect the protesters against revenge attacks or to keep an eye on the subversives?

We stopped off at La Farola, or The Lantern, an old café and bar set in an ancient building built from large blocks of stone dating from colonial times which served as a merchant's house, a warehouse and fortress. The building filled an entire block and had tall walls, a few small windows on the upper levels, covered with bars and the doors were heavy thick timbers that would resist attack. There were some modifications and shop fronts and windows had been knocked into the lower sections, but the basic outline of the original building was still discernible.

The café was a more recent affair dating from 1916. It had a high ceiling and was tastefully decorated and worth a visit just to see the inside. They make some excellent cocktails and the girls were working their way through the list. They also have a speciality on offer. Tequila has a special definition of origin but the spirit made from cactus outside of that area is called mescal. Jacob Lozano Paez discovered in the 1940 s that adding a worm to the drink improved the taste and so 'mescal con gusano' or 'spirit with worm' was born. If I could drink sour toe cocktails in Dawson I wasn't going to be defeated by a worm so I had to try one. I don't know what it tasted like before the worm was added but if you drink spirits, it's pleasant enough. I also suspect that it is a marketing gimmick and does nothing to the taste.

I had wanted to leave the party and go home for an early night but on opening the heavy door, it was pouring outside and there was a two-metre-wide river of water rushing down where the gutter should be which was flooded by a dark foaming mass. I was easily persuaded to shut the door and settle down for another mescal con gusano.

In the morning, we were picked up by Betsy and driven up a mountain overlooking the town. This was Monte Alban, the site of the Zapotec civilisation and a UNESCO World Heritage Site. Work on the site started about 800BC and was the centre of Zapotecan civilisation for the next thousand years. They started by levelling the top of the mountain to give a large flat plateau on which to build their monuments. This is thought to have reduced the peak by between 80 to 100 metres.

We visited the small but informative museum and waited in the café at the entrance for our local guide to take us around the site. We were taken up to the site and had the history explained and the many buildings interpreted. There are a few trees on the top but the massive square squat pyramids stand out. Low walls of buildings show where they were in relation to and dwarfed by the pyramids.

In the centre of the main square is the only building that is not aligned in a neat axis with all the others. This was to do with the sun's summer and winter equinoxes and this building was aligned to the equinoxes. There was a pelota court which is a game played throughout the area, seemingly by most civilisations in the area; whichever era you are visiting.

Back in the city of Oaxaca I planned to do a whistle-stop tour. Going past the student protesters' camp in the Zócalo, I visited the cathedral and then went across the road to The Museo de Pinturas, an art museum. Up the road there is the Temple of Santo Domingo, a monastery and a museum. The Botanical Gardens were on my list, but I looked through the gate and there were only a few plants and a lot of open space and at 50MXNs it seemed a bit expensive for what I could see from the entrance, so I saved some time and money and moved on to the Museum of Contemporary Art.

I find contemporary art as a genre difficult to appreciate at times as sometimes it is brilliant and I would love to have a piece in my house, and other pieces are just bits of junk or a waste of paint. But I was here less to see the art and more to wander about the building, which is a lovingly restored colonial merchant's house and worthy of a visit, just to see the architecture.

The last building on my list was the Opera House, a turn of the century building with the lower storey built of grey-green stone, the upper storey white stucco with red stone window surrounds, columns, balustrades, statuary and decoration with finials on the roofline under a copper roof. It was an unusual mixture of styles but a fascinating piece of architecture.

That evening we went to the Zócalo. A traditional band was playing and couples were dancing to the music. There were only six of us, John, Clare, Seb, Tracey, Zoë and myself who all went into Casa de la Abuela overlooking the square, as I wanted to try the local specialty. These were described to me as grasshoppers but that is saltamontes, meaning literally 'jump mountains'. They are locally called chapulines which might be better translated as crickets or baby grasshoppers. They weren't on the printed menu but I knew that the restaurant served them, so I asked the waiter and was told that they were available, so I ordered them.

I was dreading there being two or three giant grasshoppers staring up at me, but no, there were small red insects a hundred to a forkful covering the centre of the plate with some salad. Ignoring the fact that they are insects, they were served lightly fried and were pleasant enough but didn't have a strong distinctive flavour, and texture-wise, they had a slight crunch.

I had joined the ranks of coffee drinkers and I was up early to get my morning fix. The local Oxxo wasn't open, so I tried the market behind the hotel. I had passed it the day before and noted the intricate brickwork at the entrances but other than that adornment the rest of the market was functional and workaday. Stall holders were already setting up their stalls and there were women selling hot food and drinks. They had coffee but it was a thick black local version with enough sugar already poured in to make a teaspoon stand up in it by itself.

It was kept hot in a saucepan on a small gas hob. It was far too sweet for me and there was no milk available but no other coffee was available so I went back to the bus empty handed. We were due to pack the back locker at four forty-five a.m. and leave at five a.m. for the all-day drive to San Cristóbal de las Casas. As it was we had left by four fifty-four a.m. a record for being ahead of time for an early departure but it was dark and cold and no one wanted to hang about. Everyone just wanted to get on the bus and go back to sleep.

It was a tough drive for Seb who started driving that morning in the dark to get out of town on the right road. It was dark as it was before dawn and dark in the town as there were no street lights. Dawn broke whilst we were still in the mountains. We stopped at a café, no more than a truckers' stop to get that cup of coffee. We followed a river down its valley and the mountains retreated. The forests in the mountains had now changed to rolling countryside, agricultural land interspersed with natural scrubland with palms, showing that we were getting towards warmer climes.

After another two hours' driving we pulled into a petrol station with an Oxxo to get diesel, coffee and hot tamales from a street vendor. There were more vochos as the VW beetle is called locally and unlike other areas in Mexico that we had travelled through, here there were a proliferation of tuk tuks. Lunch was a brief affair at a roadside café in Tepanatepec just a few kilometres from the state border and we were joined by the resident dog, a cat and two parrots all waiting for some titbits from the table.

Along the main road we came to a standstill with no traffic coming in the opposite direction. We could see some tree branches and several tuk tuks across the road ahead of us. We walked forward to see what the problem was. This was a demonstration by tuk tuk drivers at proposed legislation that would effectively put them out of business. I had mixed messages and I was not sure whether it was safety enhancements or emission standards or both, but the drivers were adamant that the effect would be the same, making it uneconomic to make a living. I asked whether I could take some photos and they were very happy to pose for the camera.

It was a relatively good-natured affair with lorry drivers just sitting in their cabs reading, sleeping, or playing with their phones, irrespective of schedules to keep. There were street vendors selling cold drinks, hot food and ice creams to waiting motorists and tuk tuk drivers alike. Tuk tuk drivers were still making a living, as passengers got off their buses on one side of the blockade, walked through the road block and continued their journey by tuk tuk. A couple of local buses just pulled up at the back of the queue of traffic and swapped passengers, turned around and went back the way they had come with a new coach load of passengers.

The blockade was intermittent and the modus operandi was that the blockade was lifted for ten minutes every two hours or so, in order that some traffic could get through before it was shut again. But we were quite a long way back from the head of the queue and unsure whether we would get through. A bucket was being passed about for contributions and Zoë engaged them in conversation and made a generous donation to ensure that the unforgettable yellow American registered school bus driven by a woman with loads of multinational gringos, might stand a chance of getting through the blockade when it was next lifted.

The traffic inched forward and we were moving. We all leaned out and cheered and waved as we came up to the barrier. We could see some tuk tuk drivers ready to drive back into the traffic and others holding the branches ready to stop traffic. They smiled and waved back as we passed through the chicane and just a few more vehicles squeezed through the chicane before it was shut and the blockade was re-formed. The ruse and generosity had paid off and we were through.

We went through Arriaga where we left the Pan American Highway and headed north east across some mountains to cross more rolling countryside over a plain to the Sumidero Canyon River with its muddy brown waters and we started to climb up into the mountains. It was late in the afternoon when we reached the truck park where Betsy was going to be parked for the next few days. She was big and both Zoë and Seb were experienced and very good at driving Betsy through narrow gaps, but the narrow-cobbled streets of the old colonial city of San Cristóbal de las Casas were just too narrow and many roads were pedestrianised and restricted to public vehicles and taxis only.

We would make the last part of the journey from the truck park to the centre of town and our hotel, La Hotel Casa Margarita by taxi. We had a charming hotel converted from a traditional merchant or nobleman's house. There was a central courtyard with a column- lined walkway around three sides and the hotel rooms opened off this courtyard. There were other rooms on upper storeys and another smaller courtyard at the back rising to three storeys plus a roof terrace with views across the city. The main courtyard had since had a modern canopy added and kept off some of the fierce sun and occasional rain.

San Cristóbal de las Casas has been the administrative centre of the Chiapas region since colonial times and is renowned for its colonial-style architecture. It is home to both Tzotzil and Tzeltal Indians who still show their tribal origins through their varied traditional costumes and customs. However, it had been a long drive and a long day since starting before dawn, made longer by the tuk tuk demonstrations. It was dusk and there were other things on our minds. First job was dropping off our laundry to be washed and collected the following evening. The second job was to go out for a hot evening meal.

Some of us had booked a river tour along the Sumidero Canyon, which is a designated national park. Taxis picked us up and dropped us outside the old city next to the coach that would take us there. We drove down the hill back to the bridge over the Sumidero Canyon River that we had crossed yesterday, and upriver to the jetty. We donned bright orange buoyancy aids and boarded our boat for the tour of the canyon.

There was the usual safety briefing but a couple of rules were made very clear and repeated for extra clarity in both Spanish and English. These waters harbour crocodiles so keep well back from the edge and do not enter the water; do not put your hand in the water and don't lean out over the edge of the boat.

We went downstream under the road bridge and kept hard to the right-hand side. Up on the cliff was a ranger station with a ranger peering over the edge of the rails. We were told to hold up our tickets so that he could check that we had the necessary ticket. I doubt whether he could have seen the ticket from that distance, let alone the date on it, or even whether it was a ticket and not a piece of newspaper. I doubt that he even bothered to count thirty heads and thirty tickets but we did as instructed and he waved us through.

The walls of the canyon towered above us with various plants clinging onto tiny cracks in the rock face. We soon saw our first crocodile. Or his eyes and the ragged line of sharp pointed teeth-like plates running down his back as he floated low in the water near the bank. Others lazed in the sun on the foreshore, some with their heads on the ground, others with raised heads. There were a variety of sizes as well as small youngsters, born that spring to a fat giant male several metres long.

There seemed to be dozens of the ugly and dangerous animals along the banks and the prey must have been plentiful to support these many predators. Further down the canyon the walls grew higher and steeper and in places there was no foreshore at all, as the cliff face just plunged straight down into the muddy water. High above us near the canyon rim, there were birds circling using the upward air currents to gain height and save energy.

The captain told us what they were in Spanish but I didn't recognise the name or the bird. Except that if I could see them several hundred metres away above us, they must have been big birds. After the captain had finished his spiel, I was asked what he had said about the birds and what they were. I just had to say that they were condors.

We passed a grotto with a statue of the Virgin Mary and a memorial plaque to Dr Miquel Alvarez del Toro who created the park who died in 1996. Around the corner was a spring high up on the cliff face, that dripped its water down from high above the water level. It fell onto the cliffs below and great downward facing fans of green algae had built up, looking like the branches of a Christmas tree weighed down with green snow.

The river brings down the inevitable detritus of modern living in the form of plastic packaging, paper, glass and plastic bottles and anything else that floats. It collects in certain eddies along the canyon and where it opens out into the lake. There are special boats fitted with nets that work their way through these eddies straining out the rubbish to be disposed of on land elsewhere.

The canyon opens out into a reservoir created by a massive dam across the river. It generates a considerable amount of energy that serves the local population and some is exported to neighbouring Guatemala. As we approached the upriver dam site we were approached by enterprising boat-owning locals who sold sweets, snacks, cold drinks and ice cream to the tourist boats that come down the canyon.

On the way back to San Cristóbal de las Casas, we stopped at the picturesque market town of Chiapa de Corzo near Tuxtla Gutiérrez which hosts La Fuente monumental de Chiapa de Corzo, a beautiful mudejar style brick-built fountain. It is a mixture of Baroque and Moorish styles unique to late 15th and 16th century Spain, and the fountain is built in the shape of a crown. It was built in 1562 by the Dominican friar Rodrigo de León and according to historians and archaeologists, it is unique in Latin America. It was badly damaged by earthquakes between 6th and 9th December 1975 and is just finishing a period of restoration. There is also a clock tower in the same style nearby.

We were dropped off on the outskirts of the old city of San Cristóbal de las Casas and rather than take a taxi, we were happy to walk through some more of the old city, so we were pointed in the right direction and we set off. There were plazas surrounded by open sided colonnades, churches aplenty, official buildings in several different styles but by far the most popular was the colonial style from which the green, red and white Mexican national flag fluttered in the slight breeze.

Saturday was another free day but Zoë and I were going horse riding. We were picked up near the hotel and driven up into the mountains and off the road to where our horses were waiting and already saddled and ready to go. We had a guide plus another couple, Jose Luis and Erika both from near Tijuana, Baja California. Neither of them had ridden before but were happy to join in the experience.

The horses were small and Jose Luis reminded me of Laurence riding on the Paricutín Volcano as the stirrup leathers were too short and it was a small horse and he too looked as if he was crouching, rather than sitting on his horse. Also, beginners have a natural tendency to slouch forward, emphasising the crouching position and I remember my first riding lessons many years ago, being told to relax and sit up.

We set off and walked along a path between fields into the countryside. There seemed to be a long section so having checked with our guide, Zoë and I kicked our horses into a gallop. The horses were well matched but she was lighter than me and whatever her favourite flower may be, her horse would pull ahead and I was not able to catch up.

We reached the outskirts of San Juan Chamula and left the horses in the shade of some trees on the outskirts of the village and walked into the centre. We had two hours to find some lunch and do whatever sightseeing we wanted to do, whilst the guide went and did his own thing, which meant visiting friends and relatives.

In the centre of the plaza was a church, a plain white stucco building with a bit of ornamentation around the doors and windows. It was St Matthew's Saint Day and it was being celebrated in local style. There were occasional fireworks. A rocket would soar into the sky and make a loud bang with a puff of smoke high above our heads in the clear blue skies. Inside various ceremonies were being conducted. There were rushes on the floor and statues of saints sitting behind glass doored cabinets. There were a host of candles burning, adding to the heat of the day.

There wasn't one main service but small gatherings of people in various parts of the church taking part in rites. There were also people moving from one group to another and small groups just sitting and chatting. They practice a mix of both Roman Catholicism and pagan beliefs that hedges their bets for both camps, but without a knowledgeable local guide, I wasn't sure what was happening.

We met some helpful locals who welcomed us to their church and answered some of our questions but I didn't understand enough of their mixture of Spanish and local language to try to explain some of the detail. I thanked my host and added a monetary contribution to the array of other offerings on the floor in front of a statue of St Matthew and left.

There were many people dressed in local costume. Men wore a black woollen over-garment which resembled matted fur. Women wore a black lace dress that ballooned from the waist with a broad belt, a blouse and a shawl plus a head scarf. I had understood from our conversations in the church that the different combinations of dress show whether they are married or not.

We returned the way we had come with a bit more galloping for those that wanted a bit more of a ride than just sitting on a horse walking through the countryside. We had made good time and took a diversion along a stream through some trees. The branches scratched our faces as we followed the narrow track through the trees. There were a few steep sections down to and through the stream with the horses kicking up great showers of water as they walked through the stream. We finally got back to the road and to our lift back into town.

Zoë and I met up with Seb and Tracey and went to a sushi restaurant, one of Seb's favourite types of food for a snack and some wine. Later we met Clare and stopped off in a local café where we had been the night before, to catch up with what each had done over the last couple of days. No one had a plan for the rest of the day but time was marching on and after another bottle of wine we decided that we really ought to do something on our last day in San Cristóbal de las Casas so we walked up to the cathedral. A wedding was in progress so we could view the outside but could only glimpse the inside and some of the ceremony from the door.

All the way there and back I had started taking pictures of every vocho that I could find. I had the inspiration to take a photo of every colour, combination of colours and conversions to open tops or buggy, that I could find. We soon ended up back in the same café. We had been such good customers that they gave us a complimentary bottle of wine. They had also plied us with so many local equivalents of tapas that we weren't hungry for a meal but another bottle of wine would never go amiss to help wash down the tapas.

It was Sunday morning and another early start for a long drive day to Frontera Corozal, setting off in the dark long before dawn. We passed through many quiet and sleeping villages until sunrise and then through a larger village that had a café that was open and we stopped for coffee. There was a sign with a large black E standing for Estaciones or parking and a red line through it meaning no parking. Next to it was a garage door on which there was painted another sign saying 'Se ponchan llantas gratis' meaning 'we puncture tyres for free' emphasising the message not to park in front of the garage doors.

We went through some rugged terrain past plunging cliffs and forested slopes and over innumerable sleeping policemen across the main road. In the late morning, we stopped at Cascades de Aqua Azul. This is a wonderful place for a visit just off the main road down a winding side road. As the name suggests there are a number of cascades and pools and the water really does look blue.

You can swim in the pools but sliding down the cascades looked like it might be great fun but is strongly discouraged. There are a series of cascades and the path winds its way up the side of the river. Needless to say, there are innumerable cafés, restaurants, bars and trinket shops all the way along the path. It was a wonderful place to break the journey and spend an hour or two to relax and stretch your legs.

We had another stop in Palenque before heading along the last stretch of road, more of a rough track along the border between Mexico and Guatemala. The last 160 kilometres took five hours with many speed bumps and occasional delays due to animals crossing the road, including a herd of cows and crossing the road ahead of us, a glimpse of a large wild carnivorous cat, probably a jaguarundi, a black panther or jaguar-type animal. We had stopped for a natural break and just one vehicle came past. There was jungle with a thick mass of undergrowth beneath the trees with lots of birds shrieking, monkeys shouting and the noise of crickets and other insects flying past your ears so that if you stood still for too long they landed-on and bit you.

Finally, we reached Yaxchilán deep within a national park and our camp for the night. This was an unusual camp stop as we laid out our sleeping bags on the top floor of the Escudo Jaguar Hotel under a palm frond roof with no walls. Upgrades were available to palm frond roofed cabins but these were horribly expensive. A mid-range alternative was individual rooms but these only had walls but no ceiling but collectively a large single roof over the ceiling-less individual rooms. But at least they had beds and some people took advantage of these more affordable upgrades.

We walked the short distance from the hotel to the banks of the Usumacinta River where a boat was waiting for us. We were due to see the Mayan ruins at Yaxchilán which means 'green stones' in Mayan. There are no roads to reach this remote site so we needed to take a boat up the river which forms the border between Mexico and Guatemala. At its zenith, the city was dominant over other nearby cities and ruled over lesser kingdoms such as that found not far away at Bonampak.

Toucans flew overhead, easily identifiable by their large colourful bills which were great at cracking nuts but made flying strenuous when there is so much weight in front for the bird to carry. From the safety of the boat we could see crocodiles resting nearly submerged near the bank or basking in the sun on the beach. This was another river where you kept your hands well inside the boat.

We gingerly and quickly made our way from the boat and up the bank to the entrance to the ruined city of Yaxchilán, ready for when the gate opened at eight a.m. There were various ruined buildings and we were taken around and had the significance of each building explained by our local guide, Jesus.

To reach the Gran Plaza, we walked through an underground tunnel through one of the buildings. There were bats hanging from the walls and ceilings and giant spiders hunting for their prey on the floor and walls. We came out into the sunlight overlooking the Gran Acropolis, a large, flat, open area of grass. Most tourists stay on the coast and make this a day trip but we were on the doorstep so we had the place to ourselves, as tourists wouldn't arrive from their coastal hotels for at least another couple of hours.

We walked up through the jungle with monkeys calling from the tree tops as we passed, before arriving at Los Templos del Sur. Then returning the way we had come, we made a detour to the Pequeña Acropolis.

We took the boat back to the village and then set off on the return journey to Palenque. However, fired with our recently acquired knowledge of Mayan architecture, we would be going past Bonampak which was just a short distance off our intended route. It wasn't on our itinerary, but there was a democratic vote and a majority decision in favour of an additional stop even though it would delay our arrival at Palenque.

Bonampak, also Mayan was a vassal state of Yaxchilán and is a much smaller site. Although very close to Yaxchilán the architecture is noticeably different. At other sites, new kings would build new structures, but here each king would build on top of the existing structure, thus although it was a poorer state and it only had one major building, its height was on a par with Yaxchilán. Another striking difference is that here some of the fine stucco has survived as has some of the artistry that decorated the stucco walls, so this really is an architectural gem and often missed as it is such a small site in comparison to better known sites. Fewer tourists visited it so despite being in the afternoon, we had the place to ourselves.

Finally, we reached Palenque and our camp ground which was within the grounds of a hotel which also had a variety of cabins on offer. Steve had decided that he would upgrade whenever he could so he had a nice modern room to himself. Nicole and Katie shared a modern cabin with en suite facilities. Laurence had signed up for camping so he was determined to camp. I was undecided until I discovered that one of the cabins was a stucco walled single room with a palm frond roof which was so low that I had to bend double to get through the door. It had no facilities and no ceiling, just a view of the underside of the palm frond roof, but it was rustic so I took it.

The site was well spread out and quiet. Within the grounds of the hotel was a side less palm-frond-roofed mess area for our sole use. Better still it had a large swimming pool and we made full use of it. Zoë couldn't find her bikini so she stripped off to one side of the pool and swam naked. I joined in and took my swimming trunks off as well. It was a great feeling of freedom and a feeling of bravado. However, it seemed that a woman swimming naked was quite acceptable, both to the men and the women in the group although I sensed that a man swimming naked was greeted with a lesser sense of acceptance. No one said anything or obviously avoided me but I felt it best to surreptitiously slip back into my swimming trunks to preserve decorum.

That evening there was a storm with heavy rain, thunder and lightning. We were in the pool again and despite the rain it was not cold so we continued to swim and thought it better to be wet in the pool in the rain than be on land and get drenched. The lightning was spectacular with bolts hitting the mountains around us and sometimes just great flashes across the skies between the clouds above. We felt, rightly or wrongly that being in the water was safer than standing on the grass nearby as we were lower and any lightning bolt would hit the trees or the ground around the pool before it hit our heads.

A very short drive just up the road from our campsite, so short that we could have walked it in ten minutes was the entrance to the ruined city of Palenque, set on a hilltop in an area of dense, hot and humid jungle. The site hosts the most impressive series of Mayan ruins. There had been people living here for centuries but the ruins visible today date from the golden era of the city's power between 250AD – 900AD when the city was abandoned. The temples are superb relics of the Mayan culture, and there are many ruins here still un-excavated and hidden in the surrounding jungle.

In the Templo de las Inscripciones, the excavators found an intact funerary crypt containing the sarcophagus of the Sun God. They also found lots of other artefacts which are preserved in the nearby museum. We walked around the site by ourselves and stopped at whatever feature caught our eye. After a while of wandering, I left the main site and walked down the hill from the ruined city towards the museum. Unfortunately, there was a power cut so the museum was closed. So, I just continued down the road to get back to the camp site a lot earlier than intended. That was no big issue as I was part of the cook group that evening, together with Steve, Clare and Katie and I had proposed chilli con carne and we had got most of the ingredients so I could have a leisurely start to cooking the evening meal whether the rest of the cook group were there or not.

I had thought that this was a local dish and that finding ingredients, sometimes difficult for specialist dishes in foreign countries, would be simple. How wrong can you be? We could not find any kidney beans in tins in any of the local shops. There were plenty of beans of different qualities and sizes available but all dried which would need soaking overnight, and there were none ready to just put in a pot and warm up that evening.

I was resigned to using bolotti beans and then was told that someone didn't eat beans so that these had to be cooked separately. I had already developed an alternative to those who didn't like spicy food by cooking two batches, one mild and one medium but with extra chilli available on the side for those who, like myself, liked their food spicy and hot. Luckily there were no vegetarians on this leg, otherwise we would have had a problem with not enough hobs or pots to cook the increasing number of different dishes needed.

After washing up and getting ready for breakfast we could relax and have a swim. Zoë got out her violin and gave a personal rendition to the assembled crowd outside Nicole and Katie's cabin. The rest is only recounted on hearsay, but to my everlasting shame, I sat down and succumbed to violin-induced necropsy and I fell fast asleep while she was playing.

When she finished her piece, her attention was drawn to a somnambulant figure in front of her, lying in a deck chair. She approached, playing quietly at first but getting louder as she neared me those two iconic notes from the film 'Jaws'… but I was still fast asleep. The next day we had a new call out for Forfeit… 'Norman', which had to be said in the same two rising notes as in Jaws and people would have to raise their straight palm up to their forehead to imitate a shark's fin.

Zoë's a wonderful woman and despite my faux pas at falling asleep during her recital she was also very forgiving. I helped her with the last few chores while all the others went to bed. I went to my one-room rustic cabin and a short while later, she ducked under the low hanging palm fronds over the door and let herself in.

CHAPTER 8
A big hole in the ground

Feliz dias Independencia para Mexico! Or in English, Happy Mexican Independence Day! It was Wednesday 16th September, and after a long and bitter struggle against their colonial overlords, Mexico achieved its independence in 1824. It is a bank holiday in Mexico and a time for celebrations but for us it was another drive day to Mérida, the capital of the eastern state of Yucatán.

We left Palenque before dawn to watch the sun rise across the flat landscape and raise the temperature outside, compared with the relative comfort of the bus. We stopped for a natural break at an Oxxo and to pick up some coffee. There was a new Forfeit call following my slumber through Zoë's violin recital the night before of 'Norman' and I duly joined in the fun and knew that I wasn't going to live this down any time soon.

Lunchtime found us overlooking the Caribbean Sea at Champotón and we had completed a trip from Sayulita on the west coast of the continent to the east coast of the continent. There was a little harbour with pelicans and other birds fishing in the sea a short distance out from the coastline. In the early afternoon, we crossed the state border from Campeche into Yucatán. A short while later we were flagged down by an army check point and told to pull over. They inspected our papers both for the passengers and the bus and then ordered us all off the bus. Then they wanted to search our bags and the bus. A senior officer and a couple of soldiers went on board and started to look through lockers, under seats and in the overheads. Meanwhile a junior officer and another couple of soldiers quizzed us on what we were doing, where we were going, where had we been and ordered us to empty our pockets and gave each of us a thorough pat down. Then we were ordered to get our hand luggage off the bus one by one and have that searched.

Things were getting out of hand but Zoë had a word with the senior officer on the bus who seemed quite satisfied that we really were tourists and not smuggling guns, people, or drugs. He overruled the hitherto very officious and thorough officer on the ground, and we were free to go ahead, but not before having wasted nearly an hour of intimidation.

I was looking out for signs of a meteor crater. A meteor hit this area of the Yucatán sixty million years ago and was responsible for the extinction of the dinosaurs. The impact caused a nuclear winter for decades and created a massive impact area. This is known as the Chicxulub crater but it's not on any tourist itinerary. I had an estimate of where the rim would have been but after so many eons of erosion and plant growth there was little to determine its exact whereabouts as we shot past on the bus.

Our hotel was a short walk away from Mérida city centre. It was an unusual design and unique in its decoration. It was a two storey building with a central courtyard and a colonnade with a wealth of statues and plants. It had the layout of a traditional merchant's dwelling but with many art nouveau and contemporary features.

I left the beautiful surroundings of the hotel and walked into the centre of the city and visited the main plaza and the cathedral. It is the oldest in Central America, started in 1519 and completed in 1598. Outside in the plaza I spotted a light green vocho and ran across the plaza to take a photo… it wasn't a very good picture but it did capture the colour.

That evening some of us went for a meal in a restaurant which was famed for its local and unique cuisine at Los Almendros. They were about to close but there were eight of us and we promised to be quick so, they stayed open a bit longer just to serve us. After a great meal we went into the centre to experience some nightlife. We found a large bar but it seemed empty. It was surprisingly quiet across the city centre, but the celebrations for Independence Day had been held the night before, so perhaps everyone was recovering at home.

We left Mérida and headed deeper into the Yucatán. We were at Chichen Itza ready to enter when it opened. These are famous Mayan ruins plus ruins of a later Toltec city alongside and both are UNESCO world heritage sites. Just as at Yaxchilán, tourist coaches don't arrive until mid-morning from their coastal resorts so there were few other tourists about. The stallholders had not set up and the path to the main site, which would normally be lined with vendors extolling their wares, was strangely silent and empty this early in the morning.

The first building of note was the pelota court which was the largest court that I had yet seen. By skilful design and building, the acoustics were just right, so that you could hear someone talking at the far end of the court in a normal voice, even if they were more than fifty metres away.

The games are depicted in carvings on the walls. There were two stone rings set high on the wall which served as the goals. Experts are divided on the rules of the game, but the winners were often sacrificed, a great honour, as their souls went straight to heaven rather than via the thirteen levels of heaven and hell that would normally need to be visited before a person reached the same place. Other experts say that it was the losers that were sacrificed as they had brought dishonour.

Nearby the well of sacrifice offered up treasures of jade, copper and gold as well as many human and animal bones when it was excavated at the start of the century. There are skulls carved in the surrounding stone walls. The decorations here were different from other sites. At Bonampak, the stucco walls had been painted but here at Chichen Itza there was more emphasis on carving stone.

In the centre of the site is the famous El Castillo stepped pyramid which has a huge staircase to a crypt that is guarded by a jaguar statue. The crypt housed a throne in the shape of a jaguar, painted red and inlaid eyes and spots of pure jade. The pyramid also had an interesting design feature. If you clapped your hands in front of the steps, just a second later there was an echo, not of your clap but of the sound of the call of the regal quetzal bird.

With the aid of a stick to draw in the sand, the guide explained the significance of some of the features of the design and how it reflected the Mayan astronomical achievements and how their calendar worked, which was a great achievement in mathematics and astrology despite their lack of advancement in other areas. Many of the buildings are aligned with the equinoxes and adjusted for latitude at different sites, so that they are still correctly aligned wherever they were built in the empire.

As we headed back to the entrance, some of the stallholders had yet to complete setting up their stalls but the path was lined with stalls and gave an idea of how much business there was to be had here, especially as the site hosts more than 1.4 million visitors a year.

The Yucatán topographically is a low, level area of porous rocks, limestones and excellent for building. There are no large rivers but there is plenty of water. The rocks being porous, have been eroded to create large cave systems which are filled with water. In places, the erosion had made deep shafts from the surface that give access to the water hidden beneath the surface. These are called cenotes and were known to the Mayans and are still in existence today which are popular with cave divers.

One nearby has been developed as a hotel resort. There are steps down through tunnels from the surface to a large deep pool at the bottom of the cenote. After the heat of the day, this was a good place to jump in and cool off. Sunlight penetrates the bottom of the cenote where the water level is 26 metres below the surface and creepers dangle from the walls and nearly reach the water surface. This is the Cenote Ik Kil, sacred to the Mayans and the hole is 60 metres wide and the water is 40 metres deep.

We stopped at a restaurant for a buffet meal with the added attraction of a swimming pool to cool off in before and after the meal. Then it was back on the bus for the drive to the Tulum National Park on the east coast. Tulum has a lovely white sandy beach and the campsite is right on the beach overlooking the ocean. By the time we arrived in the late afternoon, most of the day trippers had gone so it was quiet. We parked Betsy on some firm ground right next to where we planned to set up camp. We chose our pitches, on top of a sand dune for the view, between two sand dunes for the shelter or under the palms for shade. I trudged over the sand to a flat spot overlooking the ocean with marvellous views of the sea with bushes either side, to set up my tent. It was also a little way away from other tents and therefore gave some added privacy.

We set up the kitchen next to the bus which was parked near the camp facilities. They were basic, a hut in which were some toilets with doors but no locks. We agreed amongst ourselves to knock before trying a door or whistling to show occupancy. The showers were just shower heads on the outside of the building with no privacy, so showering was in public with your swimming costume on for decency.

The white beach was not the picture that the brochures would like you to see. There had been a storm and a lot of seaweed had been washed up in a great ridge along the high tide mark along the seashore. In the water, there was a lot of it floating about, so you had to wade out ten metres or more before you got to seaweed-free water. The local authorities were busy and mounds of seaweed had been gathered ready to be taken away to clean up the beach. But the water was refreshing and a pleasant temperature and nearby freshwater showers allowed you to wash the sand and salt off.

Along the beach was a headland and in the other direction were many small fishing boats bobbing up and down in the light swell or hauled up onto the beach. Zoë found some spare time and we walked along the beach together. Further along the beach were loungers and parasols, plus a few café set up under the palms above the high tide mark. Despite the unsightly mounds of seaweed, it was a picturesque beach and I noted that it was surprisingly free of the usual floating flotsam and jetsam of plastic rubbish washed up on the high tide mark around some English coastlines.

As usual Zoë did some odd jobs and was the last to go to bed, sliding into my tent half an hour after I had gone to bed. During the night, there was a lot of rain, thunder and lightning. The sea was foaming as large waves crashed against the shore, driven by the wind. The rain fell in torrents making a lot of noise as it hit the canvas of the tent or fell against the palms. The wind swished the palm fronds back and forth and added to the cacophony of noise.

In contrast by dawn, when Zoë got up and slipped away to start the chores, the storm had blown over and there was blue sky interspersed with thinning cloud. It was a brilliant sunrise with a range of reds and yellows. The sea had thrown up another ridge of seaweed along the shore, but other than that, there was little to tell that a storm had passed during the night. I went back to sleep just as some municipal workers arrived at the beach to start shovelling up the seaweed.

There had been some casualties during the night. Steve and John had shared a tent and the rain had been so heavy that the water had pooled around their tent and had got their sleeping bags wet. John had retreated to the safety of the bus. At breakfast, Steve gave an account of his version of events.

With the aid of a stick, parodying the tour guide we had had the day before at Chichen Itza, he drew maps and diagrams in the sand to show how his tent buddy had deserted him in his hour of need, saving himself and his sleeping bag, whilst leaving his tent buddy to get wet and nearly drown. John was embarrassed and didn't know what to say but couldn't help smiling at the comic delivery but he also denied all of it. It was a highly amusing spectacle and worthy of a performance at the Edinburgh Festival and delivered as only Steve could deliver it in his own unique style.

After breakfast, there were just a handful of us who wanted to go and see the Tulum ruins. After so many other ruins, you can get a bit 'ruined out' but then I suffer from FOMO and could not go and not see the ruins. Another personal trait that had not gone unnoticed was my walking pace… it tends to be fast, irrespective of the amount of time we have or the heat. Steve often walked at his own pace, slower than mine so at some sites we had never seen each other as I was way-off in front and he was taking it easy. The challenge that he set for me was to walk slowly around the site. I cannot refuse a challenge although it would be hard for me to walk slowly.

We walked out of the campsite for the short distance up the road to the entrance to the Tulum ruins. It was painful to walk so slowly but I made sure that I was in the middle of the group so that I could meet the challenge that Steve had set me. Tulum was a walled city, three walls on the landward side and the seaward side was open to the sea. This was the last of the major cities to fall to the Conquistadors when the Spanish invaded. At the time that it was built it was the furthest city in the east of the Mayan empire. It was also the city that saw the rising sun first so that added to its importance, but it was also a major trading city for moving goods and trading with other civilisations further along the coast.

It is a lot smaller than the other ruins that we had visited, and rather than hire a guide we made do with the information boards scattered around the site. The stonework looked a little cruder and there were no massive temples. It didn't take much time to walk around and we were soon heading back to camp. And I had successfully completed the challenge as I was not the first to get back, and so proved that I could walk at a slower speed if I really tried, but it wasn't a new beginning and I reverted to type and continued to walk at my own (speedy) pace at future sites.

There was an England versus Fiji rugby match on television that afternoon. I am not a rugby fan but it was a chance to see a bit more countryside, have a drink and hopefully access the internet. Laurence wasn't interested, he just wanted to enjoy the beach and have a beer so we left him with a cooler box and drove out to find a sports bar. We asked around town and were directed back to one that happened to be just up the road from the campsite, Mateo's Sports Bar.

Whilst the others watched the match, I had a walk along the road to look at the small collection of cafés, bars, hostels and hotels and to discover that there was not much else in the village. There was a beach on one side of the road and behind Mateo's was a climbing wall. At the top of Mateo's is the Sunset Lounge, a four-storey high open-sided wooden tower with a view across the jungle. Looking inland, it was just a mass of tree tops and nothing else as far as the eye could see.

We got back to camp to find Laurence slumped in a chair. He had been thirsty and had drunk a lot of beer. To make matters worse, it wasn't his beer that he had drunk and to make it even worse, these weren't the local beers that could easily be replaced but Zoë's special artisan beers that she had carefully hoarded from a brewery trip in Moab, Utah weeks ago and had been saving for special occasions.

When confronted with this crime, he didn't apologise or offer to pay for them, he just dug his hole even deeper by saying that he didn't care. Zoë was usually relaxed and easy going and being a tour leader, she has had many unexpected problems to face and get over. Looking after a bunch of independently minded travellers, each with their own agenda, is a bit like herding cats. In the five months that I travelled with her between Anchorage and Panama, this was the only occasion when she wasn't her usual relaxed self. The word I would use to describe her reaction to finding that Laurence had drunk her beers would be 'incandescent' with rage. She calmed down quickly to her normal relaxed self, but the rest of us were not going to let him forget this event too quickly or easily.

CHAPTER 9

Belize it or not...

I was up at four a.m. for a five a.m. departure and in the dead of night we drove through Tulum. It was so early that the local Oxxo was not open yet, so we turned onto the main road heading south. At sunrise, we stopped at a garage that also had an Oxxo. There were some strange emotions as we knew we were leaving Mexico after several weeks and that this would be our last Oxxo stop. It was like saying goodbye to an old friend. We watched the sun come up through the trees until it eventually rose above the tree line and started to warm the cool dawn air.

We stopped again at Bacalar to make breakfast in the main plaza. It is just a small town but it does have the Bastion de San Joaquen, a small stone built Spanish colonial fort which was interesting from the outside but not open to the public this early in the day. I had spotted a vocho up a side street and went to take a photo. Just as I approached the vehicle, the owner and his wife came out of the house opposite. I did the polite thing and asked his permission to take a photo which he was delighted as someone was taking an interest in his pride and joy.

We ate breakfast which was a bit of an odd selection of food as we were crossing the border later in the day and knew that some foodstuffs were prohibited. Therefore, we gave away what fresh food we had left, which we couldn't take with us. I don't think that the local that was passing that we gave it to, could quite believe his good fortune to be given several days' worth of groceries for his family and that we were not asking for anything in return.

We reached the Mexican border at Subteniente Lopez. There was the inevitable paperwork and visa stamping but it was quick. Then we went over no man's land and I took what may have been my last photo of a vocho in Mexico, a lovely dark blue one, parked awaiting clearance from the Belize border control.

We entered the Belize border control at Santa Elena and filled in various forms and had our baggage scanned. After only speaking Spanish for a while it was gratifying to be welcomed into the country in English, the official language of this tiny Central American country and another one of the British Empire's many former colonies.

We were welcome but Betsy was not. Being a commercial vehicle, the border was closed for the weekend and her papers and driving permit would only be processed when the commercial border control opened on Tuesday morning (and not Monday as this was a bank holiday).

Zoë worked her magic with the border police and we could go back to the bus to ensure that we had everything that we might need for three days without Betsy, and then our bags were searched again. Then we boarded our last-minute alternative transport that Zoë had organised to continue our journey, two local minivan taxis for the trip to Belize City. Meanwhile Seb had driven Betsy around to a secure truck park where she would sit until her papers could be processed on Tuesday morning.

We drove around Orange Walk and stopped for a natural break and to stretch our legs. There was a notice in the toilets. For the last few weeks whenever you went to the toilet, there had been a basket lurking in the corner for used toilet paper, as the sewage system was not sufficiently robust to take paper as it clogs up the works. In this toilet, there was no basket lurking in the corner, just a message neatly written in black felt tip pen on the underside of the lid of the toilet were the words, 'Please flush your shit paper'.

We hadn't been in the country for two hours before the jokes started, such as incorporating the name of the country into phrases such as 'Belize it or not...', 'You wouldn't Belize what happened to me today...' or 'You'd better Belize it'.

We reached Belize City, the former capital of the country and went straight to the port where we were due to board a high-speed ferry. The Belize Cayes are a group of islands a short distance from the mainland that lie along the great barrier reef, which stretches along the Caribbean coast line of Central America. The island that we were heading for was Caye Caulker, where scuba diving and snorkelling are about the hardest work to be done all day.

The boat flew the Belize flag. This has a background of blue that denotes the sea and the colour of the ruling People's United Party with a red band at the top and bottom to represent the opposition party whose colour is red and to appease them. In the centre is a white disc, with the coat of arms depicting various tools in the top two thirds and a ship on the lower third to signify its link with ocean trade.

The coat of arms is supported by a mestizo and a black man also holding tools, and a mahogany tree standing behind the coat of arms to represent the mahogany trade, which was significant in the country's history. Around the edge of the white disc is a continuous vine with fifty leaves which represents the year 1950 when the PUP came to power. It is a curious but distinctive flag and the only one of three national flags that depicts humans as a major element in the design. Always useful to know it to get top points in pub quizzes (the other two are Malta and Montserrat).

After 45 minutes passing several islands, the ferry slowed and drew alongside a landing stage. All along the coast were one and two storey buildings and an occasional three storey building overlooking a narrow stretch of beach and the blue sea. We picked up our luggage and walked the short distance to our hotel.

There are no private cars on the island, the only things faster than a bicycle were electric golf carts which act as taxis should you need one, but this is unlikely as the island is only five kilometres by one kilometre at its widest, and there is only one road, with a few branches off it, but even the main road stops halfway along the length of the island. The police also have an electric golf cart, complete with a blue light. I couldn't think why they would need one, but just in case they need to chase a speeding taxi. The roads are not tarmac, just compacted sand and mostly bumpy but no one worries about the holes as the pace of life is slow in true Caribbean style.

Most of us had upgraded given that the cost was low. Tracey had the penthouse apartment on the third storey of the hotel. I did well as I had a king size bed, a bathroom with a shower, a kitchen area with a cooker and a fridge plus a seating area. I also had a large balcony overlooking the sea, with several reclining chairs on it, and enough space to get lost.

Belize is a country of many different influences and amalgams of cultures and despite English being the official language, a raft of other languages are spoken, despite having a population of only 320,000. The country also has the lowest population density in Central America.

Belizean cuisine is equally diverse with influences from British, Mexican and Western Caribbean culinary styles, so rice and beans are the main base for a dish and mixed with chicken, pork, fish, coconut milk and a wide range of vegetables, to create a delectable tropical taste. That evening in the restaurant there was a marvellous array of dishes but one caught our eye and was unbelievably cheap… lobsters, so we ate like kings, but for a fraction of the price back home.

It rained during the night, a tropical downpour and everything was wet. It had stopped shortly after dawn but there was still a lot of water everywhere. I had a walk along the main road, avoiding the puddles. I was amused to see sleeping policemen, Caye Caulker style, being a piece of thick rope nailed to the compacted sand of the road surface. I went south along the main road as far as the landing strip, which was only big enough for small planes and it stretched the width of the island, with beaches at either end, so no room here for overshooting the runway and not getting your feet wet. The road crossed the runway and ended in an exclusive resort.

I turned around and made a small detour to the industrial port on the other side of the island from our hotel. There were two landing craft beached here and this was where deliveries from the mainland would be brought, including building supplies and heavier items. There was also a power station with its associated generators, sub stations and fuel oil storage tanks.

Walking the other way up the main street, I reached the other end which finishes at the Split Bar and a stretch of water between the southern part of the island and the northern part. This channel is called The Split as a hurricane came through Belize and cut the island in two, or so the guide book tells you. It is partially true, but there was still a spit of sand between the two halves after the hurricane, but fisherman wanted to go from one side to the other side without having to go around. They dug out some sand and used this as a short cut until the current between the two islands eroded the wider and deeper channel that you see today.

Despite the detour and stopping to take photos I was back at the hotel in under an hour, so I went to the little Starbucks coffee shop just 100m from the hotel, for breakfast and the inevitable cup of coffee. We were due to have a boat trip and go snorkelling but, due to the rain and storm, the departure was put off for a couple of hours. It was better to have a delay to ensure that there was visibility, since the storm had created strong currents and the sea was a bit murky in places.

Time passed and the sea cleared, so we boarded and set off in a large sailing boat called the Ragga King, followed some way behind by the Ragga Prince with another load of snorkelers. The captain and his two-man crew put the sail up but the wind was weak so we also had the motor on to get to where we needed to be.

The first stop was snorkelling on the reef. The captain described what we were about to see and we all dived in and he pointed out the fish and corals, sometimes surfacing to add to the narrative and then diving again. There were fish of all shapes, sizes and colours, with some the size of a man's forearm. On the seabed were a mass of different corals and as many and varied as the fish. Parts of the reef were separated by just sand, covered by sea grass and we saw some large sharks and manta rays before we found another colourful outcrop of coral reef and an abundance of fish.

Back on board we moved to another part of the seabed between two large reefs. This was a known favourite feeding ground for large turtles. This was a marine reserve and we were under strict instructions not to get too close to the turtles as they are a protected species. However, if they came to us we were to just stay still and let them swim on by. The boat moored some way away from the site and we got into the water and swam along the reef and out to the feeding grounds.

There was a lovely sight of a turtle grazing on sea grass just a short distance in front of and below us. We stopped and watched it graze for a while. Then it swam up to the surface right in front of us to take some air and then swam back down to graze again. Its shell sparkled in the light coming through the water and the patterns on its shell were fantastic. No wonder they had been hunted nearly to extinction for their beautiful shells in the last century but so much better to see them alive, than as static ornaments in people's living rooms.

We had some salad as we motored to another snorkelling site. This time it was sharks, big sharks, not the giant whites but large brown ones, but they were a similar familiar shape. They congregate in this area, partly because it suits them just here and because any scraps left over from lunch are thrown overboard. Whatever you throw never hits the water. They jump out of the water to grab it before one of the others gets it. There was just a boiling mass of shark bodies as they all competed for our left overs. Beyond the shoal of sharks were other large fish, large enough not to be eaten, but not large enough to muscle in on the action, but they hung around on the periphery hoping to pick up any scraps missed.

It was snorkelling time again, although swimming with sharks was a bit intimidating and we didn't exactly rush to be the first in the water, but slowly one by one, once we had seen that the first diver hadn't been mauled to pieces, others followed and dived in. It was fascinating seeing these sharks feeding from beside and underneath them. Larger sharks swam in deeper water 40 or 50 metres away and manta rays came sweeping across the sea grass to catch any titbits that had survived the shark's attentions.

Then it was all over and we were sailing home. Out came the rum punch and we celebrated a great day's snorkelling. It was also good rum punch, with a kick of rum rather than flavoured fruit juice, although soft drinks were also available. More jugs followed as we made the long trip back to shore.

The sail was up with a bit of a breeze and I asked if I could pilot the boat. The captain told me where we were going, past several islands, told me to give a wide berth to the last one and then after passing it to turn to head for the landing stage. Then he gave me the tiller and left me to it, and I was on my own to sail us back to our harbour for a couple of hours. I had some fun steering and sailing past the various islands and making my way back towards the landing stage where we arrived around dusk.

There was no time to waste as it was the day before 21st September and Belize was celebrating its Independence Day with fireworks that evening, set off from the basketball court right next to the dock. It was spectacular followed by the whole island going out to bars and restaurants as everywhere was busy afterwards.

It rained again during the night and it was still raining in the morning. My plan was to do nothing but sit on the balcony in the sun, take a stroll along the beach, lie in the sun and have a swim, followed by a snooze on the beach in the sun. With the rain and the overcast skies, this plan looked like it was to be re-duced to doing nothing.

There are many amazing places in Belize to visit. Just up the coast is The Great Blue Hole near Ambergris Caye, the next big island up the coast which is a breath-taking sight of a 300-me-tre-wide cenote flooded by rising sea waters after the last ice age and the only place like it in the world. But then nothing looks its best on a wet dull day. There was nobody about in the hotel and no one on the streets as if everyone had been out too late the night before celebrating Independence Day.

I retreated to Starbucks whilst I waited for the weather to im-prove and drunk several cups of coffee. I caught up with emails and downloaded some photographs. The battery on the comput-er was running low so I left it and my coffee on the table and ran back to the hotel to get the mains lead. A passing local shouted at me to, "Relax man, its Caye Caulker, what's the hurry?" in a slow Caribbean drawl.

It was also a time to reflect on a few personal issues. Zoë was such a nice person and ticked all the right boxes. She was good looking, nice eyes and even white teeth that you couldn't help but notice when she smiled. She had a good sense of humour and was both good fun and good company to be with. She was relaxed, honest and didn't have issues or baggage. We seemed to have similar interests and outlooks. Nothing seemed to be too much bother, she was intelligent, multi-lingual and a good organiser. She didn't have any annoying little habits. And we felt for each other. She was almost my perfect woman.

Almost. The single drawback was the difference in age. A few years wouldn't matter when you are younger but it played on my mind. I had stopped work to travel, but her lifestyle was the travel industry and I could see her working abroad until her pension age. By the time she stopped working, even if I was still alive I might be a bedridden geriatric with Dementia just when we could have some time to be together and not be working. Right now, things were great and I was on top of the world but the long-term future played on my mind. I was not her long-term catch. I suggested some time apart. The daytime was bad but that evening I was the loneliest person in the world. It was a horrible feeling and one of my most difficult decisions ever.

By early afternoon the rain had stopped and the sun was trying to come out. At three p.m. there was a large boom as a firework the size of a dustbin went off, along with various sirens and the carnival began. Everyone was dressed up in bright and colourful outfits to represent clubs, societies, businesses and public bodies and all parts of the population were represented.

The procession eased its way along the main road with loads of banners, streamers and whistles. The island's sole fire engine was in the parade and the whole of the island police force must have been there, all five of them plus the entire traffic police, both of them riding in a golf cart. It was the Rio carnival and mardi gras rolled into one. Caribbean islands know how to celebrate!

Seb had missed all the carnival as he had taken a ferry back to the main land to travel to and stay up at the border overnight, so that he could get the paperwork processed to get Betsy over the border first thing in the morning. Then he had to drive all the way down the country to pick us up in Belize City. The original plan was to catch the morning ferry and move onto our next stop. There would be an inevitable delay as Seb drove down the country so we opted to stay on the island until we knew that he was on his way and could co-ordinate our meeting in Belize City.

Whenever a ferry was due to leave we would send a text to see whether he had got Betsy out of hock as it were. Reception was patchy and we wondered whether his mobile was receiving or had run out of battery life. We had hung around the hotel pretending to relax in the sun, but mentally pacing up and down like an expectant father. We had let several ferries go, but at one-thirty p.m. we wondered whether he had left or not, it couldn't be too much longer so we caught the ferry anyway.

We arrived in Belize City harbour just as we discovered that Seb had just left the border so we had another two hours or so to kill. Several people had no thoughts of doing anything or going anywhere, so I left my bag with a heap of other people's bags under scrutiny of those not going anywhere, for which I am truly thankful, and headed off for an impromptu but by necessity, whirlwind tour of Belize City.

The first stop was the Taiwan Embassy, and is there anything significant about that? But of course, as some countries fear allowing diplomatic relations with Taiwan, thus incurring the wrath of China which regards Taiwan as a break-away rebel state left over from Mao Tse Tung's liberation of the Chinese mainland to communist forces. But the victorious army had never got around to capturing the little offshore island, now an independent state and a member of the UN.

An untidy loose end or an inconvenient truth to communism's plan for world domination? Taiwan is eager to have as many friends as possible, when it has such a bully as a neighbour whilst China's attitude to Belize, a country the size of one of its smaller villages, is that it is not likely to tip the scales in the global struggle for the balance of power.

I doubt that trade between the two countries amounts to a row of beans. Belize exports crude oil, fruit, largely bananas, seafood and sugar cane, making up 80 per cent of exports and their top five trading partners are the USA, Canada, EU, Mexico and the Caribbean Community. Neither is there any notable presence of Taiwanese tourists so the ambassador must have a quiet life. But then any country willing to accept a Taiwanese embassy, will be welcomed with open arms by Taiwan.

Next was the Fort St George Lighthouse. King George had a lot of things named after him, as he ruled during a very turbulent, expansionist and dramatic period of British and European history. His actual input to government policy was minimal as he liked to party and leave actual government to the civil servants. There is nothing left of the fort and the lighthouse is just a light on top of a tower.

Overlooking the ocean is the tombstone of Victor Bliss 1869-1926. He inherited the title of the 4th Baron Bliss. After the First World War, he retired and indulged himself in sailing and fishing. He was taken ill off the coast of Belize and died having never set foot on the soil. But he had seen it from his ship and being a wealthy and eccentric chap had bequeathed his fortune of almost £1 million to a trust fund for the benefit of Belizeans who have received help from his largesse ever since, for which they are forever thankful.

Crossing over Haulover Creek that flows through the centre of the city is the swing bridge. It is the only one of several made in Liverpool to this design and installed here in 1923. It has a central column on which the bridge rests and it can be turned to allow ships through, although it can interrupt traffic for an hour. It is now only operated by special request.

I passed the courthouse used by the public but was not open to tourists but it was a fascinating piece of English colonial architecture. Next was Broodies, a typical merchant adventure. They imported goods from the home country and anywhere else when they could turn a profit to satisfy both local demand for basic goods and to fashion the local expat population with the luxuries that they expected. Meanwhile they would export whatever the local economy produced to whoever would pay a decent price for it.

Government House was next, a sombre colonial building set in its own grounds, with a high fence and several high-end cars outside, with chauffeurs awaiting their next call. Opposite was the cathedral, a brick-built and modest affair in international terms, but huge for the area and the oldest brick-built protestant cathedral in Central America. It was built using bricks made in England and shipped out to Central America as ballast. It is not magnificent in cathedral terms. It is purely functional with a square four-storey tower with louvered arched windows with the top storeys made from different coloured bricks, suggesting that it was completed over many years using different batches of bricks.

Then it was back to the harbour to wait for Seb and Betsy. I felt sorry for those still sitting around but then it was their choice whilst I would not have been good company as I would have gone insane had I sat around and did nothing for a couple of hours. I am not very good at an enforced session of chilling out and doing nothing.

Seb and Betsy duly turned up and it was a short drive to our next destination but being so late in the day, there was only one hour of light and then an hour of darkness before we arrived. This is always disappointing as part of the travelling experience is to see the country, which is not achieved when it is pitch black. We passed the new capital Belmopan and then turned off the road and had followed a track through the jungle. We climbed up the track into the hills and we bumped along being thrown from side to side with every jolt over the uneven surface.

After a long and bumpy journey through the jungle, we arrived at the Mountain Equestrian Centre close to San Ignacio, locally known as Cayo and checked in. I was sharing a palm frond roofed hut with a shower and toilet with Laurence. We had a marvellous meal provided by the Centre and crashed out.

We were there for several nights. The Centre was a ranch set in the jungle with a few fields hacked out of the surrounding jungle. There was a host of bird calls and from the veranda we could see several colourfully plumed birds, including a toucan which is the only one that I could positively identify. The ranch encourages the wildlife and feeds the birds. This includes sugar water feeders which humming birds fed from during the day showing off their iridescent plumage. At night bats flutter-around and drink the sugared water.

All the buildings were built out of local materials, round wooden beams, palm frond roofs, stucco and wall panels made from interwoven palm leaves and a lot of open-sided or waist high walls. Some windows had louvered shutters, such as the cabins set under trees in the nearby jungle, but just as many were just holes in the wall without glass. There was a small butterfly farm a short walk back towards the road. If you didn't walk or ride, there was nothing to keep you entertained but it was so quiet that it was a good place to relax. Being on a ranch with horses, I was in heaven.

John, Nicole, Seb, Zoë and I had signed up for a day's riding and we picked up our horses from the stables opposite the main ranch house. We were going to be led by Riego, one of the ranch hands, and with him in the lead, we set off along some jungle trails. Various trees were pointed out together with their uses, the tecoma tree, their nuts used for oil, the tapaculo tree with its medicinal benefits, the shaba tree useful for its nuts and edible leaves which is also drought, disease and flood resistant. The kapok tree had multiple uses providing useful timber, medicinal uses, stuffing and oil from the seeds and the cohune palm is useful for its oil and is one of the many local palms which make the best roofing material.

The jungle thinned and we joined a wide rough track where the jungle was interspersed with fields and the occasional building. At the side of the track was a Mennonite church. There is quite a large Mennonite community in the area, although they tend to keep to themselves. They are traditionalists and don't use modern machinery.

We stopped at a rudimentary saw mill. It was open sided under a wooden frame and roofed with canvas. There was a large bandsaw powered by a horse which would be harnessed to an arm that powered a belt and via a series of pulleys, belts and gears the horse would walk around the central pivot to turn the band saw and a few other woodworking machines, simple but effective.

The local Mennonites tend to be self-sufficient farmers but they have an excellent reputation for woodwork and furniture making, cutting their own trees and creating whatever is requested which is one of the few times that they interact with people outside their own community. They also plant teak on their land, as it is a valuable wood and acts as an investment. Land prices reflect how much useable timber is on the site, so it improves the value of the land or provides useable timber for woodworking or construction.

Some of us galloped ahead and reached the object of the ride, a flooded cave and near the entrance was a café for visitors. We had a swim across the pool at the opening of the cave and ventured a short distance inside while we waited for the rest to arrive. Then we hired some lights and canoes and paddled into the flooded cave. Various formations were pointed out by Riego and he told stories of how the local Indians would perform religious ceremonies in the caves.

There was one salutary tale about some youngsters having a party and one of the boys took his girlfriend in a canoe into the cave. They capsized and lost their light and became disorientated and so didn't know which way was out. They stayed-put in the water waiting for someone to rescue them but it was only morning when someone noticed the missing couple and a missing canoe. A very embaressed frightened and cold couple were eventually rescued by their friends after spending the night in the water clinging to the upturned canoe.

Everywhere there were bats roosting, hanging from the walls and ceiling and several different types. There were vampire bats, hence the marks on the horses and freshly dried rivulets of blood that we had seen when we picked up the horses that morning.

The fish bats flew along the surface of the water and hooked out unsuspecting fish. And there were plenty of fruit bats and bats that ate insects. After several hundred metres, the roof got too low to continue by canoe at current water levels so we turned around and paddled back to the mouth of the cave.

We had lunch as we dried off and got back onto the horses. We warmed them up and then galloped along the path up and out of the gorge and headed home. The ranch encourages wild life and had set up some movement activated cameras. On our return, they were checking the videos from the night before and there had been a jaguar hunting along one of the forest trails. There were some good shots of the jaguar prowling along the track, hunting for prey, where we had been riding just minutes earlier to get back to the ranch.

The next day was another day's riding but this time it was just Zoë and me with Junior instead of Riego as a guide. We rode up into the hills and came out on top of a ridge overlooking the ranch. After a pause for the view we came across a termites' nest with a string of termites making their way to and from the nest across the trail and into the jungle. These were edible termites so I scooped some up and licked them off my hand. They were crunchy with a woody, aniseed flavour.

We avoided the tiger ferns, an invasive species that out-competes all the other plants and can take over whole hillsides. It also had sharp points along the edge of its leaves like teeth, hence the local name and best not to brush against it to avoid getting ripped to shreds.

We galloped along some trails and reached some waterfalls, not the famous Thousand Foot Falls in the Cayo district of Belize, which boasts the largest waterfall in Central America which is 500 metres tall but a gentler lower local waterfall. It was a series of falls and plunge pools below, with not one fall above ten metres. Zoë climbed up the side and jumped in, which from that height created a huge splash. I was not so daring and was happy just to swim. It started to rain but it didn't bother us as we were wet from swimming. However, when we went to put our clothes back on, they had been left in the open and now they were wet from the rain.

We rode to the local summer residence of a business man from Belize City for shelter which was usually open but to Junior's surprise, it was locked. The generator house, a small shed set well back from the house was open so we sheltered in there to have our lunch. The horses stood still in the rain whilst we ate lunch. When we went to remount, our clothes were still wet and the saddles were wet but there was nothing for it but to remount and return to the ranch, galloping all the way up the drive and we got home just as it stopped raining.

We left the ranch and drove along the bumpy track until we turned onto the main mercifully smooth tarmac road and headed for San Ignacio. A new bridge was being built across the river but it wasn't completed so we took the old bridge. It was standing above the water but in the rainy season it is often impassable as the water floods over the top of the old bridge and vehicles must wait until the level drops sufficiently to ford the river by driving over the still flooded bridge. San Ignacio is the furthest up the river that the English loggers could navigate so it became a settlement and port for river traffic and transfer point. We continued to the Belize border crossing at Benque Viejo del Carmen.

CHAPTER 10
Guat's up, Doc?

In no man's land, Betsy had an identity crisis. Since Anchorage she had been registered as an Alaskan vehicle with Alaskan number plates. That was fine for getting across borders down to Belize but from here on it would be much more difficult being a North American commercial vehicle with extra paper work, taxes and other regulations. Hence a bit like a person with dual nationality and two passports, Betsy is also registered in Guatemala which, being part of the Central American border agreements with other countries, makes it a lot easier to cross borders. With all the passengers gathered about the front of the bus to shield what was happening, with a sleight of hand, she had a new identity and new Guatemalan number plates and we crossed the border at Melchor de Mencos into Guatemala.

We had a short drive stopping in Remate for lunch in the rain. Just like entering Belize, we started on the Guatemalan jokes, 'Guat's the matter?', 'Guat's for lunch?' and in a parody of Bugs Bunny, 'Guat's up, Doc?' Some people wandered off to a restaurant and I had a healthy choice of a banana next to the bus. As I ate I watched whilst a street vendor set up his stall on the side of the road and cooked crispy spicy chicken and chips. The smell of spicy chicken wafted across the road and I could no longer resist so I bought a portion of unhealthy fried crispy chicken and chips.

We waited until mid-afternoon and then drove on to the Tikal National Park which hosts the incredible Mayan ruins of Tikal, where we could camp for the night in the grounds of a hotel next to the entrance to the ruins. Some people upgraded which seemed to be rooms with three bedrooms but I was happy to camp. There was a big old solitary tree in the grounds that looked dead, so I avoided the nice and flat looking pitches near the tree in favour of one further away and not in danger of any branches breaking off and squashing me in the middle of the night.

I was happy with my pitch until Seb pointed out that it was in a hollow and if it rained it would flood... after the Tulum flooding experience of Steve's tent after which it had taken two days to dry out his sleeping bag, no one wanted a repeat so I moved my tent to higher ground. It was Seb's birthday so Tracey cooked another of his favourite dishes and her signature dish of nutty chicken flavoured with almonds followed by Normandy apple tart. It was fantastic and I always meant to ask her for the recipe but it was my loss as I forgot to do so.

It was not a great night. There was a lot of noisy talking as if the night guards were having a party. Several times they walked around the site shining their flash lights this way and that. An army lorry drove into the site during the night and it felt that they were driving past just inches from my head. There was another bout of talking and waving of lights and shouts of goodbye as they drove off again.

We were up and ready to go to the ruins when they opened at eight a.m. As usual as we were on-site, we were a long way ahead of the tourist crowds. We walked out of the Jaguar Inn and past a troop of mongooses working their way along one side of the car park with their tails pointing straight up and a few watchful eyes on duty whilst the rest of the troop foraged. And what is the plural of mongoose? Most references state mongooses but hedge their bets and say a rarely used alternative is mongeese. Neither sound right to my ear so I am just adding to the debate by calling it an irregular noun like moose or sheep where the plural is the same as the singular.

We were the first in the queue to get our tickets from the entrance office and with our guide we walked into the main site. We passed a clutch of wild turkeys pecking at the ground as we made our way through the jungle to one of the many temples. We paused at the bottom but started the long climb up the stairs to the top. This was a spot to view the sunrise and we met a Swiss couple who had been at the hotel the night before and had made the effort to be here early to see the sun rise and avoided paying the entrance fee as the ticket office was shut so they just carried on walking in the dark. Unfortunately, it was a hazy and cloudy morning so they didn't get the vista that they had wanted.

It was still a great morning with the sun struggling through the clouds but it gave an extra ambience as the warming sun drove off the last remaining wisps of mist from around the ruins pointing skyward through the remaining mist. We absorbed the scenery and then made our way down and walked across to the main plaza. But first we climbed a long winding wooden staircase to the top of one of the temples to get a grandstand view of the square below and the other buildings.

Our guide, César talked us through several of the buildings around the square and explained the significance of each. We returned to the hotel cum campsite to pack up camp and move on. What a delight to find that those who had not wanted to visit yet more stones on top of other stones in the jungle had dried our tents out and had packed them away. Many thanks especially to Steve who had packed away my tent for me.

That meant that we were ready to roll earlier than expected so everyone benefited. There was also another reason in that there was an England v Wales rugby game and it was hoped that we could get to the next destination and find a bar with a television to watch the game. We went back through Remate and made a brief stop at a petrol station with more staff and armed guards than customers. There was a general feeling that we just wanted to get to the next stop to find a bar with a television, so this was only a brief stop.

We reached our hotel and dropped our bags. It was set high on a hill overlooking Lake Flores and the town of the same name, on the far side of the lake. Several people had decided to upgrade so whilst I hadn't, Laurence and I were left sharing a dormitory meant for eight between just the two of us so we had plenty of space. These were little cabins, rooms on stilts with palm frond roofs set out under palm trees in the garden of the main communal area, which was also the home of the owner of the hotel.

We walked down the hill and took a river taxi to the island in the lake upon which the old town was built. It had an impressive cathedral sitting on the hill at the centre of the island and a wonderful defensive position but no defensive walls were ever built. There were many pleasant colourful lake side properties up to three or four storeys high with magnificent views across the lake.

We found a bar with a television. It was not on the right channel but the bar was virtually empty and no one was watching the television so we asked the bar staff whether we could watch the game and settled down to watch the match. I had no local currency so I went in search of a bank. I found myself alone with Zoë. There was another heart to heart chat and I admit that I forget the details but it seemed that I was getting a second chance, and all of a sudden, I was walking on air and the happiest man on the planet with a perfect partner.

Zoë had some jobs to do so she went back to the hotel. I found a bank and some fast food and then re-joined the group in the bar to watch the end of the game. England were ahead but the Welsh gradually caught up and overtook them and won by a narrow margin.

Kate was delighted but magnanimous despite all the goading she had taken earlier when England were piling on the points. We all went our separate ways after the match and I went first to see the cathedral and afterwards, I walked over the causeway to the modern town on the far side of the lake from the hotel. I was on a mission to find a toyshop to stock up on gifts.

Having searched high and low and walked up and down every street I still had not found a toy shop. I was walking back towards the causeway and paused at the bus station. There were a number of chicken buses and I took a few photos. Then out of the corner of my eye up an alleyway off the plaza, I saw a market and down one of its many aisles I found a whole street full of toy shops. I stocked up on bats and balls, board games and playing cards and carried my hoard back to the old town across the causeway on the island and found a water taxi to take me to the landing stage at the bottom of the hill below my hotel.

I had just paid the water taxi when Steve and Seb arrived in another water taxi. Steve had been for a coffee and Seb had bought two large batteries for the bus. They were big and heavy so he was looking for a tuk tuk. We decided to share the cost... it wasn't far to walk but a ride in a tuk tuk would be fun so we loaded the two heavy batteries and the three of us into the back of a tuk tuk for the trip up the hill to the hotel. The little two stroke engine had a struggle getting up the hill and it felt as if it might just rollover backwards, head over heels, but it managed the incline and we tipped the driver generously.

That evening, Zoë and I slipped away from the hotel and took a water taxi back to the old town. we found a nice mid-range restaurant in pleasant surroundings and I treated us to a large romantic dinner with several courses and wine. In the morning, I woke up and found a tick on my arm. I had noticed something the night before whilst having dinner and tried to wipe it off but in the atmospheric dimmed lights of the restaurant thought it was just a sticky bit of tar or oil. In the light of day, the monster truly had its head stuck in and was plump having fed all night. I wasn't too concerned as I had had a series of jabs against tick-borne encephalitis so infection wasn't a major concern but I wanted it off and quick.

Nicole came to my rescue and with a pair of tweezers successfully removed it whilst Laurence watched, poised with his camera. Care is needed to remove ticks as the body may break off leaving the head embedded in the skin and open to infection. The little beast wasn't going to feed off anyone else at the hotel as Nicole skilfully removed it in one piece and it was incinerated in a few seconds by a blast from a cigarette lighter.

Eating breakfast on the hotel balcony high above the lake, gave us a wonderful view of the water taxis crossing the lake, the fishing boats plying their trade and above the new town on the far side of the lake the sight of planes coming in to land over the town on their final descent before landing at the airport, somewhere to our left as we looked at the town. Excursions were sold all over the country to view the Mayan ruins at Tikal and some tourists flew in just for the day.

It was another free day to do as we pleased but Nicole, Clare, Zoë and I had already decided to go for a swim along the lake to a café. The attraction of this café was that it had a number of rope swings from which you could launch yourself from the shore and drop into the water.

We walked down to the landing stage and dived in and started to swim along the lake. Nicole had decided that she wasn't up for a long swim and decided to turn back after just a few hundred metres. The café was on the same side as the hotel but two kilometres of swimming to get there, so it was never going to be an easy journey.

Then I realised that we were swimming in murky waters, a favourite haunt of crocodiles in a hot country where we had already seen crocodiles. What was I thinking? We had been told that there were no crocodiles in the lake but did they know that they are not supposed to be here? Had they read the guide books? We were never far from land but I would never be able to outswim a hungry crocodile. I relied on local knowledge and the fact that Zoë was in front of me and Clare behind me so I was okay, Jack.

It took an hour to reach the bay where the café was but landfall was a welcome sight and an opportunity to get out and sit down and relax with a cup of coffee. I am glad that the proprietor never asked where you keep your money when you are only wearing speedos or a bikini. And just to be clear, I was wearing the speedos, the girls were wearing the bikinis.

We had a wonderful time jumping in from the cliffs or swinging out, holding on to a rope and dropping into the water. As the jumps got higher, the propensity to get a wedgie increased so boys had to be mindful. This was the same for the girls as for me but they had an added consideration. The speed of entry from a height also meant that they often lost the covering effect of the top half of their bikini, which would end up around their neck which needed to be repositioned before they exited the water. All part of the fun.

We played for a long time, interspersed with coffees or soft drinks until it was time to go. We could have ordered a water taxi to take us back but with a bit of egging each other on, we got back into the water for the long swim back to the landing stage and the hotel.

That evening we were back at the dockside for an evening boat trip to see the sunset on the lake. We boarded our boat named El Querubin or Cherub, a small twin hulled, rectangular decked and roofed pleasure craft. We set off up the lake following the shoreline, past exclusive resorts and large lakefront private residences. It was also Steve's birthday so we had a stock of drinks to celebrate. We found a nice quiet spot with good views towards the west where the sun would set and went for a swim, diving off the boat or just jumping in. There was also some egging each other on and ending with the removal of the bottoms of bikinis and speedos and waving them above your head. Getting them off was easy but getting them back on is not so easy as you float in the water.

We dried off and watched the fantastic colours take shape and slowly change as the sun went down. After the spectacle was finished, disaster struck, the engine wouldn't start. It was a nice spot to watch the sunset but not a lot of water taxis came this way and those that did were too far away to hail. We waved and shouted but they just waved back thinking that we were just having a party.

There was nothing for it so Zoë dived in and swam towards the nearest water taxi rank. She had a lot of stamina and determination as she had already swum at least four kilometres, but someone had to go and get help. There was also a certain amount of danger as in the failing light, a boat might not see a swimmer in the water. As it happened before she got to shore a water taxi went past her and she flagged it down. A rope was tied between the two boats and we were towed back to shore.

It was a lazy start to the next day as we had a half day's drive to Rio Dulce, a river that empties into the Caribbean on Guatemala's short eastern coast. We booked into an eco-lodge, The Hacienda Tijax which has several cabins on stilts standing in the shallow waters of the mangrove swamp, connected by board walks to each other and to the main centre, which consists of a bar, restaurant and a swimming pool.

It overlooks a quiet marina, full of boats. When a hurricane threatens, boats that can't escape from its course come to the ports and harbours along this stretch of coast and up the river as it is the safest place to be. Most visitors came by boat, their own or a water taxi but we left Betsy at the end of a long track from the road and walked down a path and then a board walk through the mangroves and approached the eco lodge from the landward side. The cabins were all named after birds or animals, and the one that I had was called Ibis.

It was still Steve's birthday… on the basis that although it was yesterday, it was still his birthday somewhere in the world and so we had a party that evening. Steve had a cabin along the river front overlooking the marina at the end of the board walk so we would not disturb anyone. We gathered for rum punch cocktails before our evening meal. There were some party games, including acting out famous scenes from various films, selected secretly by the two or three performers which the non-performing members of the group had to guess. Since it was Steve's birthday, he had to appear in every scene. He and I acted out some of the iconic scenes as Leonardo DiCaprio and Kate Winslet from the 1997 film Titanic. We had a meal in the restaurant and the staff there had baked a cake, so Steve got a cake with candles on it plus some cards and gifts.

After the meal, we went for a dip in the pool. It was only a small pool so more of a dip to keep cool than doing lengths. Zoë didn't bother to get into her bikini but just stripped off and dived in. Soon it was just her and me in the pool and a small group of young English tourists. They were drinking and chatting by the side of the pool in the weak light that spilled out from the bar. There were good natured calls for us to 'get a room' which is ironic as we had rooms but unfortunately, I was sharing with Laurence and Zoë as crew was sharing with Seb.

The next morning, we took a boat trip from the wharf next to the main buildings and first went up stream from Puerto Barrios past Bird Island, unimaginatively named, as it was a popular roost for all sorts of birds. Upstream we viewed the castle, the Busteon de Bustamante that the Spanish built under orders from Phillip II, since enlarged and now called Castillo de San Felipe as protection, where the river was narrow where it left the lake for the last section that flowed into the sea. Then we turned around and headed down the Rio Dulce to Livingston on the Caribbean coast.

The river flows through dense jungle which comes right down to the water's edge. Tropical birds nested in the trees and flew overhead. We took our time and had a few diversions to look at some of the boats moored up channels off the main river. We also looked at some of the trees and some of the flowers by the water's edge. For fauna, we saw some large colourful butterflies, some stick insects and a giant grasshopper that was the width of my hand.

At the mouth of the Rio Dulce we came to the small town of Livingston. It has no roads connecting it to the rest of the country and as such has developed its own unique character with something of a Caribbean feel. It has a large population of Garifuna descendants originally from west and central Africa. Today Garifuna people live primarily in Central America and along the Caribbean coast in Belize, Guatemala, Nicaragua, and Honduras.

They have their own language and customs but suffer from discrimination from the indigenous tribes. There was some black slave unrest in the British colony of St Vincent, which alarmed the white settlers so much that many of the slaves and the black free community were expelled and left by the navy on the island of Roatán, Honduras from which they then migrated to the mainland.

The beach was dirty from washed up rubbish strewn across it and it had never been cleared but this wasn't a tourist destination, and obviously nobody cared. Therefore, the idea of relaxing on the beach and swimming in the sea was one choice that I rejected. I walked up the main road with Zoë but there was little of interest and once we reached the edge of town and saw the endless fields disappearing away from either side of the road, we turned around and headed back.

There was no cathedral or castle to visit so that was another option out of the window. So, it was an early and long lunch, and I started with a beer and ordered tapado, a local dish of seafood soup with coconut milk. There was a shop in the little main street selling wines, beers and spirits and both Zoë and I had developed a taste for rum and coke. I don't drink rum at home but there is such a great selection locally and it tastes so very different. There was quite a range of brands on offer and as I was not an expert, I asked Zoë to choose a bottle and she chose a mid-price range bottle which I bought for the pair of us.

It was time to re-board and we set off once again for the return journey. En route along the gorge with towering cliffs on either side is a café where we stopped. Part of the café complex includes some hot springs on the bank of the river, creating a localised hot pool. The hot water bubbles up but the rising column of hot water moves as the river current swirls by so you must keep moving about until you are just in the right place to get a continuous blast of hot therapeutic water.

There were also fish swimming in the river, although it was so muddy that you couldn't see them. But they had a habit of nibbling your feet and when you cannot see them and get an unexpected nibble it can be unnerving. But at least there were no crocodiles… not just from local knowledge but crocodiles don't like clear, oxygenated and fast flowing water. This water wasn't clear but there was a fast current so I was less concerned about the possibility of crocodiles.

During the day, we had seen several fishermen throwing nets into the water from canoes made from hollowed out tree trunks. Several people wanted a photo and none of us had got the shot that we all wanted. Nearing the end of the journey we came across a fisherman throwing his net into the river. We asked if we could watch and take photos. He showed his technique with a few throws while we took photos. He had only caught one fish, half the size of a man's hand so it wasn't a good day for him. We gave him a tip for allowing us to take photos, getting the shots we wanted and he had earned more from those five minutes than he would from selling his meagre catch so everyone was happy. We carried on up the river towards the marina and we watched him continue to fish but without luck until we turned a bend in the river and he was lost to sight.

That evening we arranged to hire some kayaks to go paddling across the river to see the howler monkeys at dawn. They are at their most active then as they have woken up hungry and will begin hunting for food while also reclaiming their territory from any wandering monkeys that may have entered their patch during the night. There was no guide but as the most experienced paddler, I had been given specific and detailed instructions of how to get there and where to go, which channels to take and so on, so the heavy burden of leadership responsibility was on me.

It was dark, just beginning to lighten when Clare, Zoë and I pushed our kayaks into the water before five a.m. We paddled straight across the river and turned to follow the shore, noting the hotel and the private residence with the red corrugated roof and other landmarks that I had memorised the night before.

We came to a channel opening that led away from the river that we could well have missed as it was set back behind some trees. There was a false channel and then a fork, up which either channel the monkeys were meant to be. We heard the calls but had not seen any monkeys. Then a bit deeper into the forest we saw our first monkeys. They are noisy things but not very big. They are one of the top ten noisiest animals in the world, and given the racket that they make, it's true.

We could see dark forms moving through the canopy but rarely had a clear view, due to the undergrowth and the abundance of leaves obscuring the view. Our best view was when one must have missed his footing or a branch snapped under its weight and he fell through the canopy, through several branches and palm fronds to land with a thud on the ground. He would be dazed but not badly hurt, picking himself up and climbing up the nearest tree to get back to the safety of the canopy. We took the other channel and heard more monkeys but no good views so we headed back the way we had come.

We had to be back because the three of us plus Nicole had also booked a yoga session to take place in The Tower of the Shaman, a fifteen metre high modern tower (modern as in built within the last hundred years) that tops the mountain behind the eco lodge. It was a walk to get there crossing two long pedestrian only suspension bridges that swayed as we crossed. The view from the top was great, up and down the river and we could see the marina and the lake in the distance before settling down for an hour of yoga.

It was mid-morning when we loaded our bags back onto Betsy and set off for a drive into the mountains to San Andres Itzapa, a small village located close to Antigua. We would be staying at the Manos Amigas Centre, run by the Italian NGO 'Mani Amiche' in support of local women who have been abandoned or abused, and who are staying in the centre with their children. This is the project to which Luca, the Wanderlust 2012 Guide of the Year, donated part of his bursary. It is a worthy cause and our stay would help a little bit towards the costs of running the centre.

We took the ring road around the capital, Guatemala City, as we weren't stopping there. If the traffic on the ring road was anything to go by, the place is a seething mass of vehicles, traffic jams and vehicles throwing out pollution. It took a while to get through with chicken buses, cars and lorries all vying for space and changing lanes, hooting their horns and pedestrians weaving their way bravely through the traffic.

It was dark when we got to the track leading up to the Manos Amigas Centre. The rain had washed out part of the track and there was a large gully running the length of the road. It was going to be a bumpy ride so we stowed everything away. We all got out and walked up the road and waited for Betsy. Skilfully driven by Zoë they both made it up the hill and over the gully with nothing broken and we checked in at the centre and got our rooms and I had one to myself. But I wasn't alone for long as after supper and people had gone to bed, Zoë slipped into my room. She was gone when I woke up at dawn.

In the morning, we had a tour of the centre, the kindergarten, the school, the workshops, the farm, the hospital and the bakery led by the director. This was the reason that we had gone in search of toys for children in Flores. The cost of the stay plus a donation contributed to their funds but these were gifts from us to the centre and they were much appreciated. After paying for essentials, food, medicines, teachers and security there wasn't much left so these toys would go to the toy library to make life a little more interesting and fun for the children.

Then it was a repeat of the journey over the gully to get back to the main road, stowing everything away securely and walking down and waiting for Betsy, this time driven by Seb. She was down at the bottom with nothing worse than some paint having been rubbed off on the bank above the track.

It was another long drive day through mountains with some magnificent views until we started the long descent down to Panajachel, a small town on the shores of Lake Atitlan where we would stay in a small hotel. We descended some steep slopes down to the town and arrived in the afternoon and so had some time to explore the town, its market and to take a walk along the edge of the lake.

Our hotel had a small communal area but also a permanent resident, a large green parrot who either sat on a perch at head height or flew up and climbed around the trees in the garden. He was quiet but every now and again there would be a burst of bird Spanish from the trees above us. The mix of available rooms and people who had opted for upgrades was just right, so Zoë and I had a room to ourselves, as did Seb and Tracey.

The lake is in the caldera of a giant volcano, hence the steep descent down to the lake. The last eruption was over 80,000 years ago and it blew the top of the volcano off. There are three other volcanoes on the rim of the former giant volcano. The lake is an endorheic lake meaning that it has no outlet. The water level does vary as was noticed after one earthquake when the level fell several metres. The level is static as water flows in and seeps out or evaporates at about the same rate. It is also the deepest lake in Central America but I have conflicting reports of the exact depth, varying from 340 metres to 600 metres but the exact depth is not relevant when even its shallowest reported depth exceeds that of all the other lakes in Central America and it is immaterial if you cannot swim and you cannot touch the bottom.

We were going to just hire a water taxi for a tour of a couple of lakeside villages and to take in some sights but the hotel manager got us a cheaper deal with his cousin who owned a boat. Lake Atitlan's beautiful waters change colour to suit the mood of the weather from emerald and azure to lapis and olive. Today it was a cloudless sky with just a few wisps of cloud and the lake reflected the sky and it looked blue.

As we left the shore for a diagonal trip across the lake, we looked back at Panajachel. The town is low-rise, two or three storeys only, built up the lower gentle slopes with steep forest covered slopes towering above the town and all along the lake edge. In complete contrast were three twenty storey concrete blocks at one end of town. We had passed them on our way into town and had commented on them as being ugly. In the centre of a big city they may have blended in with a lot of other tall buildings but here, from the water it was an even bigger eyesore, and so out of keeping with the surroundings it is surprising that they ever got planning permission.

Our first stop was San Juan. We were met by a guide at the dockside who led us up the road past several trinket stands and around some back streets to a women's weaving co-operative where they were making huipiles or traditional dresses and scarves. We had demonstrations of how the thread is made and the dyes used to colour the thread; then the final part, the weaving of the material using the different coloured threads.

The colours and patterns are exquisite and the patterns are handed down from generation to generation. Villages also tend to have their own designs and some designs are unique and some villages specialise in a style. I could have bought a dozen but I rarely buy souvenirs as I would end up with a houseful of trinkets gathering dust. Besides, on a long trip there would be nowhere to store a lot of extra things and there would be problems of both weight and volume trying to get them home on the aircraft.

Everywhere we walked in San Juan we saw women wearing traditional dresses with aprons and shawls, all in striking and colourful patterns. Around the corner was a coffee museum and café. We were told the story of how coffee is grown, how it is processed, the different qualities of the beans and finally the many ways that it can be served. And of course, we all had a cup of coffee.

The Medicine Garden was a botanical garden with a wide range of plants with their names on little tags next to each plant. We were shown several plants and offered a few leaves to try and told of the uses that they can be put to. The accompanying nurse cum guide knew all the plants and answered questions on many plants that people were particularly interested in but which had not been included in the usual tour of the garden. My favourite was the liquorice plant used for respiratory diseases, stress, stomach ulcers, poisoning, breast and prostate issues. I am partial to liquorice so I had several leaves and not because I suffer from any of the problems that the plant is claimed to resolve. I just like liquorice and pocketed a few more leaves for later.

We passed the church built in 1633 and next to it an extension built in 2013 but with the same stone and in the same style, so it blended in with its much older neighbour. On the road, back down to the docks we paused in a gallery that displayed several brightly painted canvases of local people in the style of a well-known artist, Juan Sisay who had developed a unique style.

The boat then took us on to Santiago Atitlan, also called San Pedro la Laguna known for its colourful market. It is also the home to Maximón, a local idol, a mixture of a Mayan deity and Catholicism. Favours often asked for are for good health or a good crop but it is best not to anger him as he will get his own back on you. He doesn't have a permanent home but moves every year to another location. The year that I visited he was several kilometres away in another village in the hills. I had wanted to see him but the cost was daunting and there was not enough time to get there and back without delaying the boat's departure or risking the last section of the journey across the lake in the dark.

We walked through the markets and they were heaving with people. There were stalls lining either side and standing back to back down the middle of the road. We reached the end of the market and rather than fight our way back through the crowds, we took some back streets to get back to the docks. We met up with Seb and Tracey as we walked through the town so together we found a restaurant for a late lunch. Afterwards we had a wander through the market near the docks before boarding our boat to return to the hotel.

We had had a proposal about the route to take to get to our next stop in Antigua. There was an England v Australia rugby match being televised live, starting at one p.m. local time. A short walk from our hotel in the city was a sports bar with a large screen television and they would be showing the match. The proprietor who was also the chef was English. Someone had already done a lot of research and canvassing and given the 80 per cent vote in Tulum to watch a rugby match, it was a bit of a formality but changes are possible to the agenda if there was a majority in favour and not too much of a departure from the already agreed schedule.

The choice was either the scheduled six-hour drive through beautiful mountain scenery on twisting mountain roads which we would arrive at in mid-afternoon or the alternative which was an even earlier start and a four-hour drive (plus comfort breaks) along a main road to reach our hotel and a short walk into the town centre in time to see the kick off. That is how we came to be driving out of Panajachel through empty streets just after dawn to get onto the main road.

We arrived at the Posada La Merced Hotel, dumped our bags and walked the two blocks to get to the sports bar. I had a meal and then left everyone else watching the game and walked around Antigua.

Antigua is a UNESCO World Heritage Site just 60 kilometres from Guatemala City. It is the old colonial capital of

Guatemala but stays a major cultural centre and has a mixture of Indian markets and colonial buildings. The cobbled streets, the indigenous marimba music in the many bars and locals selling goods from a blanket spread on the ground creates a fantastic atmosphere. It was considered not to be a good place for a capital as there were several earthquakes that hit the city in historical times and several nearby volcanoes. Thus, the capital was moved in 1776 but the city is still dwarfed by the huge towering cone of Volcán de Agua.

The guide books also talk about an excursion to the Pacaya Volcano to watch the spectacular eruptions of the volcano from close quarters as red-hot lava explodes into the air and at night, the eruptions light the whole sky like a spectacular firework display. This would have been a major attraction for me and when I planned the trip there were eruptions taking place at several sites in Central America but by the time I arrived, they had all ceased. I have visited other volcanoes such as Eyjafjallajökull in Iceland which threw so much ash into the air that aircraft were grounded throughout northern Europe for three days in 2010. That volcano finished erupting just days after I booked my trip to go and see it in action. I have seen both the before and after effects of volcanoes but I want to see one erupting at close quarters.

I left the sports bar and walked across the plaza to look at the cathedral. Then through an arch down the main street to the main plaza with its colonial style municipal building, and the merchants' houses and colonnades lining two sides of the square. One side had an impressive double-tiered stone colonnade with decorative plaster work. Down some side streets were ruins, carefully and permanently fenced off.

Some were nondescript buildings but judging by the ornate portico of one of the buildings it must have been an impressive building in its day. Some of the buildings were churches with their walls still standing high but no roof and some buildings had large cracks in their walls. This was earthquake damage and the buildings were too badly damaged to be easily repaired and used again. They were slowly decaying even further.

I had my trip up the Pacaya volcano but it lacked the excitement that would have gone with the trip had the volcano been erupting. It was an early start but it was easy to get up that morning as there were fireworks being let off and a band was playing. This was the start of celebrations for The Virgin of Rosario which started at dawn. We were picked up early in the morning and after visiting a few other hotels to pick up other guests, we were driven for over an hour to reach the volcano and then up a twisting road to the visitors' centre. Here you could buy a T-shirt with 'I lava you' written on it inside a large red heart. The centre is at 1,900 metres but the crater was at 2,552 metres so there was still a long walk to reach the top.

Some of the more infirm visitors opted to take horses to reach the top. I might have ridden but it was more of sitting on a horse and having someone lead it on a halter up the mountain. We paused at the Mirador Majahue from which we could see several other volcanoes in the distance such as the double humped Acatenango 3,796 metres. The other two volcanoes were further away on the distant horizon, Volcán de Agua 3,760 metres and Volcán de Fuego 3,763 metres and there was a slight haze so we didn't have a good view of these two.

After more climbing, we looked down on the results of the most recent eruption. A fissure had opened on the side of the cone and lava had poured out down the side of the cone. It had pooled in a hollow and had filled it until the lava level rose high enough to flow down another slope. The cinder cone was devoid of vegetation, as was the fresh, now solidified lava flow with its cracked black surface and sharp edges. In contrast, the slopes that had formed the hollow centuries before the most recent eruption, had had time to erode and had developed soil and there were plants growing on the surrounding slopes so these were covered in green foliage.

We went down and walked across the lava. We took a diversion to the edge where the lava had stopped against the slopes of the hollow. In places, there were deep holes between some of the rocks with hot gases coming out. The guide cut some twigs from the surrounding bushes and from his pack he pulled out a bag of marshmallows. We roasted them by pushing the stick down the hole where the rock was still too hot to touch but cooked marshmallows nicely.

That evening we had cocktails on the roof terrace of the hotel before our evening meal in a restaurant nearby. As the sun set behind the mountains we had magnificent views of the cathedral and all around us, the mountains and volcanoes. After the meal, I was having a drink with Zoë in a near deserted bar when we got talking to the owner. He had his own Maximón and proudly showed him to us.

There was a glass fronted cabinet behind the bar with a mannequin about half a metre-high dressed in black trousers, a black and red striped poncho with a moustache. His nose had been burnt and blackened by offerings of lit cigarettes which had been pushed into his partially opened mouth and he had a bottle of beer in one hand. The owner also told us about another bar with another Maximón so we had to cross the old town and find this other bar.

This was a much more sinister figure, half-life sized, sitting on a chair which itself was set on a table in an alcove, partially in the dark but with a red light giving some illumination but not much. He had a black face, and dark hat, jacket and trousers. He had a cigarette hanging from his mouth and several bottles and tins of beer on the table and around his feet. He had a hunched appearance which added to the sense of sinister unease. It was getting late and we had an early start and some new members of the group to greet in the morning.

CHAPTER 11
The Saviour

The coffee shop next to the hotel was open so we got coffees to go whilst we waited for Seb to turn up with Betsy. We had some new travelling companions and we were re-joined by Roger from Australia who had been travelling with us starting in Alaska, but had left us to do his own thing in Mexico. There was Alex from Holland, Vera from Austria, Jim and Ginger from the USA, Lisa and Debs, Lear and Yvette from Australia and Kim from England. There were now eighteen of us, in other words a full busload. Jobs to do on the jobs rota may come around a little less often, but getting the back locker packed and just getting on and off and natural breaks would all take a little longer. There may be fewer upgrades available due to there being a larger group.

We drove to and crossed the border from Ciudad Pedro de Alvarado in Guatemala into La Hachadura in El Salvador. After 'You'd better Belize it', 'Guat the heck?' and even 'I lava you', it was going to be difficult to work El Salvador into a sentence and it defeated our attempts to continue the joke theme. El Salvador translates as 'the saviour' in Spanish.

En-route we stopped at Sonzacate for more supplies and arrived at our hotel on the beach in the afternoon at Los Cobanos, a fishing village away from the tourist trail. The schedule always allows plenty of time to get through border controls but we had got through quickly and had some spare time to go for a walk or lounge around the pool. Other than the owner we had the place to ourselves.

The back door of the hotel grounds opened onto the beach and there were fishing shacks and cafés along the beach and fishermen's huts further along the beach. There was a swimming pool and a communal single-storey open-sided sitting area. There were a pair of two storey palm frond roofed buildings with the rooms in them. Some were lucky and got twin rooms and the rest of us had dormitories.

We had a free morning to sit around the pool and do nothing. I walked along the beach both ways until I could go no further than the rocky headlands in both directions so I was back by the pool in under an hour. The most exciting thing that morning was to find a red land crab in the pool which we fished out and after waving its claw at us menacingly it scurried off and hid under a flower pot. At midday, we were going snorkelling to see a wreck just off the coast.

We walked along the road to the snorkelling centre and had a view of some exhibits and pictures of what you might find. A certain area has been marked by buoys as a nature reserve where fishing is prohibited but snorkelling is acceptable. We took our fins, masks and snorkels and walked back to the beach to where there were two fishing boats waiting, bobbing up and down in the swell with their anchors on long lines holding the boats against the sand of the beach. We headed out and ploughed straight through the heavy surf until we were beyond the breakers and we turned up the coast. We could see the top of the wreck occasionally as the swell rolled over the top of what was left of the wreck. There is only the boiler left on the sea bed and some of the hull, but the water was so murky that we saw nothing until the swell pushed you up against the hard, rusty boiler.

As a snorkelling trip, this was very disappointing as we couldn't see anything. We went a bit further up the coast but the water was just as bad with zero visibility. We headed back to the beach. One of the guides took a few people along the beach to a place near the headland and we did some snorkelling in a metre of water around the rocks. There were a few seashells and a small sea snake but little of the colourful coral that had been promised or any fish longer than a little finger.

We were all disappointed and felt that we should have been told that the sea was too murky to see anything and should have been given the chance to cancel. In the end, those who got off the boats and returned straight to the hotel got a partial refund and those who had gone snorkelling off the beach had had an extra opportunity to see something so had no refund.

We left the hotel and drove along the road for the short journey to the Cerro Verde National Park which has three volcanoes within its boundaries, stopping again for some supplies in Sonzacate. Shopping was quick as we had been to the same supermarket a couple of days before and knew our way around so we were soon back on the road. The last section of road up to the campsite was several kilometres up a steep rough track and it was going to be bumpy, added to which Betsy would need to keep her speed up because if she stopped, she would never be able to pull away again on such a steep slope. To lighten the load, we all got out and walked to the campsite. Meanwhile Seb waited an hour and drove the bus up after us, by which time we should have reached the campsite on foot.

The highlight of Cerro Verde National Park is the Cerro Verde, an extinct volcano which last erupted around 2,500 years ago. On the top by its crater is one of the few cloud forests in the country, located at over 2,000 meters above sea level. The Cerro Verde, along with the volcanoes of Santa Ana and Izalco form one of the most impressive landscapes in El Salvador.

The campsite was in an area of flat ground high up in the mountains. There was a conical cinder volcano in front of us, Izalco, a forest covered shield volcano to one side which was Cerro Verde and behind us was the Santa Ana volcano towering above the campsite and shrouded in mist. Some people upgraded to cabañas, whilst those who were camping set up their tents anywhere they liked on the large grassed area. There was a bandstand near the track and several people chose this area to set their tents up. I walked a hundred metres further on to a flat space overlooked by two unoccupied cabañas, and its location was some distance from any other tents which is an important consideration, as when there are two of you in a tent, the canvas is not sound proof.

We had booked a guide to take us up to the top of the Santa Ana volcano that afternoon and after lunch we duly walked back up the road and waited at the junction with the start of the track up the mountain. There was a policeman there as tourists are not allowed up without a police guard due to bandits and terrorists but the policeman standing there was not our guard, and he knew nothing about any tourist group going up that afternoon. There was also no guide.

It took a few phone calls and it turned out that the guide was not available and no guard had been booked but no one had told us of the change. This needed a rearrangement of our plans, so we fired the guide as he had not bothered to turn up, book a guard or communicate with us. We booked our own guard directly, with the local police for the next morning and would not bother with a guide.

Back in camp we had an unexpected afternoon free. Therefore a few of us walked up the forest covered volcano next to us, which has a smooth tarmac road running up the side. Near the top there is a guard and a fence as on top of this volcano are several telecommunication masts and it is closed to the public. Although we were not at the very top, there were still some magnificent views of the surrounding countryside. Back in camp we played Frisbee and used one of the Frisbees with a hole in the middle to play hoopla to try and get it over a bottle… no prizes, just for fun but we were very competitive.

We were up early and waiting again at the junction for our police guard. It had been a warm day yesterday but especially at this height it had been a chilly night. Zoë had slipped away early in the morning and without the extra body heat it was too cold in the tent to go back to sleep, so I got dressed as well. There was a heavy dew so people were keen to move to keep warm. The police guard was booked for eight a.m. and surprisingly he arrived dead on time and we set off through the forest on the lower slopes. Soon we were above the tree line and had a pleasant view of the campsite way below us and behind it to the south. From our elevation we could just see into the crater of the cinder cone.

Above the forest the volcano has less soil and there are rocks everywhere and the forest has been replaced by succulent plants that had thrown out tall stems on which were flowers or baby plants growing, ready to fall off and root themselves in the well-drained lava ash and rocks.

Finally, we crested a ridge and we were on the rim of the crater. Looking down into the crater, there were differing strata of rock of varied colours, blacks, yellows, reds and greys which had been laid down by earlier eruptions. Then the last eruption had blown a massive hole in the top of the volcano.

In the bottom of the crater was a lake of milky light blue colour. Gas rising from the depths ruffled its surface and the wind eddying in the bottom of the crater blew the foam and steam this way and that. Unlike yesterday, the sky was clear and we had good views across the national park and beyond. To the east we had a fine view of El Lago de Coatepeque, a flooded caldera with the small island of Isla Teopán, a small volcano that grew out of the bottom of the caldera but mostly our attention was focused on the deep crater in front of us.

It had taken an hour and a half to reach the top, with some stops to catch your breath and to wait for the slower walkers to catch up to keep the group together on instruction from our armed guard. We walked along the rim until the path petered out in a jumble of ragged rocks. Walking down was a lot faster and easier and we were back at the campsite by midday. Some of the people who had not climbed the volcano had packed away the remaining tents after the sun had driven off the morning dew so there were only a few personal bags to load into the back locker. Then it was a reverse of the trek to get here and we walked down the track and an empty Betsy came past and waited for us at the junction with the road.

We were driving along a ridge overlooking the caldera with views of Lago de Coatepeque below us when we came to a viewing platform. We pulled over and stopped. A pickup came past in the opposite direction and slowed. The car behind didn't brake and drove straight into the back of the pickup, pushing it forward a few metres with the force of the impact. The pickup lost some paint from its back bumper but was otherwise all right. The car however, had stoved in its front bumper, radiator grill, front wings and lights. Its driver tried to blame Zoë who was behind the wheel of the bus, but we had already parked at the side of the road when the accident happened.

It was clear that the car was at fault but he and his passengers, who happened to be policemen were adamant that it was our fault. There was a lot of shouting, finger pointing, hand waving and threats being made. It seemed best to get everybody back on the bus as the situation might soon turn ugly. The traffic was piling up on both sides of the scene of the accident with smaller vehicles creeping past on the verge but with everyone rubbernecking.

Eventually the traffic police turned up and found the underlying cause of the story. The car had been speeding and not paying due care and attention. The pickup had slowed as it could not see past the bus and the car driver was to blame. Quick as a flash the traffic police confirmed that we had nothing to do with the accident and waved us on our way.

We arrived without further incident at the lovely town of Suchitoto with its main plaza, cobbled streets and whitewashed houses. Suchitoto is a reminder of El Salvador's past, a beautiful colonial town a world away from modern El Salvador. The town overlooks the Embalse Cerrón Grande, also known as Lago Suchitlán, which is an important wetland haven for several fish species and migrating birds, particularly falcons and hawks created by a 90-metre-high dam across the Rio Lempa.

All through the town, stencilled in black on the white walls is a flower with a butterfly and a bird. Underneath is written 'en este casa queremos una vida libre violencia hacia las mujeres' meaning 'in this house we want a life without violence against women'. It was part of a movement to speak out against domestic violence and many of the houses have this stencilled message to voice their support. There are also murals in the town depicting Óscar Romero. He was the Archbishop of El Salvador and spoke out against poverty, social injustice, assassinations, disappearances and torture carried out by the corrupt government. He was assassinated by a right-wing death squad at the altar whilst celebrating mass on 24th March 1980.

We had planned to camp but decided by unanimous decision to stay at the Centro Artes para La Paz and in so doing support their work. They seek volunteers to teach local children arts and music and so promote peace and social inclusion. It was started by a nun who is still very committed to the project. They have a museum, teaching rooms, communal areas, a café, a chapel and accommodation surrounded by a neat garden and all set within a walled compound close to the centre of Suchitoto.

There were walks on offer, a sunset and a dawn boat tour to see the birds and a cigar rolling demonstration. This was a collection of elderly women gathered in a back room of a house who rolled cigars by hand using locally grown tobacco. It was a fascinating process, they chatted as they worked and their hands worked so fast it seemed to be but a blur. I don't smoke but I am told that these are excellent cigars. They are so good that purchases are restricted to one bundle per visitor per day. There are twenty cigars to a bundle, held together by thick cotton.

I went for a walk to get down to the lake shore. I found a road that went in the right direction and started walking. I had been walking for a while but I seemed to be no nearer to the lake which I caught glimpses of between the houses and trees. I had descended what seemed quite a distance and was not looking forward to the steep climb back up the hill. I began to doubt whether this was the right road and I had not seen anyone to ask for directions. Eventually I gave up and retraced my steps back up the hill. Steve and Laurence had had the same idea but had persevered and had reached the shoreline but judging by their reports I hadn't missed anything except tired legs or being a little fitter from the exercise.

For the evening meal, we walked into the main plaza and found a restaurant under a colonnade facing the plaza, with the municipal offices opposite and the well-known beautiful colonial style church on another side of the plaza. There was no menu but the owner reeled off a number of dishes that were available.

We had a local delicacy, pupusa, a stuffed cornmeal patty with a choice of fillings, washed down with a local cold beer. One of the non-Spanish speakers hadn't heard the name quite right and ordered meat stuffed babosa which means slug, but after a smile from the owner, she got a pupusa.

CHAPTER 12
The Bay Islands

Our next stop was due north in Honduras but the short and direct route was up and across the mountains on narrow often poorly maintained roads. Instead we headed west back to the border with Guatemala at Anguiatú and then north, before turning east and crossing into Honduras at El Florido and stopping in Copán. It was like driving three sides of a square so it was much further distance-wise plus two border crossings but the roads were much better and despite the border controls, it might still have been quicker and more comfortable, not to mention the very real possibility of punctures or grounding on the rough mountain roads.

Whilst at Quezaltepeque, a small town in Guatemala where we were having a break to stretch our legs, there was a street vendor selling fruit and had one unusual fruit for sale which I later discovered was rambutan. This is native to Southeast Asia and is closely related to lychee and longan. The skin is red and covered with soft hairy spines. The flesh is semi-transparent or pale pink and has a sweet flavour. The large single seed is glossy brown and is inedible. Always ready to try something new I bought some and they were interesting but I won't be demanding them from my local supermarket when I get home.

Honduras has an amazing coastline spanning hundreds of kilometres along both the Pacific and Caribbean coastlines, with some of the whitest beaches in Central America. The three islands collectively known as the Bay Islands is the place to be for snorkelling and scuba diving. The Mesoamerican Barrier Reef is the second longest in the world, after the Australian Great Barrier Reef and submerged below the clear waters lie unspoilt coral and an array of colourful underwater life. It has brightly coloured fish, manta rays, sea turtles and even great white sharks. We had seen some of this reef off the coast of Belize and there were more opportunities here.

Just as in Belize, Great Britain had had an influence on Honduras although it was never a British colony. The riches that Spain was extracting from her vast empire had not gone unnoticed and unchallenged by her rivals. Pirates, British, French and Dutch, often holding a warrant issued by the relevant government, regularly raided Spanish interests, ports and shipping and even destroyed the main Spanish port of Trujillo in Honduras in 1643.

British merchants set up timber operations along the coast using slave labour from Jamaica and elsewhere. They challenged Spanish dominance and even persuaded indigenous tribes to support them such as the Mishitu tribe. They live in the present day Mosquito Coast, which was named not after the mosquito but after the muskets that traders and settlers sold or gave to them to resist Spanish influence.

Britain recognised Spanish control of Honduras and the Bay Islands in 1786 but that didn't stop them forcibly moving the Garifuna from St Vincent to Roatán in 1797. The British reoccupied the islands in 1842 during the turmoil of political uncertainty of the Central American Federation to extend its control over the Caribbean and the Central American coast until 1859. Consequently, the islands have a Caribbean feel and English is widely spoken as a first language, although it is part of Honduras, where most of the mainland population speak Latin American Spanish.

The British were back in Honduras in the 1860s with a banking and railway scam that left the country with less than 100 kilometres of railway and a huge £6 million in debt, which with refinancing and rolling over of unpaid interest had ballooned to $125 million by the First World War. Other railways were initially developed by the banana companies which later evolved into general freight and passenger services.

There have been plans to link the Atlantic to the Pacific by rail for more than a 150 years. One link already exists and is owned by the Panama Canal. Discussions were announced in 2013 between the Honduran Government and the China Harbour Engineering Company (CHEC) to build a transoceanic railroad. Another big railway project was FERISTSA, announced in 2005. It proposed a 2,575 kilometre railway to link the Panama Canal Railway through the entire length of Central America to Mexico's rail system, but this still is just a proposal.

Away from the coastline are the fantastic mountains that soar above the country. There is some amazing scenery in Honduras and it is the place where many mineral resources are found including gold, silver, lead and zinc. The local natives had known about rich deposits and sought out free copper. The conquistadors undertook mining operations but modern mining only started in the 19th century.

The New York and Honduras Mining Company was set up in 1880 by Julius Valentine with Marco Soto, the Honduras president as a major shareholder and former owner of the mineral rights where the mine was located, who had also granted the company an exemption from paying taxes for twenty years. The company expanded and later secured the wharf and railway at Puerto Cortes on the Atlantic coast. Washington Valentine, Julius's son set up the first private bank in Honduras in 1888, Banco de Honduras, in Tegucigalpa and both Valentine and the then Honduras President, Luis Bogran held shares in the bank.

The company started mining to the east of the capital Tegucigalpa in 1880 and until the mine closed in 1955, it extracted $100 million in profits. It cut down huge swathes of forest to build its mines and to use as pit props. The mine had sixteen levels and burrowed two and a half kilometres into the mountain. It used those profits to expand its mining operations beyond Central America into North and South America, and into other fields, such as gas in Canada and oil in the North Sea. It was bought by AMAX in 1980.

The American writer William Sydney Porter coined the phrase 'banana republic', better known by his pen name O. Henry in 1904. Banana republic is a pejorative term for politically unstable countries in Latin America whose economies were dependent on exporting a limited-resource product, i.e. bananas and he was referring to Honduras when he coined the phrase. In 1892 bananas made up 11 per cent of exports. By 1903 this had increased to 42 per cent, yet by 1913 and despite exports of minerals from the mine, it was 66 per cent, and still rising to reach 80 per cent in 1929.

In 1899 the Boston Fruit Company merged with the Snyder Fruit Company to become the United Fruit Company with operations in Panama and Costa Rica, but soon acquired seven plantations in Honduras. A Russian émigré Samuel Zemurray established the Hubbard Zemurray Fruit Company, which became the Cuyamel Fruit Company which was bought out by United.

Meanwhile three Italian brothers, Luca, Felix and Joseph Vaccaro set up Vaccaro Brothers to export fruit from La Ceibo to their base in New Orleans, which became the Standard Fruit Company. Today United is known as Chiquita Brands and Standard is Dole Fruit, and both brands are widely recognised throughout the world.

These companies now controlled the banana trade and a lot of other trade, but exerted a lot of influence in the countries in which they operated. Not only by exploiting workers, fermenting labour unrest and dubious business practices, but also in politics. Zemurray supported a 1908 coup attempt against a Vaccaro friendly president. More recently Chiquita was involved in the 1975–76 bribing of the Honduran minister of the economy. Not for nothing is banana republic used as a pejorative term.

The town's steep and narrow roads were too much of a challenge for Betsy so when we arrived in town, she was parked in a friendly farmer's field on the edge of town. A fleet of tuk tuks met us and took ourselves and our luggage to our hotel in the centre of town. The numbers and rooms were just right and I was to share a room with Zoë, although I still had to wait until there was no one in the corridor before I snuck through the door. I felt like a schoolboy doing something illicit but also found it amusing.

I doubted that anyone in the group didn't know about our liaison, but Zoë wanted to keep a degree of professionalism and approachability. It also meant that she got asked a lot of questions and told the group various things and I was the last to know. Her driving partner had to know where she was when they weren't sharing a room together. Often, I shared with Zoë whilst Seb and Tracey shared a room. Steve went for upgrades so Laurence usually had a room to himself. But it had to work out at the same or fewer number of rooms. Otherwise the kitty would be paying for more rooms than necessary and that was unacceptable. Sometimes I would pay for an upgrade just so that we could be together.

After breakfast, we were met outside our hotel by several tuk tuks and went in convoy to the Copán ruins just outside of town. We were greeted at the ticket office by our local guide as we entered. A large flock of macaws also greeted us, with their bright red, yellow and blue plumage, unmissable in the trees above us and were encouraged to stay here by being regularly fed.

The site itself is not a wide-open space as at Teotihuacan outside Mexico City, nor is it nestled in jungle as at Yaxchilán, but it has just enough trees to give some shade and an idea of what it looked like when the archaeologists found it, while also giving enough uninterrupted vistas so that you could imagine ceremonies being undertaken. And whilst talking of comparisons, some of the buildings are large but not monolithic as at Chichen Itza.

The ancient ruins of Copán are the southernmost of the great Mayan sites for which Central America is famed. It was the capital city of the major Classic period kingdom and it is estimated that it had about 20,000 people and covered a quarter of the area of Tikal. People had lived here for centuries but it was at its peak from the 5th to 9th centuries AD when a vassal king rebelled and beheaded the ruling king. The city continued to see large buildings erected but it was in decline. A significant part of the eastern side of the acropolis has been eroded away by the Copán River, although the river has since been diverted, to protect the site from further damage.

This site is unique because of the 21 stelae or columns that have been found here. These are heavily carved with reliefs depicting the passage of time and the lives of the Royal families. There are also many small pyramid-shaped temples and excavated vaults. Some of the pyramids have only been partially restored so you can see the restored stepped pyramid face right alongside a jumbled pile of stones with trees sticking out of it, just like the first archaeologists would have found it.

When we had finished viewing the ruins, we hired tuk tuks and went back to the hotel. Alex and I had booked a horse ride for the afternoon and were duly picked up at the hotel by another tuk tuk and taken down the road to where the horses were waiting on the outskirts of town with our guide, a local who was curiously named Walter... not a very traditional local name.

There were just the two of us and Walter so we mounted and walked out of town over a river and into the countryside. Alex hadn't ridden before so only wanted to walk but the guide was happy for me to ride ahead, so I galloped up the path to the next junction and turned around and walked back to join them to check which direction we were going. Then I would gallop off up to the next turning.

We rode up the side of the valley and looked out over some fields in the bottom of the valley, the town and the ruins beyond. We stopped at a women's co-operative, a single room with a loom and several examples of the goods that they weave. There was only one girl there at the time but we had a chat and bought a few things.

After a ride down another path we came to a hacienda. There was an open-sided pavilion with its drapes flapping in the light breeze with views up and down the valley, which doubled as a yoga room. There were rooms for guests in separate buildings and a stable with several horses and a choice of saddles sitting on a rail. Alex and I stopped for a short break for some refreshments in the open air restaurant and it must have been a regular stop as Walter went off to chat to some of the staff.

Alex looked like he was finally relaxing on his horse and was doing very well for a complete novice. We rode back to town and stopped some distance short of the hotel but we knew where we were. We said goodbye to our horses and Walter and on the way back to the hotel, Alex and I stopped at a local café before walking through the main plaza and back to the hotel.

That evening there was an optional activity of driving out of town and going to a spa, followed by an evening meal and then driving back. This was popular with all the girls and I tagged along for the experience as the only man in our group interested in the spa.

A pickup turned up with a driver and a chef. We climbed into the back and our first stop was a supermarket for some last minute items for the chef, some soft drinks and the opportunity for those that wanted to get some wine or beer. The spa is due north from Copán up a dirt track. It is just over 20 kilometres away but would take us nearly an hour to get there over the poor mountain roads. We also stopped a few times en route as the chef was looking for some local cheese and had to ask several people before finding a farmer with some spare cheese to buy.

The track runs parallel to the border with Guatemala and connects many rural communities but only connects with other similar dirt tracks and there is no town in this remote part of the country. We were thrown around in the back of the pickup as it lurched over the uneven track and bounced on some of the larger rocks.

We still sat on the edge or stood just like the locals but made sure that we held on tight. Later it started to rain and the driver handed us a large sheet of plastic through his window whilst he was still driving and bouncing along the track. We huddled underneath and held on to the corners as the pickup continued up the track.

We arrived at the Luna Jaguar spa and hot spring resort. We left the driver and the chef to light the barbecue, set up the table and prepare the food. We changed into our swimming costumes and crossed the bridge into the spa. It was late in the day and most people had been here during the day and so were making their way home. So as time passed it was getting quieter as people left.

There were two hot springs where the water was too hot to touch. There were a series of pools interconnected by channels.

Further down the series of pools, the waters are cooler and in places mixed with cool stream water from further up the hill and there are various pools, none particularly big so it has an intimate feel.

The higher pools or those nearer the source are the hotter pools. We started at the middle pools and as we got used to the temperature we moved up to the warmer pools. We alternated between hot pools for the benefits, followed by a cooler pool for relaxation and an occasional dip in the mud pool. It is not often that you can smear yourself with hot mud and sit back to relax. I had never had a mud treatment but here was my chance. I sat in the mud pool with the warm mud up to my chest and I smeared more mud onto my face and shoulders. I washed the mud off in the next pool and returned to the hotter pools. People pay good money for such treatments so it must be of some benefit.

Under the forest canopy and considering it was late afternoon, moving on to early evening the light was failing. Our driver came with several candles and lit them so that we had some light. The spa was still open but it gave no illumination and punters were expected to either bring their own or sit in the dark.

Finally, the meal was ready and we walked back across the bridge, changed out of our wet things and sat down to a marvellous home cooked meal. We had salad, tortilla, beans, tamales and chicken. We had a great meal and chatted about what everybody had done during the day. The night air was cool in the back of the pickup after the heat of the day and the hot spa but it was still pleasant. I felt very relaxed and was sure that the treatment had left my skin smooth and glowing and feeling refreshed.

I hadn't booked any breakfast so I went in search of a coffee to take away. The stallholders in the local market were setting up and there were some cafés, but all of them only served ready-made, black, strong, sweet coffee. To find an open coffee shop early on a Sunday morning was a bit of a tall order but by sheer chance I walked past exactly what I wanted just off the main plaza.

I got two coffees, one for myself and one for Zoë as we all knew what she could be like before her first coffee in the morning and went back to the hotel. I was mobbed by coffeeholics for directions as they were all eager to get their fixes and hadn't found an open café or coffee shop. We checked out of the hotel and we got into a fleet of tuk tuks whilst our luggage was carried separately in a pickup and we went in convoy to re-join Betsy. We loaded our bags into the back locker and were soon back on the road.

We stopped mid-morning for a break at the Honduran equivalent of a motorway service station. It was a collection of cafés and shops in a row opposite a petrol station with a large parking area on both sides of the road. Whenever a bus or a mini-bus slows down and pulls off the road, a mob of street vendors would swarm around the vehicle. They were selling cold soft drinks, crisps, fruit, sweets, bags of nuts and a host of things that the hungry or thirsty traveller might want. When another vehicle slows the crowd of street vendors disperses to rush over to this new arrival, all eager to be the first to get to the vehicle and make a trade. It seemed a dangerous occupation as there were always some vendors standing in the road with traffic going past.

The mountains had turned into rolling hills as we skirted the city of San Pedro Sula, crossing the river and driving to the airport. We had chartered a plane direct with SOSA, an aircraft company and our flight to Roatán was booked for two p.m. The check-in desk told us that since we were all there and more than an hour early, they would see whether the plane could leave early. We were checked through and sat in departures.

Our flight wasn't on the public displays but that wasn't unnerving since we had chartered the plane direct with the company. There was no news and two p.m. came and went and Zoë went off to find an official from the airline to see what was happening. We had a good view of the landing strip and the apron but whenever a plane arrived, no one was in SOSA livery. There was no news and no one from the company could be found. An hour later we were still waiting without any explanation from the company, but ground staff from other companies with access to flight filings, said that there was a Roatán flight listed for a three thirty p.m. departure.

SOSA became the focus of our anger and whilst we didn't know what SOSA stood for, we made up our own acronyms such as Seldom On Schedule Airlines or Shit Operator, Shit Airline. That deadline also passed so it was past four p.m. when we were called through the gate.

We walked across the tarmac to a plane that I am pretty sure had been waiting there since we had arrived. Its livery wasn't SOSA but CMA, Compagnie Maritime d'Affrètement, part of the large French conglomerate Compagnie Générale Maritime. There was a nasty suspicion that SOSA had taken our booking and money and then went to find a sub-contractor to fulfil the booking.

It was nearly five p.m. before the doors were shut and we started to roll towards the take-off strip. But at least we were now on our way and were soon soaring above sugar cane fields and banana plantations and out across the coast. It was only a small plane and we took all the seats. It was less than a 40-minute flight and we had reached 9,000 feet when over Utila about three quarters of the total distance, when we started to lose altitude and came in to land at Roatán.

We were here at last but the next problem faced us. The plane was unloaded but not all our bags were there. The next load of passengers had boarded and the plane had left. There was no one on hand from SOSA or CMA so we began some frantic checking with officials who didn't know anything.

Then I spotted my black bag with its pink Herdy on top of a heap of other bags that were familiar in one corner of the airside unloading bay, through the rubber curtain where the baggage claim belt weaved its way from arrivals back into the restricted-air side. There were signs saying, 'no entry' and 'authorised personnel only' but if you get no help from the officials and there is no one about, sometimes you just need to use your initiative.

Ourselves and our baggage would not all fit onto one flight, so some of it had been sent ahead on another earlier flight. When no one had claimed it from the earlier flight, the airport staff had taken it off the conveyor belt and left it in a pile air-side. We were soon reunited with our bags and we set off to our posada or hotel resort via the supermarket.

There was some anxiety about getting to the supermarket before six p.m. as it was a Sunday and no alcohol is sold after that time. I was still in the alcohol aisle when security guards roped off either end. They were generous to allow those already there to finish choosing their bottles and to walk out with whatever they had in their baskets but would not allow anyone else in. Those in the group who hadn't made it in time shouted their orders down the aisle at me… a bottle of rum, a six pack of beer, a bottle of white wine. I staggered past the bemused security guard at the end of the aisle with enough bottles and cans to stock a pub or at least have a very long party.

The main centre of West End overlooks Half Moon Bay and we had a lovely beachfront resort hotel overlooking the next bay up the coast. It might sound a long way but it was 400 metres but in the heat, that can still feel like a long way. This was one of the taller buildings on the island at three storeys. Most people had decided to upgrade. Steve had gone very upmarket and booked a different hotel, ending up in the penthouse at the Beach House at Half Moon Bay, located in the centre of the bay on the beach with its own landing stage.

Tracey and Seb had taken the penthouse at the top of our hotel where we were all staying. The others were given rooms to share and I was allocated to share with Laurence on paper but as Seb was in the penthouse, I thought that I would be with Zoë and so hung about to find out which room she was in. What I was supposed to have done was to drop my bag off in Laurence's room to make it all look normal, then swear him to secrecy and move rooms under cover of darkness. As it was I was left as the last guest with Zoë and anyone watching would have known for sure and after keeping appearances for weeks, her cover was blown. Our room was at one end of the building. Several rooms looked out over the bay but I had a few treetops obscuring part of the view whilst Seb and Tracey in the penthouse had an uninterrupted panoramic view over the treetops.

The rooms were equipped with kitchenettes, balconies and hot water. The grounds were laid-out gardens with plenty of shade. It had its own landing stage stretching out into the bay with a roof over the end to give shade for some sun loungers which is where we agreed to meet up in the evening for cocktails. When I arrived, some seemed to have started and were already merry. Zoë had stripped off and was swimming in the nude. I was in shorts and T-shirt but the others egged me on. Rather than go and get changed, I just stripped off and jumped in. The swimming bit was easy but there was the difficult moment between getting out and getting my clothes back on. It was quite an evening with a few things going into the water, a mobile phone, a glass and a chair. The chair was easy to pull out but the glass and phone were not found.

Before breakfast some of us went for a swim off the landing stage. It was the same team that had started out for a swim at Flores, Zoë, Clare, Nicole and myself. We swam across the bay but didn't land as it was private property so we just swam back, taking it easy and having a chat as we swam.

There was nothing formally planned for the day so we were free to do as we wished. But certain jobs needed to be done. One was to find the local laundrette and drop all my clothes off for a good wash, except for what I was standing up in. Laundrettes were cheap and efficient. Being on the road, even if you don't wear something, it still gets dusty, creased and inevitably rubs shoulders with dirty clothes in your bag. Hand washing in cold or warm water is never as good as a hot water wash in a washing machine.

Next was a bag of ice. There was a fridge in the room but I doubted its efficacy in keeping anything cool. The dial was turned to as cold as possible and the motor was running but it wasn't cold. Besides I had become partial to a Central American standard cocktail, the Cuba Libra, a cocktail made from rum, coke and ice.

I am not usually a rum drinker and other than Bacardi couldn't name another brand at home. But locally throughout Central

America there is an entire range of both light and dark rums, different qualities and tastes and it is available everywhere. I don't like coke so I tend to smother it with rum. In a hot climate ice in a drink doesn't last long so I would need quite a bit of ice.

I walked along the sea front, partly for the walk and partly as I needed goggles for swimming. Alex and Seb are both PADI qualified divers and had gone off to find a boat to take them out for a dive on the reef. It is a great diving area with clear water and plenty of coral and fish to see. There was no shortage of dive operators scattered along the front. I had begun to regret not going as well. It was a couple of years since I last dived but with a dive master in a group, I am sure that it would have all come back to me.

I was happy to buy my goggles so that I could go for a swim using front crawl rather than keeping my eyes out of the water while doing a breast stroke. I also checked out the availability for a boat ride to go snorkelling on the reef the next day. It would not be quite as good as diving from a dive boat as they go to different parts of the reef than the snorkelers, but I would see just as much.

That afternoon we took some kayaks and paddled out of Half Moon Bay and around the headland to the bay over which our hotel looked. It might have been only 400 metres to walk but that is across the narrow neck of land and it is a lot further by sea, as seen from the air or on a map, the headland looks like a lollipop with just the shaft connecting it to the mainland.

We passed some very jagged and sharp coral that made up some of the shore line. We could see fish beneath us but difficult to make out shapes looking down through the surface of the water in a light swell and the distorting effects of the water. We reached the hotel landing stage where we had had cocktails the night before.

Someone had dropped a phone into the water and another person had knocked a glass into the water the night before. The water in this bay is not so clear as elsewhere as it does not get flushed by the sea so any murky water tends to stay around for a while. I put on my goggles and leaving someone else to hold my kayak and paddle, I dived in from the kayak to see whether I could retrieve the phone or glass.

It was surprisingly deeper than I expected and the visibility was worse at depth. I had several attempts at diving to search the seabed using my fingers but was not lucky in finding either items but at least I had had a go and felt that at least I had tried to support my friends before getting back into the kayak. This is not altogether an effortless operation whilst in the water and not recommended unless you have practiced before and know the drill with hopefully another kayaker for assistance. Yvette held my canoe parallel next to hers and head in the water, I wiggled my way, feet first back into my kayak.

That evening, since it was the second Monday in October, it was Canadian Thanksgiving which is a bank holiday in Canada. Zoë was Canadian and there was a Canadian bar and café down on the beach next to the Beach House, so our plans for the evening were simple and a foregone conclusion.

There was bunting decorating the bar, several large Canadian flags and two goals set up on the road outside for people to play ice hockey, the national game. This was a miniature tropical version of the game with a tennis ball instead of a puck, and as there was no ice, the compacted sand and gravel of the road stood in for the ice rink. There was little traffic and it was quiet most of the time and players didn't mind clearing the pitch and carrying the goal posts to one side whenever a car wanted to get past.

We had managed to find a free boat to take us in a single group to go snorkelling the next morning. It promised to be another sweltering day so we wore just swimming costumes with T-shirts and hats against the sun. Carrying water and cameras we walked along a landing stage and found our boat. We had to wear buoyancy aids which are not very flattering and are cumbersome but that was according to the local regulations. However, once out of sight of the coast guards we pulled them off. A couple of times the captain asked us to put them on again as a patrol boat came near, so we hurriedly put them back on until the patrol boat was out of sight again.

We were taken to the Blue Hole, not as spectacular as 'The' Blue Hole in Belize, but it was on the seaward side of the reef, with various formations on top of the reef and a plunging canyon that cut through the reef and out to deep water, thus a variety of habitats and different fish, ferns and corals.

After more than an hour we moved on to Black Rock. This was on the more sheltered landward side of the reef and near the base of some small cliffs. Therefore, there were yet more different habitats and fish. This had more nooks and crannies for fish to hide-in and you never knew quite what was down there. Both were marine reserves so the fish were protected but there were plenty of good sized fish that fishermen and restaurants would be happy to have. We pulled into West Bay for some lunch at a beach café before our last swim and back to Half Moon Bay.

We gathered on the beach to catch the last of the afternoon sun and to watch the sunset. Moored in Half Moon Bay is a ten-metre-long sailing boat, permanently moored out in the bay. It is distinctive as it has a wooden built staircase aft, eight big steps high, going nowhere but sticking out from the aft end of the boat and jutting out over the water. The mast is at an angle, as much as 20 degrees so that the top is over the water. There is a rope tied to the top of the mast and dangling in the water.

This is a rope swing that's free for anyone to use who can get to it. It was the usual gang of four swimmers who headed out from the beach although Nicole turned around after a while. We had great fun clambering aboard and jumping off. There was an added element of fun here as the boat was gently bobbing around in the swell.

But much more significant was that as you launched yourself off the edge of the boat hanging onto to the rope, your weight would tip the boat onto its side. If you were on board as someone else had a swing, you had to hold on otherwise you would be thrown to the deck or overboard. Zoë had gone first whilst Clare and I watched. Clare could grab on to stay upright, while I was unprepared, and I was standing right on the gunwale to watch so I went straight into the water. No one got caught out again.

We had a wonderful time working our way up the stairs as our confidence grew, until we were leaping off the top step. There was a certain skill to learning to get the jump just right. If you held the rope too low, you just went into the water while still holding the rope and as the boat righted itself, it would pull the rope up. If your legs were astride the rope, you might get some nasty rope burns between your legs. If you held on too high, you avoided hitting the water with your legs around the rope, but letting go from a height might mean a wedgie or dislodging a bikini top.

The next morning, we were flying back to the mainland and so had to eat or drink anything that we couldn't take with us. Rather than waste it and leave it or have things being squashed and oozing out in my luggage, that evening meal and breakfast were an unusual combination but at least we would not be wasting food.

There was a little confusion at the check-in as we had to pay a tax. We had to pay the tax at the bank and take the receipt to the check-in with our passports. I knew that there was a tax for international departures but didn't realise that this also applied to any departure, hence also internal flights. Luckily, we each had the correct amount in local currency to pay the departure tax, but only after a bit of lending and borrowing amongst ourselves.

We were flying back by commercial flight but the flight was scheduled to take a lot longer than the flight out. We had no sooner taken off for San Pedro Sula than we were landing again at Utila which was a half an hour stop en route. This plane was a larger plane than the one we had flown on to reach Roatán and had seating for 27 and they got all our luggage on board but this time the plane was over booked.

The air hostess asked for a volunteer to sit on the jump seat in the cockpit. This was a drop-down seat fixed to the back of the door into the cockpit. I was at the front and my hand shot into the air. The hostess was about to take me forward when I heard Steve say that he had never had the opportunity to sit in a cockpit before. I had sat in a jump seat before so I gave my place to him. It was a short flight but he loved every minute of the flight, getting a first-hand view of what it is like to be a pilot and see what they see as they took off and landed.

We grabbed our bags and walked out of the terminal and loaded Betsy. Then it was a short drive south through the mountains. We were driving up the valley which is the main road between Honduras's largest two cities, San Pedro Sula and Tegucigalpa, the capital. Towards Peña Blanca there is a huge pipeline snaking its way down the valley, with some sections elevated and visible near the road. This was a major water resource for towns and cities further down the valley and as far away as San Pedro Sula. They are a separate system from the giant hydroelectric scheme at El Cajón Dam and its reservoir, Embalse Francisco Morazán which is 50 kilometres to the east on another river.

We stopped for a break and lunch in Peña Blanca which is the gateway to Lake Yojoa which is the largest lake in Honduras with a surface area of 79 square kilometres, and an average depth of fifteen metres at an altitude of 700 metres. The lake was formed by volcanoes whose lava flows created a natural dam across the river. It is a picturesque area of scenery with steep mountains. There is the Santa Bárbara National Park to the west and to the east is the Cerro Azul Meambar National Park. The whole area is known as an area with a vast range of biodiversity with 400 species of birds and 800 plant species which have been found in the region. On the downside deforestation, cattle ranching, and development threaten the area. Some of the best coffee in the world comes from the area around Santa Bárbara.

A short way out of Peña Blanca we reached our overnight stop at the D&D Brewery, Lodge and Restaurant. They create and have on tap up to eight of their own beers and stock up to thirty imported international beers. We were due to have dormitories here but several people upgraded and there were camping facilities for those that wanted something a little cheaper.

It is a fascinating place with the cabins set in thick forest, with a small swimming pool and a restaurant, and not to mention the huge choice of beers that would take a week to get through. Plus, there are plenty of walking and other activities in the area so, it seemed a great shame not to have scheduled more time to spend here.

We had tried several of the beers and we were in danger of getting through a large number and not seeing any of the local sights, so we reluctantly left the Brewery and followed the directions to Lake Yojoa. It was a lot further than we had been led to believe. It was also muddy in places and the path so narrow at times that progress was slow.

We followed a muddy path along the edge of a river, flowing into the lake and reached the lake itself. On a fine day, there would have been something to see but the water was muddy where the river emptied into the lake and mist hid the far side of the lake and the surrounding mountains. There seemed to be few birds about except some ducks sitting on the lake some distance away. It had also started to rain so it was not a memorable trek. We got back to the Brewery and sat warm and dry in the Brewery snug.

Another very embarrassing moment for me occurred that evening. Zoë got out her violin and started to play for us. To my shame I was asleep in no time. And I have form for falling asleep during a recital, as I had done so at Palenque in Mexico. That time I was in a deck chair but couldn't be woken.

This time I was sitting in a chair and falling asleep, I was soon falling off my chair and head-butting the concrete floor. That woke me up and the manager and a member of staff got the first aid box out and patched me up. I was profusely apologetic to both Zoë for interrupting her performance, the other guests for interrupting the recital and to the first aiders, who couldn't serve beer whilst they attended to me so I should also apologise to those thirsty drinkers for depriving them of a beverage. The fact that it happened in a brewery might lead the reader to suppose that that might have had something to do with it, but I believe I suffer from an unusual form of violin induced narcolepsy and I am prepared to offer myself as a subject for further medical research in this field to dispel the notion that beer might have had something to do with it.

It was still raining in the morning as we drove on through the mountains. Low clouds obscured the mountain tops and drifted around the lower slopes. The road improved from a winding mountain road to a gentler gradient, a wider road with a good tarmac surface with broad sweeps around obstacles with cuttings, embankments and retaining walls where necessary, so that the rate of progress improved. We were approaching the capital city of Honduras, Tegucigalpa, high in the mountains and where the river Choluteca runs through the capital city and on to the Pacific Ocean 300 kilometres away and a good name to remember how to pronounce and spell it, for pub quizzes. We didn't go through the city but took the main road that goes around or bypasses the capital to the south.

The road had changed again into a dual carriageway with heavy traffic, but flowing freely. At one spot, the right-hand carriage way was blocked by cones and the traffic was diverted onto the other carriage way. A whole section of the hillside to the right had slumped and blocked the road ahead. It had pushed-over lamp posts at the side of the main road and there was debris up to seven metres deep blocking the road. The extent of the slide was significant but we couldn't see how far up the slope the damage went. But we could see the roofs of several houses which had been carried down the hillside by the slump and whose roofs now lay at crazy angles.

The ground had become saturated and unstable and had slumped down the steep slope, either under its own weight and instability or nudged by the effects of a nearby earthquake. The houses had survived the quake intact but their foundations had failed and they had moved with the rest of the hillside in a slide down the slope. The houses had kept their shape but had ended up at crazy angles and not as the neat ordered terraces that the architect had planned. The windows had been removed as had all the contents so it was just the shell that had been left.

More than twenty homes had suffered a migration caused by nature down the hillside and I could see another four-standing high on the hillside above the slump, just as the builders had intended, in an offset line working their way down the hillside. These looked abandoned and not surprising, given that their neighbouring houses had ended up disappearing down the slope. It might not be long before these houses might end up joining their friends, abandoned and resting at crazy angles further down the slope.

CHAPTER 13
Nicaragua

At Las Manos on the border there were the usual forms to complete, taxes to pay at a bank and then taking the receipt to the border officials window to prove that you had paid. Exiting a country was usually relatively easy but access to the next country was inevitably more difficult.

Entry into Nicaragua was difficult and bureaucratic. Amongst the documents, papers and stamps needed was that we had to undergo and pass a medical examination to produce the necessary receipt to the border official. We walked into the medical centre to be handed a tiny slip of paper with a photo on it of a thumb print and a stamp. There was no examination or questionnaire and everyone got the same photocopied piece of 4cms square piece of paper and was ushered out of the exit door in less than five seconds flat. It seemed that only non-locals... meaning both Nicaraguans and Hondurans, had to have this piece of meaningless paper, as only Europeans seemed to have to visit the medical centre. The procedure was pointless if you didn't have an examination to show whether you had a raised temperature or were a carrier of other diseases.

Suitably armed with our fistful of documents, stamps and photocopied pieces of paper we queued one by one to hand them into the border control and were told to wait. I could see passports and wedges of paper forms being scrutinised, counter stamped and passed to another official, to do the same thing and to be stamped again before the pile of documents were taken behind the scenes for more scrutiny.

Two hours later we were handed back our passports with just a faint 5cms by 2cms blue stamp in our passport. We had obviously passed their security measures... we were not members of a subversive political agitation, terrorist, or smuggling organisation on some list. We didn't have illegal firearms, drugs or other contraband in our luggage, nor were we smuggling people, engaged in the slave trade, prostitution or seeking to overthrow the government, money laundering, or carrying any of a host of illicit fruit, vegetables, meat, fish or shellfish products or substitutes or products derived thereof, or engaged in illegal contaminated waste disposal or carriers of a host of endemic tropical and other infectious diseases... in short we were deemed as 'clean'.

I have often wondered what might happen had you answered yes to one of those questions on the innocuous immigration slips of paper. And who in their right mind would admit to it? If you were smuggling people or bombs would you admit to it! Even if you did tick the yes box as a thoroughly honest citizen, although otherwise intent on a criminal activity, they might just think that you must have made a mistake and cross it out for you and tick the 'no box' as it was just too much trouble to investigate it further.

All the individual government ministries need your little bit of paper saying 'no' to prove that you were dishonest in completing the form should you be found out later. Never mind the fact that you are breaking international law against people smuggling, drug dealing or terrorism; or that the punishment for a criminal offence is so vastly more than a civil offence of misrepresentation on a piece of paper. You will get banged up for a long time and deported, so another four weeks suspended sentence for a form-filling error seems irrelevant. But I would not advocate anyone in my party ticking the wrong box just to see what might happen.

It was dark by the time we got through controls and we stopped shortly afterwards for a dinner break before heading to our hotel in León where we arrived in the dark and late at night.

The rugged beauty of Nicaragua makes it one of the most interesting places in Central America to visit. The origin of the country's name is in dispute. Some guides claim that it is based on the local Indians tribal chief Nicarao plus the Spanish for water, seeing that they lived around lakes such as Lake Nicaragua and Managua. A nice story... but when Gil González Dávila came to

Nicaragua in 1521 and visited Rivas he recorded the name of the city as Quauhcapolca and the chief's name as Macuilmiquiztli.

Nearer to the truth may be that Nicaragua means surrounded by water in the local Nahuatl language. A more believable claim for me is that the name stems from the indigenous words nic-alt-na-huac meaning 'here at the lake' or nic-alt nahuac meaning 'the Anahuac from here'.

The landscape is filled with many volcanoes, which can be climbed and are just waiting to be explored. The tranquil surrounding of trees and many trails means there is plenty to explore. In contrast to the natural scenery is the metropolitan centre of the city of León, Nicaragua's second largest city after the capital, Managua, is full of culture and was to be our first overnight stop in the country.

The original town was founded in 1524 a short distance away, but abandoned in 1610 after several earthquakes. The newer city had been the capital since colonial times, but in the early 18th century the capital shifted back and forth between León, favoured by liberal regimes, and Granada preferred by conservative regimes. A compromise was reached with Managua located between the two, being the capital since 1858.

There are an abundance of churches, cathedrals and art galleries plus university buildings scattered around the city. Exploring sites and learning about the culture can be demanding work, but with the wide variety of food and drink available, it is a chance to relax if you are not a culture vulture. The markets have a range of produce of beautiful shapes and colours. Nicaragua can grow tropical fruits all year round and the stalls in the markets display juicy fruits such as mangoes, bananas, watermelons, plums, dragon fruits, star fruits and passion fruits and loads of other fruits and vegetables.

Like the fruit and vegetables in the markets, the wildlife is colourful too. It is the place to find the three-toed sloth. This wonderful animal can be seen climbing through the trees, so we were on the lookout for sloths. Other animals included anteaters and armadillos. We had already seen sea turtles and spider monkeys… which are usually heard first and seen second. But first we had the city of León to explore.

Disaster had struck during the night. Betsy had been broken into and the padlock that secured the door was nowhere to be found but the thieves had carefully shut the door again, so that it appeared that nothing was untoward until the first person went to open the bus in the morning. Zoë had lost her laptop, a camera, a Swiss Army knife and a small leather bag containing cosmetics plus other items. The thieves thought that the cosmetics bag was a wallet and took it to rifle through later and would get a shock to find just personal items and nothing of real value. She was gutted at the personal loss of so much that she held so dear. When you live on the road and live out of a bag, everything in that bag is important.

I had some bottles of wine stolen that were under my seat and not surprising since both Zoë's and my things were at the front of the bus. As the thieves got bolder, they worked their way through the bus but they were inconsistent as they ignored Tracey's much more valuable ten-year-old tequila from Tequila and another bottle of spirit. They took Laurence's thick, warm and waterproof jacket, an odd choice given that Nicaragua is never that cold and he is a big chap so it was unlikely to fit the average Nicaraguan, let alone a larger local. They emptied a bag which they took with them, to use to carry their haul away but missed a wallet that fell out with a pile of dirty clothes.

They also left anything in the overheads, another couple of laptops, a coat with money in a pocket and a wallet visible in the netting, saved by the darkness. These items were missed as the thieves would have been seen through the windows from the pavement and may have been discovered. Other people had lost items, phones, or cameras and some were not discovered as missing until the owner wanted to use something and couldn't find it anywhere.

Zoë went shopping for items that needed to be replaced quickly. Luckily it was a university town and there would be electrical shops to buy a new laptop but you may not get the choice available from the internet as delivery would be difficult if you are constantly on the move. You could only buy what was on sale.

I walked into the main plaza, looking at the architecture, an art nouveau style theatre in one corner, a colonial style building and a 1930s modern minimalist style municipal building on another side of the plaza and the large whitewashed walls of the cathedral. This was a typical colonial baroque building built between 1747 and 1814 and was undergoing renovation but much of it was still open to the public and you could visit the crypt, a museum, the bell tower and walk on the roof and enjoy the views.

Just walking around some of the back streets off the main plaza there were some interesting examples of secular architecture and yet more churches. In contrast to the plain whitewashed walls of the cathedral, El Calvario church is ornate and partly red; the fine décor of La Recolocción is partly yellow and La Merced has a similar pillared façade compared with La Recolocción but is white. The streets and markets were bustling with people but somehow the experience of the grandeur of the city and its energy was overshadowed by the losses from the bus theft the night before.

Zoë had got a replacement laptop, not her first choice and no chance to recover photos or her music which were only stored on the hard drive and which are irreplaceable but the piece of electrical hardware was adequate. She had also found an optician and had got a new pair of prescription glasses.

We were driving 150 kilometres past Lake Managua also called Lago Xolotlán, Nicaragua's most polluted lake as until recently sewage was dumped in it from Managua and as it has no natural outlet the pollutants were concentrated. The lake level rises with heavy rains and occasionally overflows via the Tipitapa River into the neighbouring Lake Nicaragua.

We weren't stopping there as our focus was seeing the active volcano in the Masaya National Park. We stopped at the visitor's centre to pick up our guide and to visit the exhibition that explained about the volcanoes and some of the geological history of the country plus the fauna and flora to be found in the area.

The park is inhabited by many kinds of animals including coyotes, skunks, raccoons, opossums, deer, iguanas, and monkeys. There are many paths that lead through the park and the trekker might get to see some of the animals. We didn't have time for any trekking in the depths of the park and since animals tend to stay away from the heavily populated tourist trail, we would be lucky to see even one of the animals on the list.

Our guide joined us on the bus with a big sack and we drove up towards the rim of the crater. The jungle thinned and we were soon above the tree line with a view of the twin volcanoes of Masaya and Santiago towering above the landscape making an incredible sight. We passed old lava flows that vegetation had covered and newer flows where the plants were just beginning to gain the upper hand to cover the black jagged lava rock with soft green foliage. The most recent flows were just a jumble of sharp jagged black rocks flowing down the hillside and frozen in time.

The guide books talk about lava pools glowing red and photos in the visitor's centre showed what these looked like but activity had reduced since the guides had been written and the lava had solidified so there is no red glowing rock to see. Looking over the rim of the crater there is a vast hole with vertical sides. There is a lot of pungent sulphurous gas billowing up and obscuring the bottom of the crater somewhere below. We caught glimpses of the lower walls as the wind pushed the gas clouds this way and that as it eddied around the deep hole but we never saw the bottom of the crater.

There is a track that leads up and over a ridge to another area of the volcano which has restricted access and is only accessible to small groups with a guide. The guide produced helmets and lamps from his big sack and we tried them on for size and made the necessary adjustments. He also had a face mask and respirator but then he is down here several times a day, but there is no danger for occasional visits, only for long-term exposure.

We walked down the slope and into a hole in the ground. Here was a lava tunnel that extended several kilometres underneath the lava field above and the entrance was where the roof had collapsed. Lava flowed down the slope but the surface cooled and solidified. The lava underneath was insulated and if it had an exit further down the slope, it continued to flow. When the lava stopped flowing from the fissure, the tunnel drained, leaving a long downward sloping cave.

This has since been colonised by bats and as we walked along the top section of the cave there were bats flying about our heads. The smell from bat poo decomposing on the floor and walls, wafted up to us and was pungent, repelling and poisonous, hence only the top section is open to the public. It was nice to get back to fresh air and light above ground.

We were due to stop for a while in the town of Masaya, Nicaragua's third largest city but first we stopped for an ice cream overlooking Laguna de Masaya, a lake next to the town with steep cliffs plunging into the water. The city is known for its folklore and for its handiworks and hence the next stop was to look at the market. The market has a whole host of handicrafts and textiles, tourist trinkets and things for the home. Stalls selling similar goods are grouped together, making browsing for specific items a lot easier for shoppers. The stalls themselves are nothing fancy but the wall surrounding the market area was built of good quality large stone blocks with a date on the wall above the main entrance declaring that it had been built in 1891.

It was just a short distance to Granada where we had a couple of nights in a hostel. It is the oldest city of the 'new world' having been founded in 1524 and was registered as such in the official records of the Crown of Aragon and the Kingdom of Castille in Spain. It might be old but it is only the eighth largest city in Nicaragua.

We were dropped off with our luggage at a hostel and Betsy was driven to a truck park. Our hotel was a traditional colonial town house, built around a central courtyard where there were palms growing. The colonnade around the outside had some hammocks slung between the columns in the shade and some of the rooms opened onto the main courtyard. There was a labyrinth of corridors and other small courtyards and yet more rooms.

One of the dormitories was a former warehouse at the back of the building with a tall arched stone roof. There were communal areas, a kitchen for guests to use in another courtyard completely under cover, and another courtyard with covered areas next to the walls with open sides and with a central section open to the skies. Some people wanted a little more luxury and privacy so Steve, Nicole and Vera found a nearby hotel.

I went for a walk with Zoë to the central park opposite the cathedral. Down one side runs Calle de Calzada, a pedestrianised road where just about every building is a café, restaurant, or hotel. It was Saturday night and everywhere was busy and noisy and I wanted somewhere a little quieter. When we reached the far end, we turned right and right again to go up Calle El Caimito and ordered food in El Camello where several others of the group joined us. After the meal, several people wanted to go on and party but I was content with an early night.

I was up early the next morning. I had booked a boat for a cruise around some islands in Lake Nicaragua but wanted to take some photos of some of the buildings in the town. It was early on a Sunday morning and there was no one about and the light was just right. I retraced some of the route I had taken the night before. There was a former cinema, built in an art deco style and now a supermarket, there were plenty of fantastic colonial buildings around the main plaza and down the main streets and plazas surrounding it, as well as the cathedral and municipal buildings.

At the end of the pedestrianised Calle de Calzada is the Iglesia de Guadalupe, a church the size of a cathedral. A service was being held so I only caught a glimpse of the inside from the doorway. It has a strategic location as it was at the entrance to the city from the port, just a bit further down the road on Lake Nicaragua. It was looted several times by English, French and Dutch pirates who sailed up the San Juan River and across Lake Nicaragua to plunder Granada.

Granada was also significant in a turbulent time in Nicaraguan history at the hands of an 19th century adventurer, William Walker. It is a fascinating story of a "boys own" adventurer. He was born in Tennessee and graduated in medicine in Pennsylvania and practiced briefly in Philadelphia before moving to New Orleans to study law, before changing his career again to be co-owner and editor of the New Orleans Crescent newspaper. He had an aspiration to conquer large areas of Latin America to create slave states in campaigns known as filibustering or freebooting.

Before turning up in Nicaragua he already had form. He sought permission from Mexico to create a colony in Sonora, part of present day north west Mexico bordering California and was refused but he began recruiting followers anyway, but his ambitions now changed from a colony to setting up an independent republic with himself in control.

In 1853, he set out with 45 men and captured La Paz, the capital of Baja California and declared the new Republic of Lower California with himself as president. The Mexicans were moving forces to regain control of the area so Walker first moved south to San Cabo Luis at the tip of the peninsula and then again north to Ensenada which is nearer to the border and easier to supply. He pronounced his new republic as part of the larger Republic of Sonora, although he never actually captured any Sonoran territory. He was forced to retreat to California by stronger Mexican forces and a lack of supplies.

He was put on trial for conducting an illegal war. With echoes of the Alamo when Texas was pulled away from Mexican control for the benefit of the USA, and the Manifest Destiny Doctrine, first coined in 1845, whereby American settlers would spread throughout the continent, he and his project were popular with the public and the jury found him not guilty after just eight minutes.

Before the opening of the Panama Canal in 1914 and the completion of the USA transcontinental railway in 1869, the way to move goods and people from the east coast to the west coast, thus avoiding the long and treacherous journey around Cape Horn on the southern tip of South America was by travelling down the east coast by ship to Central America and making a short overland journey across the isthmus before boarding another ship to go up the west coast.

One of these overland routes was through Nicaragua, up the San Juan River and across Lake Nicaragua, then across the narrow strip of land, at its shortest just twenty kilometres to the Pacific coast and then to board a ship and sail up the west coast. The commercial exploitation of this route had been granted by Nicaragua to the Accessory Transit Company, controlled by shipping magnate Cornelius Vanderbilt.

In 1854, a civil war erupted in Nicaragua between the conservative Legitimist Party based in Granada, and the liberal Democratic Party based in León. The Democrats sought military support from Walker who landed in 1855 with 60 men, and was quickly reinforced with 170 locals and 100 Americans including the explorer and journalist Charles Webber and the English experienced mercenary Charles Henningsen. His Nicaraguan contribution was to oversee artillery and conducting several of Walker's battles, which is just a small chapter in his own long and interesting life.

Walker attacked Rivas, a town that controlled the transhipment route across the isthmus but he did not take it. He later captured Granada and took control of the country as commander of the army under the provisional president Patricio Rivas, and was then recognised as the legitimate government of Nicaragua by US President Franklin Pierce.

Meanwhile, Cornelius Garrison and Charles Morgan, partners in some of millionaires Cornelius Vanderbilt's many business dealings in the Accessory Transit Company had provided aid to Walker in return for Walker seizing the company assets and turning them over to Garrison and Morgan. They in turn would give logistical support for Walker's army. It was better in their view to earn some revenue supporting Walker than none, as the fighting would discourage normal trade and the steamers would be tied up earning nothing.

Vanderbilt was incensed by this treachery and sent two loyal supporters to the Costa Rican government with detailed plans on how to defeat the filibusters so that he could regain control of his assets and business interests.

Walker's exploits scared neighbours and investors alike with his ambitions for further expansion. Costa Rica declared war on his regime, emboldened by support from Vanderbilt. Walker organised a battalion of four companies. One was composed of Germans, a second consisted of Frenchmen and the other two companies were staffed by Americans, totalling 240 men in total to invade Costa Rica in a pre-emptive action. However, this advance force was defeated.

With Costa Rican troops advancing from the south, with support from Honduran and Salvadorian troops from the north and west they besieged Granada. After several months of siege warfare, in December 1856 Henningsen gave the order to burn Granada and retreat across Lake Nicaragua. Under intense military pressure from the joint armies of Central America, Walker retreated and surrendered in May 1857 to the US navy.

Meanwhile British colonists in Roatán had long-feared that Honduras would seek control over their affairs and sought Walker's help to set up a separate English-speaking government. Walker returned to Central America and landed at Trujillo on the mainland of Honduras but became a prisoner of the British navy. The British controlled the neighbouring regions of the Mosquito Coast, now part of Nicaragua and an area now called Belize. There were also strategic and economic interests in the proposed construction of an inter-oceanic canal and Walker was a dangerous and loose cannon in the area. Walker was handed over to the Honduran authorities and he was executed in September 1860 at the age of just 36.

I continued my walk down the road from Iglesia de Guadalupe towards the lake. It was already getting warm and the water looked inviting but I wasn't going to risk it. There were bull sharks in the water that swim up the river and lived in the lake. They had been hunted for their skins for use as leather, their flesh for meat, their fins for soup and anything left over was used as fish food or fertiliser. They were hunted down in their thousands and spawned a whole new industry to process them but they are now rarely seen but I wasn't tempted to test the waters.

I walked along the front and then turned inland to find a road that would take me back towards the centre of town, my hostel and my pick-up for the trip that I had booked the day before. Back at the hostel I was duly picked up and driven to a port on the lake. There is a whole string of islands just off the shore line south east of Granada, created when the nearby volcano Volcán Mombacho blew its top and threw huge boulders into the lake. Today these islands are the homes of wealthy individuals who have built up the banks of the islands, built landing stages and elaborately architect-designed houses and retreats.

The trip was a tour of these luxury homes from the water, with a host of famous politicians, actors and businessmen's names claimed to own this or that island. Lunch was at a restaurant on one of the islands, which also had a swimming pool where you could relax in the water, safe in the knowledge that you would not be bitten or worse-still eaten by one of the now rare sharks that live in the lake, before returning to Granada.

I was having an afternoon coffee at one of the restaurants along Calle de Calzada when I had a Damascus moment. I had been wary of eating at restaurants whilst sitting in the street, ever since Oaxaca in Mexico where street vendors, entertainers and beggars harassed us whilst trying to eat. I have no objection to poverty-struck people trying to make a living and can usually emotionally manage to accept it during the day as a tourist. But when relaxing for a meal, I do have trouble with emotional acceptance plus indigestion whilst trying to relax. I might be eating a meal that may be a whole days-worth of food for the less fortunate. They have sharp eyes and if you are generous to one deserving cause, you tend to get mobbed by others eager for some largesse.

My heartstrings were tugged however by some of the boys working the restaurants, by their dexterity in working simple strips of palm fronds into wonderful shapes. There was no coercion, just what I felt was genuine humanity. I was sitting at a restaurant in the street in the late afternoon with Zoë and a young youth came up and presented her with a flower made from a strip of palm frond and walked off. She called him back and gave him a small tip for the flower.

I was converted by her generosity and humility… it wasn't much in UK monetary terms, it was mere pence, but it meant a lot in human terms and it was a generous gesture. A little later another youth came over and started to make something that involved a lot of folding and knotting of the palm frond. I didn't wave him away, as I might usually do, but was intrigued and wondered what it is was that he was making. It turned out to be a life size reproduction of a giant grasshopper just like we had seen in Rio Dulce. I was smitten by his efforts and he presented it to Zoë. I thanked him and gave him a tip for his efforts.

Had another youth came over and asked what I would like him to make I would have happily paid for a whole zoo as I was so enamoured with the production and result of folding palm frond strips into interesting shapes. However, with our flower and grasshopper on the table we were left alone by other passing lads with strips of palm fronds looking for custom. The grasshopper was a treasured possession that sat on the dashboard of the bus for a long time afterwards. At the end of the trip I carefully wrapped it up and put it in a tin with some padding. I returned home with it safely wrapped in my luggage. I had wanted to bring it home as a reminder to be more generous in charitable giving to the truly needy.

I went for a walk past the market, which being late in the day and a Sunday, people had packed up and it was deserted. I was looking for a shop but I forget now what I wanted to buy but the cemetery was out this way and I wanted to see the local funerary architectural style.

I hadn't gone very far when I realised I was in the wrong end of town. There were a lot of dilapidated houses, people slumped on the side of the road, dirty children dressed in rags playing in the street, and women with big smiles and wearing too much make up and very little else but all eager to engage me in conversation.

There were groups of young men hanging around street corners and eyeing me with suspicion. Every now and again I was asked, usually by a young lad whether I wanted to buy any drugs with lots of different drugs on offer at cheap prices. I smiled and walked straight on purposefully pretending I knew exactly where I was going and turned right and right again and made my way back to the more familiar and hopefully safer central area of the city.

Granada was also a post-visit source of angst. It was only later that I discovered the theft. I had tried to get money out of a cash machine but it denied giving me any cash. I thought that I might be asking for too much so I tried with smaller amounts but still no luck. What had happened was that my account was being debited but no cash was coming out of the machine.

The other more significant theft was harder to explain. I avoid ATM's in supermarkets or in the street and prefer to go into a bank to make a transaction. Most of the local banks have 24 hour-access and a security guard on duty. I also like to see that other people have used the machine before me so that I know that it works and that other people trust it.

Somehow my card details had been stolen and money was extracted from my account in California, whilst I was in Nicaragua. I lost several hundred pounds before my bank thought that it was suspicious activity and barred further transactions. Several other people lost money in the same way, and one poor individual lost $8,000.

As Betsy couldn't get down the narrow streets of the old city, we carried our luggage up the road to a main road where Betsy was parked to get on board. On one side was a church with an open space in front of it and on the other side of the road was a hotel and on the whitewashed wall next door, there was a blue plaque proclaiming that this was where William Walker stayed during his time in Granada.

On the way out of town we passed the cemetery that I had started to walk towards the day before. I was sitting on the same side of the bus as the cemetery and I could see over the fence and had a view of the gravestones. I got to see some ornate edifices but would have liked to have had some time to explore and take photos, rather than just a glimpse as we drove past.

Our destination was Rivas where we left the road that runs parallel to the shoreline of Lake Nicaragua to reach the port where ferries dock. We would take a ferry from San Jorge to Moyogalpa, a port on Ometepe.

Ometepe is an island formed by two cone volcanoes. Its name derives from the Nahuatl words ome and tepetl meaning 'two mountains'. The two volcanoes are Concepción and Maderas which are joined by a low isthmus to form one island in the shape of an hourglass. It is the largest island in Lake Nicaragua and the taller of the two volcanoes, Concepción, at 1,610 metres makes Ometepe the world's highest lake island. The soils derived from volcanic ash are rich and are therefore very attractive to farmers despite the constant threat of a volcanic eruption.

There is a vehicle ferry but we would leave Betsy on the mainland and take the more frequent and cheaper foot ferry. It might be meant for passengers but a number of motorbikes were wheeled on board and lashed to the railings for safety. An hour later the ferry docked at the single simple landing stage and we disembarked. It was a short walk to our Hotel Ometepe as the hotel entrance is opposite the exit from the landing stage.

This is a charming family-run hotel with many rooms opening on to a long communal balcony with hammocks and arm-chairs to relax in. There was a pleasant restaurant area open to the public, next to the entrance opposite the landing stage. The website suggests that it has a swimming pool in a beautiful garden setting. The beautiful garden setting was there and all around the hotel but the swimming pool was another matter. It was half full, not of water but of garden waste.

There were various tours and activities on offer. One option was a trek up the volcano which is the one that I opted for, as I just cannot get enough of walking and volcanoes. It is a long walk, at altitude, in the heat and would take several hours. It also left at four a.m. in the morning for an early start to avoid some of the heat of the day. The tour needed a minimum number of guests and a long arduous walk with an early start so it was not going to be that attractive and I couldn't summon up enough interest from the other members of the group for this to be a certainty. It was obvious that this was not an attractive option for most people. I didn't get my guided walk up yet another volcano.

What was popular was a trip out to Punta Jesús María to see the sunset. It was a bumpy ride in pickups down the coast to the point. This was a sandy spit of land on the western edge of the island formed by waves washing sand along the beach to accumulate in a long spit sticking out into the lake.

We walked out to the end of the point and watched as the sun set behind the mountains on the mainland more than ten kilometres away. The water shelved deeply on one side but was shallower on the other side and we went for a swim. Thoughts about shark attacks seemed to be far from our minds as we dived into the water.

We stopped at a local restaurant on the return journey for an evening meal. There wasn't a menu, they had one dish on offer and the choice was to take it or leave it. Thus, we all had roast chicken and rice with a piquant sauce.

Having missed my preferred option of a trek up a volcano I had an easy morning and walked around town. Other people had taken a bus to a spa, a bus around the island or hired mopeds for the day. Zoë had finished writing up her reports, booking rooms and taxis for the next leg of the journey, researching travel times and routes etc. by lunchtime and was eager to go exploring. I had done nothing all morning and was looking for something to fill in the afternoon so we walked up the road and hired a motorbike.

There was no checking of licences or experience but we did ask for helmets and I was surprised that there were some available. It had been a while since I rode a bike and we had had an idea to visit a museum and the spa. I was ready to try a bike again but not confident that I could drive across the island without getting a bit of practice in first and then get to see what we had planned to see before dark.

Time was marching on and I didn't have the luxury of time to practice so I found myself holding on to Zoë's waist as she drove a dirt bike out of town over the rough roads. I was a bit tense at first, but soon relaxed since she had already driven me safely thousands of kilometres from Anchorage in Alaska and I knew that she had had plenty of experience driving bikes. I would have loved to see where we were going ahead of us but I was conscious that if I lent to one side to see past her head, it would unbalance the bike so I was content to look just sideways.

We stopped at a museum just off the main road around the island. There was just a rough track from the main road to the entrance, just a pair of parallel tyre tracks over a meadow. If you can see where you are going you might be prepared for every bump in the road, but for a blind passenger it was uncomfortable so eventually I got off and walked while Zoë drove the trail bike over the rough ground and thoroughly enjoyed herself. It was a fascinating place with examples of petroglyphs, pictures, money and stamps but we didn't spend much time there. It was back on the bike and off to Ojo de Agua, the spa that was the destination of our ride that afternoon.

We were stopped at a police roadblock but our papers were in order and try as they might to search our bags, they found no guns, drugs or whatever they were searching for and satisfied that we weren't international terrorists, smugglers or whatever we set off again. The sun that had shone all morning had been obscured by clouds and it had started to rain.

As we entered the car park there was a long line of mopeds, so we had arrived at the same time that the others were visiting. When we reached the spa itself, they were huddled under the shelter of one of the buildings surrounding the pool preparing to leave. I am also sure that it had been described as warm water so I was disappointed to discover that it was a cold-water spring. It might have been lovely in the heat of summer but it was cool and the trees overhead gave plenty of shade but this late in the year it did feel cold.

I still had an enjoyable time, going for a swim and trying to cross the pool on a slack line and falling in every time before I made it even half way across. Cocktails were being served in coconut shells with straws and umbrellas, inevitably incorporating rum and coconut juice so I just had to try one.

It had started to rain so everything was wet as we got back on the bike and started to make the return journey. The rain stung the skin as we drove along the road so I wasn't missing the ability to look forward and sat in the lee of the wind and rain behind Zoë as she negotiated potholes, cows and children on the road home with me hanging on for dear life.

CHAPTER 14
Sloth country

We caught the eight a.m. ferry back to the mainland. Then it was a drive to the border with Costa Rica at Peñas Blancas. Exit and entry was not unduly troublesome to the seasoned traveller as we always expected the worst so we had built plenty of time into the schedule. However, we queued at two different windows and some of our party didn't speak Spanish and obviously didn't answer the question correctly or hadn't specified what was needed. We discovered that some of us had a 30 day visa whilst others had only a five day transit visa which was not adequate as we would be in the country for more than five days.

It was a bureaucratic nightmare to get the first visa cancelled and a new correct 30 day visa re-stamped into passports. It cost nothing in cash terms but took hours to negotiate with senior officials to cancel a visa and re-issue one to get the right pieces of paper. Personally, I couldn't understand why they just couldn't give another stamp but apparently once the stamp has been put in the passport the official in front of us wasn't authorised to stamp it a second time. Eventually we were through the bureaucratic maze and we continued our journey to arrive at the Hotel Cabanitos on the outskirts of La Fortuna.

La Fortuna is a small town situated just a few minutes away from Costa Rica's most active volcano, the majestic Arenal which was visible from the hotel grounds but the peak was obscured by clouds. The kitchen, restaurant and bar were near the entrance to the hotel site whilst the rooms were individual cabins with twin or double beds, set in their own grounds and all the communal garden areas were beautifully manicured with lush neatly trimmed grass and a blaze of colour from the flowers planted in the borders. I shared a cabin with Zoë at the far end of a row of similar cabins.

The guide books say that the Arenal Volcano is regularly spewing smoke and ashes and is beautiful to behold as the hot lava lights up the dark night sky with its red glow. However, it was not erupting when I visited which was another disappointment on the volcano front. It was erupting when I booked the trip but it had settled down to dormancy by the time that I arrived on site which was a recurring theme. All the volcanoes that had been active when I had planned the trip had all since quietened down so the goal of seeing an eruption eluded me.

We walked into town that evening to the offices of an adventure activity company where various trips were on offer. As usual there were a minimum number of people needed to book a trip for it to be a confirmed departure. Since there were so many different tastes, unsurprisingly several people were disappointed in not getting their hopedfor first choice of tour.

I would have gone up the volcano but I knew that no one else would want to do that. Also, I wasn't feeling well, not that I could put my finger on anything specific but that I just didn't feel right. An early night and some rest would do the trick and nip it in the bud before it turned into something more serious.

I had a lazy morning and luckily whatever it was the night before, I now felt perfectly fine. I spent the morning sitting around the swimming pool and having the occasional swim. In the afternoon, I walked into town and explored some of the side streets. Feeling much better, I was ready for the next adventure. That evening we were picked up in a taxi and taken to the Baldi hot springs and spa which also has a hotel and restaurant on site where we would have an evening meal.

This was a much more up market spa than the last spa that I had visited in Copán. This was set in its own grounds with artificial waterfalls, subtle lighting, bars and several water slides. It was remarkably quiet but we enjoyed a couple of hours of fun in the different pools before changing and having our choice of evening meal in the restaurant.

We drove out of La Fortuna and up the road to Laguna de Arenal created by a dam. We saw our first sloth, perched in a tree by the side of the road fast asleep. We strained our necks to peer into the canopy. He was quite a way up the tree and we didn't get a clear view as there was so much foliage but it was a sloth.

The road continues across the top of the dam but we stopped at the beginning of the dam with the lake on one side and the forested valley on the other side. This lake was expanded in 1979 with the new dam and its hydroelectric plant initially produced 70 per cent of Costa Rica's electricity but with increasing electrical power usage in the economy and expanding production, this has dropped to 17 per cent.

The towns of Arenal and Tronadora were both relocated to new sites with the old towns now on the bottom of the lake which is up to 60 metres deep. We were taking the direct route to Monteverde but Betsy was too big to manage the steep twisting mountain roads so Seb would drive her to the far side of the mountains on a long circuitous route and take a taxi to re-join us in Monteverde. We got off the bus with our hand luggage and boarded a ferry to cross the lake. We were met on the far side by minibuses which ferried us through the mountains to the town itself where we arrived at around lunchtime.

It was Jim's birthday so we had a birthday cake with candles on it for lunch. Jim and Ginger cut up the cake and handed round plates to the assembled crowd and for those not there, they missed out as the whole cake got eaten. Rooms were allocated in the main hotel building which we were told had marvellous views across the valley and down to the centre of town further along the valley. However, it was foggy and the view was obscured. Seb and Tracey and Zoë and myself weren't in the main building but had self-catering flats in the house next door and Steve and Laurence opted for an upgrade and got a flat.

That afternoon I went on a coffee and cocoa plantation tour. We were picked up by the Don Juan Minibus and taken to the Don Juan Coffee Plantation. We were taken through the entire process from planting the beans, looking after the bushes and harvesting the beans. Then we were shown the drying process followed by the roasting process.

They also grow cocoa and we were shown the plants, the pods, the process of separating the cocoa beans from the pulp of the fleshy part of the pod. Then the processing of the cocoa into chocolate to eat or to drink. Needless to say, the tour ended at the gift shop and café where we bought chocolate and drank several coffees.

Monteverde and the cloud forests which surround it are considered the top destination in Costa Rica and certainly one of the top eco-tourism destinations in the world. The bulk of Monteverde's rainforest and cloud forest can be found in the Reserva Biológica Bosque Nuboso Monteverde which attracts vast numbers of visitors each year. The area has an incredible diversity of flora and fauna and the area is one of the best in Central America to view the indigenous bird, the quetzal.

We picked up our guide at the hotel and were being driven to the reserve in two minibuses when the guide asked the driver to stop. There was a sloth asleep in the trees. With the help of a long lens on a tripod we all had a chance to see this animal curled up, asleep in the nook formed where a branch joined the main trunk. We would be seeing other sloths whilst in Costa Rica but the best place to see sloths is at the sloth sanctuary which is located on the Caribbean coast. Unfortunately, we were not going anywhere near it so this was not on our agenda so we had to make do with whatever sloths we came across.

We arrived at the reserve's visitors' centre and started our guided tour through the forest. There is plenty to see and lots was pointed out to us by our expert guide. The calls of the birds alerted the guide to what birds were around us. There were many humming birds, all sorts of insects and flora. We were also lucky enough to see a quetzal bird with its colourful plumage in the trees above us. He also obligingly demonstrated a short flight as he flew a few metres to another tree, again well within viewing distance.

On offer was a canopy tour, however, having had a guided tour on the forest floor, I was not interested in a canopy tour. Also on offer was a visit to an adventure park with multiple zip lines. It claims to have the longest zip line in the world but this was an activity that didn't interest me so I went for a walk around town for the afternoon. But those who went off to do the zip lines had a wonderful time whizzing down the wires high above the tree tops and through the jungle and as a bonus also got to see the forest canopy at close quarters.

The morning was cold and damp as we got into two mini-vans and headed out of the mountains. All except Seb who had taken a taxi two hours before everyone else in the dead of night to pick up Betsy and meet us on the main road. It was only thirty kilometres but due to the twisting and steep mountain roads it took an hour to reach the junction. When we turned the last corner to reach the junction with the Pan American Highway, there was Betsy and Seb waiting for us and we were all reunited.

Where the road crossed a bridge over the Rio Grande de Tarcoles, there are signs both of a viewing point for crocodiles in their natural habitat and warnings not to go near the river. There was other advice such as not to get within fifty metres of a crocodile, to exercise caution and a reminder that safety is their concern but your responsibility. This was a popular haunt for crocodiles.

From the safety of the bridge above the muddy brown waters of the river, you could peer over the edge and look straight down on more than a dozen crocodiles. They were lying in the water, completely submerged except for their eyes and a few rows of raised osteoderms or teeth like structures that run in ridges from their heads along the back to the end of the tail. This was clearly one river that was not to be used for swimming.

We left the Pan American Highway as it cuts inland through San José, the capital. We turned off and followed the coast road until a side road that leads down the hill to the small beach resort of Manuel Antonio right next to the entrance to the Manuel Antonio National Park. Our hotel was El Faro Beach Hotel which was a stone's throw from the park entrance, less than fifty metres. A visit to the park was scheduled for the next day but we had arrived early so we decided to visit that afternoon and therefore leave the whole of the next day free to do as we liked.

The park was set up in 1972 and is Costa Rica's smallest park at just 1,983 hectares but it has been voted one of the prettiest parks and hosts a mass of biodiversity, a stunning variety of both fauna and flora. It has four white sandy beaches and several rocky islands just out to sea. It has a tombolo or sandy spit of land that separates two of the beaches and connects one of the rocky islands to the mainland. It does have its drawbacks as there are crocodiles in the area, the monkeys are known to grab bags and cameras off unwary visitors and there are strong riptides making swimming dangerous.

We had a biologist as a guide and although it is a small park and just a short walk he was busy pointing out flowers, palms, iguanas and other lizards, chameleons, racoons, colourful birds and some bats roosting in the trees. It has several types of monkeys but what people most wanted to see were the sloths, and there are both two and three toed sloths in the park. We were duly rewarded with some sloths contentedly sleeping in trees and not too obscured by foliage. It may be just a small park but it packs a lot into that tiny area.

With our free day, most people were up early to be picked up for a cruise. It was on a large catamaran with a swimming pool on board and the opportunity to top up your tan on the sundeck. It would cruise along the coast with opportunities to go for a swim, both in the sea at designated stops or in the on-board pool. There was also a free bar on board offering as much rum as you could drink. So, there was something for most people. If it had been a smaller boat I would have gone as well but as it was a big boat with dozens of guests on what was a booze cruise it didn't appeal to me so I opted to go for a long walk around the local area by myself whilst Zoë wrote reports, did accounts and booked hotels and upgrades for the next few days.

We met up for sunset cocktails at a bar some distance back up the road which links the resort with the main road. There were plenty of hotels, cafés and other bars throughout the resort but with so many you need something extra to stand out. El Avión has it in bucket loads. Its centrepiece is a C-123 Fairchild cargo plane that has been converted to a bar and restaurant. It is so popular that the public area has expanded all around the plane. We had some drinks and of course had to pose for photos around the plane. Most popular was climbing into the cockpit and leaning out the window.

Down the road is another restaurant that has a railway carriage in which you can dine called El Wagon. Yet another has some of its walls made from different shaped and coloured glass bottles. We had to go to those as well and bearing in mind that some people had already been on a booze cruise it had become a bit of a drunken and raucous group on a pub crawl. Things could have got out of hand as there are plenty of other bars but being the low season, our livers were spared as some of the cafés and restaurants were shut.

In the morning, we returned to the Pan American Highway and followed it southwards to the border with Panama at Paso Canoas. There were more queues to join, forms to fill, unsmiling border guards, taxes to pay and papers to be checked. We had to pay an exit tax and were directed to a minibus. It looked suspicious with two girls with laptops sitting in the back of the minibus plus what was either a plainclothes armed guard or the girl's civilian minder with a partially concealed weapon standing outside. It just didn't look authentic so we went back to the main building.

After checking again in the main building, this really was where you paid your six dollars exit tax. The automated payment system within the building looking something like an ATM didn't work and so the minibus, girls and guard were the back-up system. I was first in the queue and handed over a ten dollar bill and was given three dollars change. I complained that the change was incorrect but was told that there was an extra dollar added as a 'handling fee' so that the six dollars exit tax costs seven dollars. I complained and asked whether there was an alternative method to pay to avoid the handling charge Yes, of course, she answered with a beguiling smile and directed me to the ATM look-alike in the main building that was not working.

The money was stuffed into a biscuit tin under the seat and I got a receipt that was written in ball point pen on a scrap of plain paper but with an official looking stamp. I was told to move on and make way for the next customer. I went back to the border control and that little piece of paper seemed to satisfy the border guard behind a grill in the main building who added it to a pile of other slithers of papers, stamped my passport and waved me through.

At last we were through exit procedures but had to repeat everything on the Panama side of the border. This time we were taken to a room with our luggage. This chap was a "jobs worth". The form had to be filled in precisely correctly, in the same colour ink, spelt correctly without any crossings out, or illegible words so those with poor handwriting had extra problems. Addresses had to be exactly right, in the right order and a post code. No one got away with just their first attempt, and the average number of attempts was three. Then one by one we had to stand next to our luggage and have everything searched, pulled out and wash bags and cosmetic bags opened and examined.

We had been there for an hour and not even half way through. Then the "jobs worth" was called outside and another border guard took over. He collected all the forms, spelling mistakes and crossings out ignored. His idea of a search was to just open the luggage and have a quick look at the top. We were all out in five minutes. Outside, Betsy was parked in the same place and there were several lorries, buses and cars pulled up behind her and ready to drive on, having passed all their border requirements, but were unable to get past Betsy who was blocking the road.

At last we were over the border and in Panama, it was our last border and the tenth country on our trip from Anchorage. We were on our home run.

CHAPTER 15
The Canal

Panama is the southernmost country of Central America and links Central America with South America via its border with Colombia. However, land travel between the two continents is difficult due to the Darién Gap and the security situation within it. This is an area of dense impenetrable jungle and swamps. For a long time, it was a refuge for guerrillas fighting the Colombian regime. It is also a drug production and trafficking area so several different armed groups roam the area, vying with each other and the army, the border security forces and drug enforcement forces for dominance.

In contrast, Panama is a safe country to travel around with a stable economy and is one of the largest gross domestic products per capita countries in Central America, despite its small land area. Its key geographic location, with its canal linking the Atlantic and Pacific oceans and its history, it separated from Colombia with American support in 1903 has helped its development. Democracy is now strongly emerging in the country as Panama puts behind it the political turmoil of the Noriega regime which saw American troops invading and occupying the country in the late 1980s and early 1990s, in support of the Panamanian people who were being repressed by the corrupt government.

One job that needs to be done after every border crossing is to get hold of the local currency. Most people travel with a wad of an international currency that is easily exchanged for local currency such as euros, American dollars, or UK sterling, but it does need a money changer or a bank that is both open and that transacts currency exchanges. Most borders have a fistful of entrepreneurs with pockets bulging with currency to buy or sell local currency and major internationally recognised currencies.

The drawback is whether you are getting a good rate, receiving forged notes or suffer a sleight of hand in counting out the notes. An easily manageable alternative is to use an ATM, although there are drawbacks and my experience in Granada in Nicaragua is a salient reminder that even these are not foolproof.

Panama does not produce any banknotes of their own national currency, the Balboa, but instead use the American dollar. However, they do mint coins which are the same weight, dimensions and metallic composition as US currency and both types of coins circulate in the economy freely.

In 1941, President Dr Arnulfo Arias created the El Banco Central de Emision de la Republica de Panama with authority to issue banknotes. In due course on 2nd October 1941, 2,700,000 balboa notess were issued, named after the Spanish explorer and conquistador Vasco Núñez de Balboa. Just one week later on 9th October 1941, Dr Ricardo Adolfo de la Guardia Arango replaced President Dr Arias as president in a coup. The new government closed the bank, withdrew the bank notes, and burned all the remaining stock of balboa banknotes and the country has used American bank notes ever since.

We had a short drive along the main road to the city of David where we turned off the Pan American Highway and up to Boquete in the mountains. The area is famous for outdoor activities and the nearby Volcán Barú, the highest point in Panama. The town is also a gateway into the La Amistad International Park, not just a national park as it straddles both sides of the Costa Rica-Panama border. It is a remote area in the mountains and includes Volcán Barú but its range of biodiversity is not fully researched but it is a vital link in the Mesoamerican Biological Corridor and is a designated UNESCO World Heritage Site with about twenty per cent of the region's biodiversity.

After breakfast in the hostel where we were staying, there was the sound of a band playing at the end of the road. A local school was practicing for a carnival and a procession around the town in a week's time, to celebrate Separation Day, a bank holiday in Panama to celebrate its separation from Colombia on

3rd November 1903. This closely follows celebrating Halloween and the Dia de los Muertos or Day of the Dead. Everywhere there were effigies of witches and ghosts decorating shops and front gardens.

There are lots of celebrations undertaken in November with five bank holidays. The 4th November is Flag Day and 5th November is Colon Day to celebrate Panamanian efforts to stop the Colombian army from attacking Panama City during its fight for independence. The other two holidays are 10th November to celebrate an uprising against their original Spanish rulers led by Rufina Alfaro in 1821 and Independence Day on 28th November when Colombia, of which Panama was a constituent part, gained independence from Spain in 1821 and hence November is also referred to as Independence Month. In total, there are fourteen bank holidays in Panama compared to just seven in England. It is not surprising that Panama has so many as Spain, its former colonial master from whom it inherited some of its national identity, has twelve national holidays plus a host of added regional bank holidays.

Despite all the activities on offer, I just wanted to go for a walk, check out the town and relax. I had been travelling for five months and had done lots of activities throughout the trip. I only had a few days left before I reached the end of my trip in Panama City. Had this been part of a two-week summer holiday out of my annual holiday allowance from my employer, I would have made an effort to go and do something, but I was in a reflective mood after five months travelling, ten countries, covering over 15,000 kilometres and I would have to say goodbye to both my fellow travellers and more importantly to Zoë, with whom I had shared so much. But that was a few days away.

But there was still a poignant moment for me in the afternoon as I sat drinking a beer in the communal area of the hotel, whilst I watched Zoë working, doing accounts and writing reports. It might seem glamorous to be a tour leader and travel the world but there is also a lot of challenging work and jobs to be done while the clients have some free time.

It was a long drive day to get from Boquete, back to the Pan American Highway with a stop for lunch in Santiago. It was a chance to buy some snacks and for the cook group to get everything that they needed. I also saw some Swiss Army knives and bought one for Zoë to replace the one that had been stolen from the bus in León.

We carried on down the road in Betsy to reach our last campsite before Panama City at Playa Santa Clara on the Pacific coast. In the USA and Canada, we had spent most nights camping. In contrast through a lot of Central America we had been spoilt as we had stayed in hotels or hostels. This was our last camping night and there were no upgrades available.

It was a basic affair. There was a beach café that served food and drink during the day but closed in the evening. There was a little stream that flowed into the sea but its mouth was filled with a bank of sand washed there by the constant coming and going of the tide. The water from the stream built up behind the bank and just seeped away through the sand.

There were a couple of showers, or rather shower heads sticking out of the side of a building. The original intention was just to wash sand off after a day on the beach, rather than a cleansing shower for campers so no walls for privacy had been built but that wouldn't bother us. There were some palapas or beach umbrellas made from palm fronds. And of course, a lot of sand. You pitched your tent on the sand anywhere above the high tide mark. At least the ground wasn't hard, it was flat and it was easy to drive the tent pegs into the ground. Most people had pitched their tents close to the palapas but I selected a site further along the beach. I never noticed how she did it despite keeping an eye open but Zoë's sleeping bag, blanket and things would appear in my tent as if by magic.

The last camping night also meant it was our last night to cook for ourselves. There was a bit of a party atmosphere. Some people were flying home and would leave as soon as they arrived in Panama. Some were going on to Colombia as part of a north and south American trip, flying on to Colombia to avoid the Darién

Gap, including Zoë whose contract was for several more months leading groups through South America. Seb would be driving Betsy back to California where she was due a major overhaul and Tracey would be going with him for the ride. Some had booked other hotels in Panama City so this was also the last night that we would all be together.

The party atmosphere was added to by the need to drink all the beers and spirits that were on the bus as we would be staying in a hotel in Panama for a couple of nights but Betsy was going back to California. There were also orphan drinks, drinks left by passengers who had left the trip but not drunk all their hoard and it would be wasteful to throw it away. Many thanks to those unknown passengers who nobly donated some drink to our final farewell beach party.

The cook group cooked and several of us helped prepare the food. I think the cook group included Steve and Tracey but there was such a feeling of comradeship and so many helpers, that I wasn't sure who was in charge. The sea was rough but it didn't stop us having a swim. Zoë and I stripped off and swam naked on our little patch of beach away from the palapas but going past them to wash off the salt before getting dressed for dinner.

After the meal Zoë got out her violin and played. So as not to repeat my embarrassment of falling off a chair as I had done at the D&D Brewery, I sat on the sand and leaned against a palapa. But true to form, I fell asleep whilst Zoë played. I woke up a short time later but found my glass of Cuba Libra and the bottle of rum had disappeared. Zoë had got her own back on me and had helped herself. Serves me right for falling asleep during a recital yet again.

It was also the last time that we had to pack the back locker, but after so much practice it was second nature. We were back on the road by the scheduled time and just an hour short of Panama City. The road crossed a high-level bridge above the Panama Canal, the Centennial Bridge on the Pan American Highway. There were magnificent views up and down the canal. It is a main road with no footpath and stopping is obviously forbidden, otherwise it would be a permanent traffic jam as people took photographs.

The Panama Canal is an amazing engineering achievement being 77 kilometres long that connects the Atlantic and Pacific Oceans and it is a key route for international maritime trade. There are locks at each end to lift ships up to Gatun Lake, an artificial lake created to reduce the amount of excavation work needed for the canal, whose water level is twenty-six metres above sea level.

There had been talks about a canal ever since 1534 shortly after Spain discovered and started developing Central America. There have been many schemes suggested, alternative routes and different combinations but it took hundreds of years before the current scheme was operational. It is an obvious answer to avoiding the dangerous sea journey around Cape Horn at the southern tip of South America and the extra cost of transhipment of goods over land from one side of the isthmus to the other.

William Walker interrupted the transit of goods and people between the two oceans on another route via Nicaragua, but demand for an easier route increased in 1849 with the discovery of gold in California. Prospectors wanted to get there and merchants wanted to import goods to satisfy the demand from the increasing population. The Panama Railway was built to cross the isthmus and opened in 1855, fourteen years before the first transcontinental railway route opened in the USA.

The French success in building the Suez Canal and the profits it generated encouraged planning for a canal to cross the isthmus. In 1877 Armand Reclus, an officer with the French Navy, and Lucien Napoléon Bonaparte Wyse, two engineers, surveyed the route and published a French proposal for a canal. The first attempt to construct a canal through Panama, then part of Colombia, began on 1st January 1881. The project was inspired by the diplomat Ferdinand de Lesseps, who was able to raise considerable finance in France because of the huge profits generated by his successful construction of the Suez Canal.

De Lesseps wanted a sea-level canal as at Suez but the plans didn't consider the rainy season and the Chagres River which now feeds Gatun Lake and the lake level rose ten metres in one season. Neither did it take account the much higher mountain terrain that lies on the proposed route. The equipment rusted in the tropics and the jungle was alive with dangerous snakes, insects, spiders and disease.

The plan was far too ambitious and the engineering equipment not up to the job. The death toll from yellow fever, malaria and a host of other tropical diseases took its toll on the workforce, which needed constant new drafts of men. In 1884 the death rate was over 200 per month. Finally, the company went bankrupt in 1889 and 22,000 people had died and there was no canal.

In 1894 the Compagnie Nouvelle du Canal de Panama was created to take over the project. There was only a minimal workforce to run the Panama Railway and undertake limited work on cutting the canal, not a major effort but just enough to keep their franchise. The excavations required for a sea level canal was overly ambitious and a compromise of locks to raise ships to get the canal through the mountains was more realistic.

Meanwhile the USA was interested in pursuing the canal project and after the failure of the Colombian government to ratify an earlier agreement, it gave considerable support to Panama to break away from Colombia and its warships patrolled offshore to intercept any marine-borne Colombian military forces trying to intervene in Panama's attempt for separation. In 1904, the French equipment and excavations, including the Panama Railroad were sold to the USA and work restarted on building the canal but this time with locks across the isthmus. It took another ten years and a further 5,600 deaths from disease and accidents before the canal was opened to traffic on 15th August 1914.

The US continued to control the canal and the surrounding Panama Canal Zone until the 1977 Torrijos-Carter Treaties provided for handover to Panama. After a period of joint American-Panamanian control, the canal was taken over by the Panamanian government in 1999, and is now managed and run by the Panama Canal Authority, a Panamanian government agency.

Annual traffic has risen from about 1,000 ships in 1914 to 14,702 vessels in 2008. In 1934, it was estimated that the maximum capacity was 80 million tons per year. However with upgrades to operating systems, 299.1 million tons passed through the canal in 2009.

There are restrictions on the size of ships that can use the canal, decided by the size of the locks. The largest ships that can use the canal are called Panamax. This is typically a ship with a deadweight tonnage of 65,000–80,000 tonnes, but its actual cargo is restricted to about 52,500 tonnes because of the 12.6 metre draft restrictions within the canal so ships cannot be filled to capacity.

The Panama Canal Authority set tolls based on the vessel type, size, and the type of cargo carried. The average toll is around US$54,000. There is inevitably a queue to get through the canal but for a fee you can jump the queue. Priority passage can be bought via the Transit Slot Auction System. The largest amount paid was $220,300, paid on 24th August 2006, by the Panamax tanker Erikoussa, to jump a 90-ship queue waiting for the end of maintenance works on the Gatun locks, a delay otherwise of a week. The normal fee would have been just $13,430 but the ship owners obviously thought it was worth the extra money. It normally takes six to eight hours to pass through the Panama Canal.

An expansion project has been under construction since 2006, and after some slippage in the schedule, it was due to open in 2016. The larger locks plus increased dredging will allow bigger ships to use the new cuts and locks and then go through the existing Gatun Lake. The maximum level of the lake has been increased to ensure sufficient water for the new locks to operate at the same time as the existing locks. The new dimensions of ships using the new locks instead of the existing locks will increase by 25 per cent in length, 51 per cent in beam, and 26 per cent in draft, as defined by the New Panamax metrics.

Just over the Centennial Bridge is a reminder of that terrible death-toll to build the canal. On the right next to the road is a sign proclaiming the Cementerio Frances, the crossed flags of France and Panama plus the dates 1880–1899. Behind is a grassy slope surrounded by trees where there are severl graves. There are several of these cemeteries scattered along the track of the canal and it is a poignant reminder of the cost in human terms of the early attempts to build the canal.

Just a short distance further is the visitors' centre opposite the Miraflores Locks. From the multi storey building you can stand on one of the viewing platforms and watch the ships going through the locks. There are also educational films, a museum on the construction of the canal plus the usual cafés and gift shops. Amongst the many facts thrown at you, I was intrigued to discover that the sea level on the Pacific side is about twenty centimetres higher than that of the Atlantic side due to differences in ocean conditions such as water densities due to salinity, temperature and weather.

We were just in time to see the MV Isla Bella, registered in San Juan which is the world's first LNG powered container ship on her maiden voyage through the canal on her journey from the Pacific to the Atlantic Oceans. It is incredible how these massive ships negotiate the locks with just literally inches to spare on either side between the ship's hull and the concrete sides of the lock. Admittedly there are tugs on duty and there are locomotives with long hawsers to guide the ship through the locks but there is still only a wafer thin margin of error.

We watched as several ships negotiated the locks. Then there was a delay as the direction of traffic reversed and ships were leaving the central section of the canal from the Atlantic Ocean through Gatun Lake and then negotiated the locks down to reach the Pacific Ocean.

After a while it was time to move on so we boarded the bus and drove into the centre of Panama City. We unloaded all our individual possessions from Betsy and waved as she drove off and disappeared out of sight around the corner to a truck park nearby. I was sharing a room with Zoë but there was an elephant in the room. It was what I called the Panama Moment. As an analogy, at university, you sign up for a course and you know that in three years' time, there will be an exam to test your knowledge.

From the moment, you sign on to a course, the clock is ticking and whatever happens in the meantime, the exam will happen.

After Panama, Zoë would fly on to Colombia and continue to take people on tour through South America as per her contract. I had a flight via Portugal to get home to the green countryside of West Sussex. We never talked of our aspirations or fears of what we would do after our enforced split by circumstances when we both left Panama on our separate roads. That was the elephant in the room and an unresolved issue.

Panama City has two centres, the modern, high rise centre where there are shopping malls, head offices of local companies and the finance, commerce and banking centre of the country. This is where multinationals have their local offices in tall concrete towers thirty or forty storeys high. Just two kilometres along the beachfront is the old traditional centre, mainly two or three storeys high, with the cathedral and a series of old buildings. This is known as the Casco Viejo or Old Quarter of the city. The original centre of the city was first established in 1519 but was looted and burnt to the ground by the well-known pirate and British admiral Henry Morgan in 1671. There are some beautiful buildings but many dilapidated ones as well but gradually the area is being renovated.

This is where La Rana Dorada is located, a mini brew pub where some of us started with a few tastings of the beers available. There are several restaurants and one, the Restaurante Casa Blanca, where there was live music where we gathered for our last meal together. I had already had a moment of reflection in Boquete and had said some personal goodbyes, knowing that the parting of the ways was fast approaching for me and some were easy and some were very emotional goodbyes.

We had had some great times travelling together, some magnificentsights, lots of fun and many memorable moments. I had been travelling with some people who turned out to be great company and good friends but now we had to go our separate ways. Some had been travelling with me for just a few weeks. Others I had met up with in Anchorage months before. For yet others, this was just another stop on a long trip through the Americas, around the world or just another part of life's great journey.

Seb drove Betsy up to the front of the hotel and those flying to Colombia to continue their journey to South America got aboard. Seb with Tracey would drive them to the airport and then drive Betsy back to California for a major refit. There were many farewells but my emotions were running deep and wild and I was having a great problem keeping them in check and not being seen to be too emotional or bursting into tears at saying goodbye to Zoë.

Zoë was the last to get on board Betsy but we had a cuddle and a kiss before she turned and climbed the steps and shut the door behind her. Seb pulled away from the kerb and drove down the street. There was a lot of hand waving from both the pavement and from the windows of the bus. Tears were welling up but with great determination, I held them in check. At the end of the road, Betsy turned the corner with Zoë on board and I was once again all alone.

Acknowledgements

FOR ZOË.

Other books by the same author

K2, The Savage Mountain Travels in Northern Pakistan
This is the story of travels in northern Pakistan using Gilgit as a centre. It is the story of the journey westward to the fascinating Kalash Valleys and a surviving unique culture struggling to live and maintain their identity in the harsh and rugged mountains bordering Afghanistan.

The story continues to Baltistan and up through the Karakoram Mountains and the infamous Karakoram Highway that links the country to China via the Khunjerab Pass, the highest road border crossing in the world. The journey goes eastwards across the Deosai plateau which has an average elevation of 4,000 m and the disputed areas of Jammu and Kashmir. Finally there is the ascent to base camp of K2, the world's second highest but most deadly mountain.

Overlanding the Silk Road
This is the story of a long journey following the Silk Road overland from Europe to China. The journey starts in London and a dash across Europe. The real journey starts in Istanbul and winds through the history and countryside of Turkey. Then over the border into Iran to experience its rich history and architecture.

There are the bizarre experiences of the beautiful, modern but empty city of Ashgabat, the capital of Turkmenistan. Just north of the city are the Dervasa Gas Craters located in the middle of the desert.

A trip to the disappearing Aral Sea is followed by an immense amount of empire building, architecture and history across a land fought over by Alexander the Great, Tamarind and Genghis Khan.

There is an enchanting wander through the mountains of Kyrgyzstan. This country of beautiful mountains and lakes is known as Asia's little Switzerland.

The scene slowly changes as the Muslim influence gives way to Han Chinese dominance, the Great Wall of China and the end of the Silk Road at the ancient capital of Xian and its famous terracotta army.

The Klondikers

The Klondikers was the name given to the people that had heard about the gold that was to be found around what was to become Dawson City. It was just sitting there waiting to be picked up by anyone who could make the challenging journey to get there.

This is the recreation of the journey that one farmer from the wheat growing areas of the prairies around Calgary may have experienced to get to the gold. It is the story of crossing the Rockies to the western seaboard, travelling up the coast and making landfall. Then the intrepid potential gold panner had to cross the Rockies on foot and brave blizzards and freezing cold.

When the weather and the ice had melted, he then had to paddle his way down 800 kilometres of river to the goldfields. Once he arrived that was the least of his problems.

Crossing Russia on the Trans Siberian

Russia is a vast country that covers more than a third of Europe and stretches for nearly nine thousand kilometres across northern Asia. The journey takes the reader on a tour through Russian history and geography starting in the Imperial city of St Petersburg with its spectacular palaces and museums.

A voyage by ship leaves St Petersburg to follow rivers and canals crossing several lakes through the northern pine forests past wooden cathedrals and monasteries to join the Volga to reach Moscow. There is the Kremlin and Red Square plus many other sights including one of the largest and ugliest sculptures in the world.

After Moscow is one of the longest railway journeys in the world on the Trans-Siberian railway to pass through birch forests, over grassy steppes and through the Ural Mountains to reach Vladivostok on the Pacific coast.

There are stops en route at Yekaterinburg where the Imperial family were murdered by the Bolsheviks, horse riding in the Altai Mountains to reach Mount Belukha, Siberia's highest mountain and at Irkutsk near Lake Baikal with its unique biodiversity and the world's largest volume of fresh water before finally reaching Vladivostok in Russia's far east and its port on the Pacific.

EIN HERZ FÜR AUTOREN A HEART FOR AUTHORS À L'ÉCOUTE DES AUTEURS MIA ΚΑΡΔΙΑ ΓΙΑ Σ
...ANTA FÖR FÖRFATTARE UN CORAZÓN POR LOS AUTORES YAZARLARIMIZA GÖNÜL VERELI
...IONE PER AUTORI ET HJERTE FOR FORFATTERE EEN HART VOOR SCHRIJVERS TEMOS OS
...RE SZÍVÜNKÉRT SERCE DLA AUTORÓW EIN HERZ FÜR AUTOREN A HEART FOR AUTHORS À L'É
...CORAÇÃO ВСЕЙ ДУШОЙ К АВТОРАМ ETT HJÄRTA FÖR FÖRFATTARE Á LA ESCUCHA DE LOS A
...TEURS MIA ΚΑΡΔΙΑ ΓΙΑ ΣΥΓΓΡΑΦΕΙΣ UN CUORE PER AUTORI ET HJERTE FOR FORFATTERE
...ARLARIMIZA GÖNÜL VERELIM SZÍVÜNKÉRT SERCE DLA AUTORÓW EIN HER
...OR SCHRIJVERS TEMOS OS CORAÇÃO ВСЕЙ ДУШОЙ К АВТОРАМ ETT HJÄRT

The author

Norman Handy was born in 1957 in Beckenham, Kent in the south east of England. He went to school in Beckenham and later went to boarding school in Cranbrook, Kent. He studied Business Economics and Accountancy, plus Law for Accountants at Southampton University.

During his studies, he also travelled and after finishing university travelled and worked abroad. He returned to the United Kingdom and after some time working in a riding school, followed a career for thirty years in the financial services sector in London, including periods working overseas.

He has two children and is a keen horse rider, walker and skier and of course, writer! He spends his time between his home in West Sussex and travelling.

novum 📖 PUBLISHER FOR NEW AUTHORS

The publisher

*He who stops
getting better
stops being good.*

This is the motto of novum publishing, and our focus
is on finding new manuscripts, publishing them and
offering long-term support to the authors.
Our publishing house was founded in 1997, and since
then it has become THE expert for new authors and
has won numerous awards.

**Our editorial team will peruse each manuscript
within a few weeks free of charge and without
obligation.**

You will find more information about
novum publishing and our books on the internet:

w w w . n o v u m - p u b l i s h i n g . c o . u k

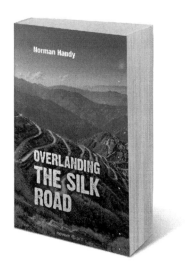

Norman Handy

Overlanding
the Silk Road

ISBN 978-3-99048-708-2
354 Pages

Overlanding the Silk Road is a real page turner, taking you on journeys you never thought you'd go on! From London to places like Kyrgyzstan, known as Asia's little Switzerland. Sit back and enjoy the beautiful scenery and experiences this book will take you on.

Norman Handy

The Klondikers

ISBN 978-3-99048-714-3
246 Pages

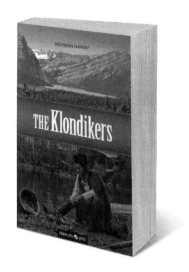

Have you ever wondered how gold is really found? Well you're
about to find out as Norman Handy recreates the journey
that one farmer from the wheat growing areas of the prairies
around Calgary, may have experienced in his quest to find
gold!

Norman Handy

K2, The Savage Mountain

Travels in Northern Pakistan

ISBN 978-3-99048-716-7
262 Pages

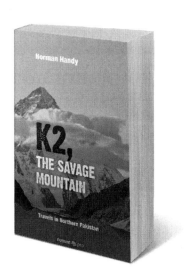

Strap yourself in for this one as you're in for quite a ride! This is the story of one man's travels in northern Pakistan. The final challenge comes for the ascent to the base camp of K2, the world's most deadly of mountains. A definite must read!